LA SERENISSIMA

The Last Flowering of the Venetian Republic

ALFONSO LOWE

CASSELL · LONDON

CASSELL & COMPANY LTD
35 Red Lion Square, London WC1R 4SG
Sydney, Auckland, Toronto,
Johannesburg

First published 1974

ISBN 0 304 93899 8

Printed by Hazell Watson & Viney Ltd, Aylesbury, Bucks

F 1273

LA SERENISSIMA

Contents

Illustrations

Illustrations

Plates not acknowledged are in the author's possession

Preface

Venice in the eighteenth century was a paradox; in some respects an anachronism, in others she was before her time. Her life was prolonged because of the liberty she offered; yet she lost her own freedom because of her alleged tyranny. Her importance may be inferred from the number of foreigners who visited her, attracted by her music, art, pageantry or gallantry. And just as she was quietly declining, deprived of her empire, incapable of protecting herself, she astonished the world with an explosion of energy—intellectual, spiritual, musical and artistic—that has made a unique contribution to civilization. This is the subject of my book.

My task has been made easier by the kindness of Professor Filippo Donini, late of the Italian Institute of Culture, London, whose recommendation opened many doors for me in Italy, and of the various Italian officials in libraries and museums who showed their interest in my problems, especially Professor Zanussi of the Belluno Civic Museum. I also offer special thanks to the authorities of the British Museum and the Victoria and Albert Museum (Libraries and Print Rooms). My publishers have been most helpful and I specially wish to thank Esther Eisenthal for her competent elimination of irrelevant material from the manuscript.

ALFONSO LOWE

San Pedro de Ribas,
Barcelona 1973

Note: The map overleaf shows the eighteenth-century Venetian Republic in the context of Northern Italy today.

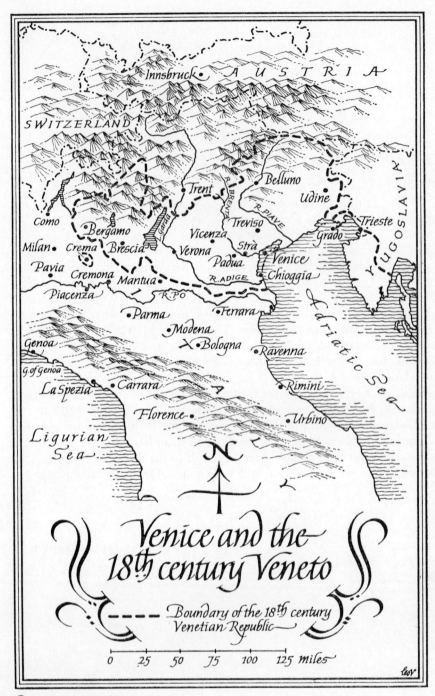

Venice and the
18th century Veneto

- - - Boundary of the 18th century
Venetian Republic

0   25   50   75   100   125 miles

© Cassell & Co Ltd 1974

Part One

THE PEOPLE

I

What went before

Once did she hold the gorgeous East in fee,
And was the safeguard of the West: the worth
Of Venice did not fall below her birth,
Venice, the eldest child of liberty.

Wordsworth's strophe is as concise and accurate as all great poetry. At Nauplia in the Peloponnese you may wander through two Venetian forts, part of a chain that once extended from the Adriatic to Asia. Here, in 1694, died Morosini the conqueror, and with him Venice's last hope of reviving her Eastern Empire. The decline of what had once been the richest Mediterranean power since she helped to destroy Byzantium was only the prelude to a flowering of art and intellect that was but thinly disguised by Venice's superficial frivolity. Beaten by the Turk, envied and hated by the great powers who profited by supplanting her sea-borne commerce, impoverished and alone; 'Yet amid all this', says Brinton, 'the banner of St Mark still floated over Venice and her subject cities, and the form of the great republic, the "Serenissima", remained unchanged. Alone in Italy Venice remained unconquered by the alien, had stood beside Mantua in her hour of agony against the Imperialists, had held their own against Spanish domination; and now, out of this strange fantastic life of pleasure, there comes to bloom a new art which has its own fascination.'

What, we may ask, is the connection between power and culture? Does a state at the peak of the former necessarily attain the zenith of the latter? By no means. Art, Reason and other triumphs of the spirit tend to outlast military and political glory. It was so with Athens, the Carolingian Empire, Caliphate Spain, the France of Louis XIV. The arts may even flourish side by side with a liberty that can fairly be called licence. And so it happened here too: by the eighteenth century, to use Chambers' words, 'Venice was not rising, but on the other hand not sinking . . . .' Existing on a lower level, tapping new sources for her livelihood, she astonished a world that was looking for enlightenment through the mind, rather than through the senses. In an age when the pursuit of happiness was esteemed by philosophers and officially bracketed with life and liberty in an emerg-

3

ing state, she consciously set an example of pleasure that drew admirers to visit her and think of her as a paradise for every class. From the middle of the seventeenth century the government encouraged, as a matter of policy, anything that would attract tourists—splendid theatres, diverting spectacles and unrestrained carnival.[1]

In France the death of Louis XIV had released a frivolous court from its unnatural restraints. Pomp gave way to light-hearted enjoyment of life and, as usual, the mood of man reacted on his environment. Ponderous, over-emphasized Baroque buildings, furniture, pictures and plays yielded to increasing lightness and elegance. Freed from their shackles, the nobles of Versailles celebrated with an exuberance that was reflected in more delicate structure, lighter colours, fragile ornament and looser morals. Along with the reaction against grandiosity came the intellectual revolt against ponderous philosophy, for seemingly arid enquiries into ideas had led insensibly to the study of human relations. Hobbes and Locke made way for Voltaire and Rousseau; behaviour was scrutinized instead of beliefs. The heavy drama of Corneille gave way to Molière and the *Comédie-Française*; Poussin and Lebrun surrendered to Watteau and Fragonard, Boulle to J. A. Meissonier, and orthodoxy to scepticism.

Perhaps the change of outlook spread like an infection from France to the rest of Europe; perhaps conditions everywhere called for it simultaneously. But whatever the mechanism, the Age of Enlightenment and the bright flame of the Rococo had arrived, the latter to reign until it was quenched in blood and mud. In Venice we have the opportunity of seeing the ferment at work in a state which at once had a pleasure-loving population and a reactionary government.

It was not yet the age of the common man, but Venice was the home of the vulgar patrician, the shrewd merchant and the happy-go-lucky workman. Here were no benevolent monarchs to be thanked for their condescension, no restraints of clergy to be circumvented. Without benefit of encyclopaedists the Venetians followed their own path in the pursuit of happiness. Their ideals may have been less than spiritual and their wants material; but the change that was spreading over Europe produced a revival of science and art which has made humanity their debtor. This is not to say that the rest of Italy took no part in the flowering: Rome's Spanish Steps and Trevi Fountain will readily come to the mind of the casual sightseer. But nowhere else was their such a symbiosis of arts, crafts and sciences; only in Venice did material achievement find the literary, dramatic and artistic masters needed to record for our delight this golden interlude. In the century of Watteau, Fragonard, Hogarth, Gainsborough and Reynolds her artists were invited to every corner of Europe; in that of Haydn and Mozart musicians came to Venice to listen; in that of Voltaire, Algarotti became the favourite and counsellor of Frederick the Great; and

4

Canova, like Praxiteles two thousand years before him, earned the plaudits of the civilized world while his republic was sinking to its end. It is tempting to call the period a renaissance; but the term must be regretfully passed over, for there was no consistent attempt to recapture the glories of a classical heritage.[2]

I have mentioned the vulgar patrician. Government was the concern of an upper class, whose families had for centuries been inscribed in the Golden Book. As these grew fewer and the State poorer other families, including nobles from Venice's mainland possessions, the *terraferma*, who were often exempt from taxation, were invited to buy their admission; one such offer, without obligation to buy, was made in 1775 and found only nine who aspired to the honour.[3] New patricians, like the 'New Christians' of Spain, were still looked down on by the others. Another problem was set by the poorer nobles; their families had risen through commerce, they were being submerged through indolence. Living squalidly in the parish of St Barnabas, whence their name '*Barnabotti*', they drew a small government pension which they supplemented by gambling (presumably as bankers at basset or faro), pimping and selling their votes in the Grand Council. And yet, in spite of these obvious defects, the government was a good one and, by comparison with the rest of Italy, singularly good.[4]

Hale stresses the social harmony and the co-operation of all classes that aroused more amazement and more envy than any other feature of the Venetian way of life. Quoting Pullan, he makes it quite clear that there was no social friction between upper and middle classes and that a rudimentary welfare service saw to the comparative contentment of the proletariat. I say 'comparative' advisedly, for, if there was occasional discontent, there was none of the permanent resentment that found its expression in Revolutionary France.

If you consider this praise too qualified, reflect that Louis XIV asked Venice, as the least corrupt uninvolved state, to act as mediator at the conferences which preceded the Treaties of Utrecht (1713) and Rastatt (1714). Her main preoccupation at home was to avoid any form of tyranny, so the Doge himself was a prisoner, even if an almost divine one, and members of the government, however highly placed, were subject to discipline by the Council of Ten. It is unnecessary to detail the forms of government. The nobles, which is to say adult males who were listed in the Golden Book, formed the base of a pyramid; they elected the equivalent of committees for various purposes. The apex was the elected Doge and next to him in rank were the appointed *procuratori*, usually seniors who had deserved well of the State. Their official function was to administer the Basilica of San Marco, but their influence as former office holders or ambassadors was considerable. Rule by a minority class, of which every member could attend 'parliament', was nothing new when it was practised in Athens, where the word 'democracy' was invented; there, though, one must concede in all fairness that the voters amounted to over five per cent of the population, a far larger proportion than in Venice. It is worth recording, however, that when the Council of Ten threatened to become tyrannical, it was in turn brought to obedience. Strict security was always maintained; hence the French ambassador's dispatches used to be opened by the Venetian authorities while Rousseau was employed at the embassy. The swarm of spies which is often mentioned is in all likelihood imaginary: Casanova was the only one for a while though three at a time were employed earlier in the century. The prisons, whose very mention used to inspire a thrill of horror, were almost empty when the Republic fell in 1797; the *Pozzi* or 'wells'—dungeons which we should call 'tombs'— were little used; the 'leads' under the roof of the Ducal Palace were insufferably hot in summer, but Balzac[5] remarked that Paris had 10,000 inhabited attics that were less comfortable. The *Bocche di Leoni*, the stone lions' mouths into which secret denunciations were slipped, were also less sinister than one is led to believe. Unsigned letters were ignored and the rest investigated simultaneously by the three State Inquisitors, who bore no resemblance to those of the Spanish Holy Office. If the charges were not proved the informer was severely punished.

Horror tales may have served to scare potential criminals, or they may have been invented by those who needed to justify the overthrow of Venice. Much misinformation was inspired by an anonymous book, published in 1769 and now attributed to Goudar,* *The Chinese Spy*. In it one may read, 'Silence is the emblem of this government. Everything is secret and mysterious. Politics are shrouded in dense night. Chatterers in Venice are buried alive in a tomb covered with lead. A man who has talked once is condemned to eternal silence . . . it is a great tyranny.'

On the other hand another adventurer, Casanova, an exile since his dramatic escape from his attic prison under the 'leads' of the Doge's Palace, upheld Venice's reputation for liberty when Voltaire disparaged it.[7] A foreign lady confided to Isabella Teotochi Albrizzi that she had a secret fear of the State Inquisitors and a perverse longing to see one; upon which her hostess pointed to her kindly, tranquil husband and said, 'Here's one.'[8]

On the whole, then, government was fairly benign, so long as the subject of politics was avoided. We see the same attitude of cautious tolerance in modern states that rely on tourists for much of their income.

* Angelo Goudar was a well-known Venetian adventurer; 'philosopher and politician, rogue and spy, prolific scribbler who deals with Venice in certain tracts published either anonymously or under the name of the beautiful Sara Goudar, who passed for his wife and was picked up by him in a London tavern and transformed into a lady of taste and fashion.'[6]

6

In her dealings with the Church, La Serenissima made it quite plain who ruled in Venice and, though she would be the last to repudiate the Catholic faith, she was never backward in defining the Church's sphere of influence and in opposing any trespass on her own. The Pope's political power in Venice was therefore negligible and when we read of the Inquisitors it is state officials who are meant.

An aristocratic republic, as Montesquieu called it, had to resort to subterfuge in certain cases. Thus the public arrest of a resisting individual was not allowed,[9] but I know of no case where effective private restraint could not be imposed. Where considered necessary, La Serenissima had powers that extended beyond her frontiers: in 1754 the Council decreed the death of two glass-blowers who had fled to foreign capitals with the secrets of their art. Poison was to be the weapon, but in case it failed the assassins were empowered to use the dagger. This was perhaps the rarest, as well as the most extreme measure taken to preserve respect for the government, rightly regarded as of supreme importance. External appearances were therefore stressed and all patricians had to wear a 'toga' of appropriate colour during sessions and in public; it is even said that no one, of whatever civil condition, could cross the Piazza of San Marco unless wearing a cravat. At the same time, though, sumptuary laws were passed; while the Doge paraded in cloth of gold under a golden umbrella and nobles followed in scarlet silk and purple velvet, women were forbidden to wear jewellery in public after the first year of marriage and were subjected to other, comparable restrictions; it does not surprise us to read that they defied the proclamation and were successful in their revolt.[10] In any case, as aristocrats, they would be immune from the Council of Ten, while prostitutes, regarded as a tourist attraction, were also treated with respect. Politically, in fact, Venice was a model of toleration, long before the English sent to seek instruction for a constitutional government.[11] It may be conceded that in the eighteenth century Venice's system was perhaps not inferior to the British, which was also an oligarchy, though of a different and more elastic kind; but Venice had been a constitutional state for at least two centuries.[12]

Her mainland possessions, the *terraferma*, proved to be of the utmost importance, in that they helped to feed and finance the dying state. They had been conquered by the doges Tomas Mocenigo and Francesco Foscari during the first half of the fifteenth century, against considerable opposition from the Venetian government. Though Vicenza, Verona, Padua and other towns contributed to the welfare of the State and guarded its international trade routes on land, there were disadvantages too; the greatest of these became a matter of life or death and Venice's fall was partly caused by her inability not only to protect her mainland possessions, but to prevent others from fighting their battles on them. Venice anticipated

Clemenceau in believing that war was too serious a matter to be left to soldiers. Her army, in fact, was negligible and her defence remained on the sea, even when her distant possessions had been lost. Though she held aloof from all European disputes in the vain hope that she would thus be permitted to continue existing, she still gave the world examples of her old skill and bravery at sea. In 1716 Corfu was successfully defended against the Turks: in the following year prodigies of valour marked a major engagement at the Dardanelles; another took place off Lemnos, where a Venetian captain Lodovico Flangini beat off a superior force in five hours' combat and then, mortally wounded, ordered his men to carry him up to the quarter-deck, so that he could 'die in battle'. In the last third of the century Angelo Emo bombarded the Barbary ports so thoroughly that the pirates agreed henceforth to respect the Venetian flag. Even in a decadent state the old, proud spirit survived: the inhabitants of Conegliano defied a whole Austrian army when they were accused of sheltering deserters. Galleys, or the galleasses that began to replace them for economy, were manned largely by volunteer rowers, significantly including a number of deserters from the Venetian army. The arsenal still employed 3000 workers but, though Venice possessed 184 men-of-war at the time of her fall in 1797, there was so little work in the shipyards that they were idle except in an emergency, when they would work day and night—for double wages.[13] Their patron saint was most fittingly Noah, whose boat building is illustrated in a mosaic in the narthex of the Basilica of San Marco.

Towards the end of the century such officials as were not too busy gambling and wenching paid attention to reports from abroad that Venice was losing her ancient prestige. Doge Alvise Mocenigo knew that fighting would not save the state; regeneration must begin at the roots, by restoring her ancient prosperity.[14] A treaty with Portugal made the merchant navy free of harbours in the Atlantic; efforts were made to encourage trade with Denmark and Russia; the Doge approached Britain, proposing that Venice be used as a station on her commercial route to the East; a Chamber or Council of Commerce was formed—according to Casanova it was given precedence over the Inquisitors of State—and was instrumental in starting a postal service to Austria and improving transport by road and canal. Reforms of every kind were in the air, from the foundation of technical colleges to the protection of the city against the storms of the Adriatic. One of Venice's most impressive works, in fact, was undertaken and completed between 1774 and 1782: the sandy bar which separated the lagoon from the sea was reinforced by the tremendous walls, or *murazzi*, of Pellestrina. Nor was pride allowed to diminish; the two ambassadors extraordinary who attended the coronation of George III in 1762 were informed that they were to be honoured with knighthood. Learning that this would involve kneeling before the Sovereign, they maintained that it was impossible for two Procurators of St Mark to kneel, except before the Majesty of their own country. But though a few patricians still showed evidence of the old spirit, they could do nothing against the apathy which the pleasure-loving majority opposed to every scheme for improvement. And so *la dolce vita* is blamed for the inevitable end.

Is it possible always to define the causes of an empire's rise and fall? Should we not rather remember that empires have always fallen? And, in the case of Venice, that she remained a world power for six centuries, in contrast to the three of Spain and England, and the two of Holland? To the contention that lax morals and so-called 'degeneracy' are necessarily the preludes to extinction, remember that Rome in the first century of our era is still notorious for the behaviour of profligate emperors and citizens and for pandering to the mob with bread and games. Yet the age of Caligula, Nero and Domitian was but a prelude to the century of the Antonines, of which Gibbon wrote: 'If a man were called to fix the period in the history of the world, during which the condition of the human race was most happy and prosperous, he would, without hesitation, name that which elapsed from the death of Domitian to the accession of Commodus.'

2

Grand Tourists

The stage is Venice and her mainland domain; the time is the turn of the century. The seventeenth, *le grand siècle*, that began with glory for France on the field of battle and the insistent triumphs of literature and Baroque art, has passed away in an atmosphere of boredom. Science still holds out the promise of a better, or at least a more interesting future; kings, the Church, the art of war and other, less destructive, ones, the social order, all appear immutable in the eyes of a weary world. The nobility pass the time in frivolity while philosophers try to explain what is wrong with the world. Of the lower orders it is only natural that the wealthier merchant class should be the first to gain a modicum of respect; hence the eighteenth century is remarkable for the rise of the bourgeoisie. Only at its end did the eruption of the masses in France threaten for a few years to put the proletariat in control of affairs. Until then it was kept obedient by threats or by entertainments (*Plebes novarum rerum cupida*) and, in England at least, by the humanity of such as the Wesleys. In Venice there was at first no social classification other than the entries in the patrician Golden Book and the gentility in the Silver; otherwise the nature of their work distinguished what would formerly have been called guilds—the gondoliers', the shoemakers' and so on. The bourgeois, according to Jonard,[1] alternately supported the nobles of the *terraferma* and the workers, the latter being the first to feel the poverty that accompanied Venice's decline. Travellers all stress the good behaviour and humility (perhaps these meant the same) of the lower classes; most of them recorded their experiences after a few weeks' stay among the patricians. But in the newspapers of the second half of the century we can read of the increase in theft and of insurrections of starving peasants on the mainland.

A truer picture can be gained from the accounts of nobles carelessly spitting out of their theatre boxes on to the occupants of the pit and from reading the works of Goldoni and the Gozzis. It is probable that Jean-Jacques Rousseau learned much when, as secretary to the French embassy, he compared the Venetian government with those of France and Switzerland. Nearly twenty years later his *Social Contract* would call hereditary aristocracy 'the worst of all governments' and would hint at a democracy of *suitable*, but not all citizens. He disagreed with the *philosophes* who were desperately trying to save something of the world of privilege, while Frederick of Prussia, Joseph II in Vienna, Charles III in Madrid and Catherine of Russia all strove to show the virtues of an enlightened despotism. Goldoni was another shrewd observer of life at all levels. When he was fifty and at the height of his powers and popularity, he wrote three plays which brought the middle class into prominence. The same was being done in England by Gay and Lillo, by Hogarth in painting and by Richardson, Fielding and Smollett in the novel.

In *I Rusteghi* Goldoni portrays the eternal bourgeois materialist; he had already satirized the nobility often enough without being detected. Four elderly, middle-class characters are shown, critical pessimists, bad-tempered, argumentative and cross-grained, petty tyrants in their homes. 'When I was a boy,' says one, 'my father asked me, "Would you like me to take you to see the New World★ or would you rather have twopence?" I chose the twopence.' As an observer of everyday life Goldoni is superior even to Pietro Longhi the painter. In his plays, Pantalon† ceases to be the stupid old man, everybody's butt, and becomes the power behind the play, the master who makes his puppets dance. In real life the bourgeois merchant had the calm assurance of the self-sufficient[2] and in the play *Il cavaliere e la dama*, Pantalon, in the part of Anselmo, says: 'Commerce is of use to the world, necessary to the life of nations, and one does not say "plebeian" of him who engages in it honourably, as I do. That man is plebeian who, by inheriting a title and some land, passes his days in idleness and thinks he can trample on the rest of the world while living on his superiority.' But commerce and trade are not always the same and of course the man who sat in the inner office looked down on the man behind the counter.

The government was not insensible of the problem. As early as 1706 public lectures on humanities and sciences were given and the College of Physicians was authorized to confer eight degrees in Medicine each year. Concern with public enlightenment naturally extended to education in the families of the *Barnabotti*, for they would be included among the future rulers, if that is what you can call the equivalent of a member of parliament. Meanwhile the poor were becoming poorer and beggars so numerous that they were an embarrassment to a state desirous of attracting tourists. As Voltaire said of the social strata in England, comparing them with the national drink, 'There is froth at the top, dregs at the bottom, but

★ A diorama portraying the wonders of America. A painting of owner and audience by Gian Domenico Tiepolo hangs in the Ca' Rezzonico.

† Pantaleone was the commonest man's name in Venice, after one of its favourite saints, Pantaleone of Bithynia. When trousers came to Europe from the East, they entered through Venice where they were first worn. The French therefore nicknamed the trousers *pantalons*, whence our 'pantaloons', which survive exiguously as 'pants'.

good in the middle.' And, as the Venetians have always been a softly spoken people and averse from violence, no harm was done by the increasing signs of poverty. For the froth continued to bubble and a minute element of Venice's population sustained her reputation for gaiety and laughter, wantonness and frank misconduct, earned the reproofs of Rousseau and Addison[3] and attracted the largest influx of visitors to descend on a single town since the end of the medieval pilgrimages.

The Grand Tour is first mentioned in 1677[4] but its participants increased in the following century. As the bourgeoisie was becoming more influential, it is clear that they formed an increasing proportion of the visitors. France, Germany and the northern continental states sent their share, but that of England possibly exceeded all the rest together; in fact, according to Levey,[5] it was particularly an English idea. By 1770 '... where one Englishman travelled in the reign of the first two Georges, ten now go on a grand tour. ...' Italy was the country to make for and then, again in Beckford's words, 'straight to Venice'. Germany and France were frequently at war and were sometimes looked at on the way there or back, though the former had appalling inns and merciless taxation, but the goal was still Italy.

Does this not suggest that her studious abstinence from war may have produced in Venice, not only a glut of tourists, but the tranquillity which is possibly the antecedent of many 'renaissances'? If we think of man's spirit as forever striving for, and wars with other calamities as occasionally combating the flowering of genius, may we not regard these 'rebirths' in the light of a resumption of normal human progress? But whether or not it was cause and effect, we know that Venice was at peace, that the arts flowered there as rarely before and that hordes of visitors came to be captivated. Her notable broad-mindedness may also have contributed; it was common knowledge in England, for instance, that Milan was a difficult place for Protestants.

In the eighteenth century Addison was the first English visitor of whom we know, his tour lasting from 1699 to 1704. As befitted a dean's son travelling on a government grant, he disliked foreign 'goings-on'. He disapproved of the French and of much that he saw in Venice. It is possible, of course, that he felt so awe-stricken that he asserted himself by defensive disparagement. We find that the fullest accounts of life in Venice are those of the French visitors, perhaps because they were less inhibited. Montesquieu was there in 1728 and was the first, but not the last to complain that foreigners were charged double for everything. He saw the people of Venice as easy-going; creditors could be put off by threats of a beating when they came dunning. The English especially, but other visitors too, had taken everything from Padua, as well as from the rest of Italy. Practically all that is left are the pictures in the churches; the rich nation takes everything to herself. The President* de Brosses is an observant, as well as an amusing traveller. He reflects the tastes of the age, which held that anything other than Classical was simply barbaric; there is therefore no admiration of Venice's beautiful mansions, less than none of the Basilica of San Marco or of the Doge's Palace and, in Verona, 'San Zeno is worth seeing, if only to appreciate the bad taste of those days'. Apart from his adherence to fashion, he is broad-minded and witty; writing to a friend and referring to the news of the death of a third person's youngest son, he adds, 'I console myself thinking that it is a loss which can be made good in two minutes.' And again, when he is shown an authentic chastity belt in the ducal museum, designed to ensure the honour of the inventor's wife, he adds, '. . . judging by its width, his wife's honour must have been pretty broad'. He is also an observer and credits the Venetians with such sweet and gentle dispositions that their canal bridges are quite safe, even without a handrail. If there is an occasional ducking, it happens to a foreigner who misses the path.

La Lande the astronomer takes us into the second half of the century; he is a thorough materialist, but a reliable witness. His judgment on paintings is worthless by modern standards, but he is one of the few to mention John Law's tomb (of which more later) while it was still in the Church of San Gemignano. One of his anecdotes is also worth repeating: an English 'milord' remained standing in church during Mass; a senator next to him told him that it was not seemly to make himself conspicuous. 'But I don't believe in trans-substantiation' said the Englishman. 'Neither do I', replied the senator, 'but get down on your knees like me or leave the church.'

When Samuel Sharp, and Gibbon[6] a short time after, crossed the Mont Cenis Pass, their coaches were taken to pieces and carried over, and the passengers likewise transported in wicker chairs. A supply of sturdy porters was always available, recruited from the local peasantry and happy to be rewarded with a small coin. The Grand Tour was becoming organized and the souvenirs brought back by earlier travellers undoubtedly helped to swell the numbers. 'There are few gentlemen', writes Small, 'who are not, in some degree, apprized of what they are to expect from the views they have seen of this place, painted by *Canaletti* [sic]. . . .' The English, who were the best customers (as observed by Montesquieu), were especially well treated; they were often lodged in the ducal palace or with patrician families, though the chief hotels, such as the Leon Bianco and Albergo Reale, were highly esteemed; in 1770 a Mrs Miller is recorded[7] as staying in a rented *palazzo*, while many others awaited tenants. Though visitors to Venice included a pope, five kings and five dukes,[8] the Doge himself usually found time to take young Englishmen on a personally

* Of the Dijon Court of Appeal.

conducted tour. Venice was an international meeting place and Horace Walpole tells of his calling on the widow of John Law in 1741. Law, a Scot, had been financial adviser to Louis XIV; his 'system' was simply an anticipation of today's and could easily have succeeded. He was unfortunate in that a rash speculation—in itself no serious matter—led to a run on the bank, which had issued far more paper than he had gold coverage; he had to leave all his possessions and live out his days of poverty in hospitable Venice. He died in 1727.

Law's tomb is under the flagstones of the central nave of San Moisè; on the diamond-shaped surface is carved a Latin inscription, which tells us that the ashes were placed there in 1808 by the *adjutor Napoleoni maximo, gubernator Venetiarum, Alexander Law Lauriston*. Following up, I found that in fact Law's great-nephew, named here, had been Napoleon's aide-de-camp at Marengo and was one of his favourite generals. In 1807 he was made governor of Venice and it was during his governorship that the old Church of San Gemignano, facing the Basilica of St Mark, was pulled down to make way for the new wing of the buildings that almost surround the square, the *ala Napoleonica*. Lauriston must have been informed that his great-uncle's ashes were buried there and personally arranged for them to be transferred. To crown the display of family unity Lauriston died twenty years later in the Place Vendôme house built by his great-uncle in the far-off days of his prosperity.

Walpole calls the widow 'Lady Catherine Law'* and says of John Law, that he had 'an excellent head of him in crayons by Rosalba, the best of her portraits'. I have seen a crayon portrait of the period which shows a young man who could well be Walpole as he was in his early twenties, dressed in Venetian carnival style with the white mask, still secured under the three-cornered hat, resting over his left ear. One would hardly take him for the brilliant letter-writer, though it is easy to imagine a somewhat disdainful attitude and a tendency to pass judgment with little hesitation. We need not be surprised that the chief impression of Venice he has left us is of 'the pestilential air of stinking ditches'; perhaps he was sitting by an open window while Rosalba worked on his portrait. Fortunately for us, this aesthete was an insatiable collector. Strawberry Hill, his fanciful, Neo-Gothic country residence at Twickenham, contained, among other furniture, a printing press. Like other travellers, he delighted in bringing home *objets d'art* to remind him of the Grand Tour. His paintings, furniture and tableware might be Rococo, but they went with the equally ornate late medieval ornamentation and interior decoration.

Another to complain of the smell was Mrs Piozzi, Dr Johnson's Mrs Thrale after her second marriage. The Rialto Bridge and St Mark's

* Law had eloped with Katherine Knollys, daughter of the third Earl of Bunbury, while she was still married to a Frenchman.

Square were 'covered with stinking chicken-coops, and all about the ducal palace is made so very offensive by the resort of human creatures for every purpose most unworthy of so charming a place'. Small has no need to be genteel: the streets are used by the 'nasty fellows' who 'let down their breeches wherever and before whomsoever they please, so that many open parts, including the Piazza and outside the ducal palace, are dedicated to *Cloacina*, and you may see the votaries at their devotions every hour of the day'. Not, one would think, too abnormal a state of affairs in an age when sanitary buckets were carried down the marble stairs of Versailles and English gentlemen kept a chamber-pot in the sideboard, for use before joining the ladies.

Dr Charles Burney, the musician, was not disappointed in his Grand Tour and left valuable reports about the state of music in Venice, as well as a daughter Frances (Fanny, Madame d'Arblay) whose fame has outlived his. Beckford was another helpful observer and I give two excerpts from his letters that are especially shrewd: 'Whether he [a Venetian] visits a Countess, or a courtesan . . . is equally indifferent to the Government of Venice, who have more good sense than to meddle in matters which do not concern the welfare of the state', and 'The art of ruling is to keep the people in good humour and the rulers of Venice are expert in this'. Perhaps the most important visitor, to judge by results in England, was Richard Boyle, third Earl of Burlington. The present Burlington House, seat of the Royal Academy, is the result of a short visit to Venice and the *terraferma*, which aroused his interest and indirectly produced many of Britain's finest country mansions.

Goethe was among the last and brightest lights that fell in love with the city whose buildings seem to rise so eerily from the mirror of the still waters of the lagoon. He, like de Brosses, was steeped in Classicism, reinforced at this late date (1786) by the work of Winkelmann, that left no room for admiring medieval or modern art. Apart from his obsession with Cagliostro and grotesques, he seems to have been of a sentimental turn of mind; he describes movingly how the women on shore sing when they see the fishing fleet bringing their husbands back in the evening, and how the stanzas, sung alternately by men and women, carry far over the still waters. One cannot but think of 'Moby Dick': '. . . in Salem, where they tell me the young girls breathe such musk, their sailor sweethearts smell them miles off shore. . . .'

Horace Walpole could sneer at 'those learned patrons of taste, the Czarina, Lord Clive, or some Nabob . . .' and at Boswell, who did not omit Venice from his lustful tour. His vindictive side serves to introduce us to Lady Mary Wortley Montagu. This aristocratic and intelligent woman had lived half her life before she came to Venice. La Serenissima sheltered many from pursuit; in this case it harboured her quarry.[9]

Francesco Algarotti was Venice's leading representative in the Age of Enlightenment; she met him in England when she was nearly twice his age; there was a short but passionate (at least on her side) love affair and Algarotti left for Venice. After three years she followed him, only to find that he had left for Prussia. Nevertheless she stayed in Venice for a year; she established a salon there and experienced the kindness and good taste of the Venetians. She found living cheap and entertainment abundant, even in the absence of a lover; box-owners in every theatre in Venice made her welcome. She was as enchanted with the attentions paid her by the Venetian ladies as she was bored by the English who passed through on the Grand Tour, particularly the men, of whom she wrote, 'Inundations of them this carnival; their whole business to buy new clothes.'

Horace Walpole's scurrilous lines addressed to her coach and his description of her when they met in Florence take us too far from our subject; but we may remember that the doggerel was written shortly after he had enjoyed her hospitality.[10] For those who like to peep at the end of a story I may add that she and Algarotti lived together for two months in Turin, when she was fifty-two; they quarrelled and parted and sixteen years later she wrote of him sarcastically and possibly astutely, 'A. is at Bologna, I believe, composing panegyrics on whoever is victor in this uncertain [i.e. Seven Years'] war'. 'Horry' Walpole's malice is usually accounted for in one of two ways: that Lady Mary was one of the many who spread the rumour that he was illegitimate; or that she had befriended Miss Skerrit, who had supplanted Walpole's mother and whom the first Earl of Orford duly married after his first wife died.

But it is unnecessary to continue the long register of those who made the Grand Tour; so many that Dr Johnson once remarked wistfully, 'A man who has not been in Italy is always conscious of an inferiority.' Those who could afford to travel made for Italy, and those who arrived in Italy made haste to reach Venice. Such was their pride in having visited this queen among cities that there was '. . . a great output of fakes of Titian, Tintoretto, Veronese and others to satisfy people on the Grand Tour, who like to come home with "genuine" works of art, many of them by sons of the famous.'[11]

It is only fitting, in view of the large proportion of British tourists, that the leading patron of arts of eighteenth-century Venice should be an Englishman, Consul Joseph Smith. The details of this remarkable man's Venetian career are summed up by Adrian Eeles, whose note deserves to be quoted at some length.

Joseph Smith was one of the greatest collectors of the eighteenth century. He was responsible for amassing an outstanding group of works by Canaletto* and for this reason alone his life and character deserve a short notice.

Joseph Smith was born in about 1676.... Some time at the beginning of the eighteenth century he settled in Venice, was apprenticed to the Consul, Thomas Williams, and apparently earned his living as a merchant and banker. All through his life he had a keen interest in finance and it is clear that he was a successful businessman.... Smith's first passion was book collecting. He was interested not only in collecting old books if they met with his fastidious standards, but also in contemporary book production in Venice.† To this end he launched the publisher G. B. Pasquali and gave constructive support to the production of fine books, many of them illustrated. In the years before 1730 he was also buying paintings by contemporary Venetian artists such as Rosalba Carriera, Sebastiano Ricci, Marco Ricci and G. B. Piazzetta.

Smith not only commissioned works for his own collection, but also acted as agent for other patrons.... After 1740 when the number of Canaletto's commissions diminished, Smith filled the breach by commissioning the series of views of Rome.... Also at this time Smith ordered the thirteen decorative overdoors. The series of etchings are also dedicated to him.‡ Directly and indirectly, Smith had proved himself to be Canaletto's most assiduous patron. When the artist left Venice in 1746, Joseph Smith sent word to Owen McSwiney in London, asking him to help Canaletto to find employment. Indeed it might have been Smith who, having given substantial support to Canaletto in difficult years, suggested that a journey to England would be profitable.

In 1744 Smith was appointed consul. By this time he was a well-known figure in Venetian society. His palace on the Grand Canal, housing a unique collection of books, gems, paintings and drawings, was open to any visitor sufficiently curious. He had many acquaintances and yet few people liked him. Contemporary diarists like Horace Walpole§ and Lady Mary Wortley Montague [sic] were consistently critical of him (resentment, perhaps, that a tradesman should have such good taste?).[12]

The rest of the account describes how negotiations for the sale of his collection were begun with the Prince of Wales, then aged eighteen, and completed in 1764, after the purchaser had become George III. It now forms part of the Royal Collection at Windsor. Smith lived to be well over ninety and was buried in the Protestant cemetery on the Lido. His

* Now in the Royal Collection at Windsor. A.L.
† De Brosses mentions rare incunabula. A.L.
‡ There is a complete series in the Carrara Academy, Bergamo. A.L.
§ Who called him 'The Merchant of Venice'. A.L.

grave survives in a poor state of preservation, having escaped the fate of the rest of the cemetery, which was incorporated in the airport. Goethe found it and wrote, 'To him I owe my copy of Palladio and I offered up a grateful prayer at his unconsecrated grave. . . .' He adds that it was half buried in sand and soon no one would be able to find it. I am glad to add that Her Majesty's British Consul has launched a fund for the preservation and removal to a more suitable place of his predecessor's grave, for he seems to have been a remarkable man, gifted with both artistic apprecia-tion and shrewdness. Thus, when the Venetian government banned the export of works of art for a while, Smith exported the artist, Canaletto, to England.* This, at least is how it strikes me.

The Windsor Collection by no means exhausts the list of Smith's works of art. In the catalogue of a sale at 125 Pall Mall, formerly the premises of the Royal Academy, on 10 December 1789, we read of paintings 'of a gentleman, long resident in Italy, purchased from the celebrated collection of Joseph Smith, Esq., late British Consul at Venice'.[13] Molmenti says that Smith employed Giovanni Sasso and Luca Breda to restore canvases and that he especially encouraged new artists. (The official restorer of canvases was Pietro Edwards, a frame-maker who opened his own studio in the Monastery of SS Giovanni e Paolo in 1728. The name, but not the man, crops up again in our story after many years.) With regard to Smith's detractors: we must remember that works of art fetched a high price, that he often had to gamble on the strength of his judgment and that at least once he was known to be in low water. I see no reason to grudge him any fortune he may have made. He was a worthy representative of a country whose travellers were foremost in appreciating the arts, in a city which at the time was outstanding in their production.

---

* But it is possible that the ban applied only to the Old Masters.

3

Daily Life

The reader will have concluded that accounts of daily life in Venice during the eighteenth century are many, but that those written by visitors are liable to be one-sided. I shall take Molmenti as representative of the Venetian historians' views about the lower classes, and Bailly of the French. Both, of course, have had access to the same sources and differences may therefore be attributed to prejudice. Bailly, for instance, regards Venice as decadent and fossilized, intent only on preserving her mode of government, and wants to explode the myth of a docile, sweet-tempered proletariat. It is agreed by all that the government was determined to preserve the old order, but it seems more likely that the populace in the city (but not necessarily in the *terraferma*) was equally conservative and proud of their nation. It is not only in the upper classes in most countries that the champions of liberty find opponents; they meet them also, and in greater numbers, among the very class they propose to liberate.

In Venice it is true that some of the proletariat's apparent contentment arose from the lavish entertainment they were offered; but it is usually French authors who draw attention to this and stress the tyranny of the oligarchs, as though to excuse the republican rape of the Serenissima. They often ignore the fact that the French republican general had already sold her secretly to a far more despotic state. Molmenti, however, pictures town life in Venice as that of 'a great family that never left the house; the canals and *calli* were its corridors, the little squares its anterooms, and the larger squares its saloons. . . .'[1] The impression he leaves is indeed that of a cosy family more occupied with its day to day activities than with questions of state or with class-conscious resentment. Whom are we to believe? The only factor that might sway our judgment is Molmenti's obvious, profound acquaintance with the Venetian dialect, which is recorded as used in the streets, the shops, the home, the theatre and even the Senate; against this it is only fair to add that Jonard and other Frenchmen seem to know it too, rely on many Italian sources and show the love of Venice which affects all who study her history and achievements. We cannot quarrel with Jonard when he remarks that most travellers arrived in Venice with their ideas ready-made, without the time to learn the

Venetian dialect nor the opportunity of being received by a patrician family. But this, he continues, does not stop them giving their opinion on a city through which they have passed hurriedly, guide-book under arm. Again, we have to discount human foibles in our informers. Casanova, a son of the people if ever there was one, who bluffed his way into every class of society and became an insufferable snob, writes about France, of '. . . the best society, except, however, that of some provinces where the nobility, whom one mistakenly calls good society, allows its character-istic hauteur to be broached a little too much'.[2]

Even contemporary Venetian observers may be unconsciously pre-judiced. Jonard draws attention to the *Gazzetta Veneta* of Count Gaspare Gozzi, a conscious imitation of the much admired *Spectator* of Addison. The latter's remarks about Venice make it clear that he regarded criticism as part of an essayist's duties, and so Gozzi, too, felt that he must criticize. Again, Gozzi was a member of the poorer aristocracy and had therefore been brought up to think of himself, his family and his friends as apart from the masses. Did any patrician ever forget that his family was inscribed in the Golden Book?

When we read travellers' letters and the numerous books that describe eighteenth-century Venice, it is important to keep in mind that ninety-nine per cent of the writing deals with the activities of one per cent of the population. To use Voltaire's simile again, though the froth provides the material for what follows in this chapter, the makers of the last flowering were drawn largely from the beer in the middle; a few from families in the Silver Book but most from below. Strangely enough to our minds, even Molmenti devotes nineteen pages of his chapter on family life to the patricians and only five to the rest. This introduction is an attempt to put into their proper perspective the many accounts of life in Venice which I quote. The famous 'liberty' (or licence) of Venice that is so often referred to may after all be nothing more than the shop front dressed to attract the customers.

Another complication which we could well consider now arises from the accepted and much repeated belief that the fall of Venice was the result of a century of immorality. I have always thought it strange that, if Venice's downfall was the direct consequence of *la dolce vita*, the judgment of Heaven should need at least four generations to get going. It would be as reasonable to maintain that Austria's decline into a third-class power in 1918 was the result of the 'immoral' waltz that entertained the Congress of Vienna in 1814. Later I came across Damerini's political explanation of this facile, puritanical view:

Meanwhile there occurred a remarkable event. After the fall of Napoleon the Austrian government, for obvious reasons, were not disposed to associate themselves with a public opinion born of French accounts; they had even favoured, at the early collapse of the Italian Kingdom [that of Napoleon], the rebirth in Venice of a consciousness of its splendid past, attributing to Napoleon all the responsibility for the suppression of the Venetian Republic. Since this showed that Venice had not deserved its fate politically, there was born the critical view that sought for the cause in the debased private and public behaviour of the eighteenth century.

The Austrian government had nominated Cardinal Flangini as Patriarch of Venice—the same who had been one of the most vociferous critics of private life and had procured the closing of the gambling halls in the eighteenth century. Hence the gradual adoption of the idea that saw the Venetian Gomorra punished by God.

In the mind of the foreigner eighteenth-century Venice was a topsy-turvy world where features were concealed by masks for half the year; where the gondola assumed the offices of sedan chair, link boy and house of assignation; where entertainment, flirtation and possibly more could be sought in convents, while courtesans contributed to the feast of reason; where the Most Serene Republic (feminine) annually wedded the Sea (neuter in Latin, masculine in Italian) with a ring in token of real and perpetual mastery. 'By the eighteenth century', says Phillips, 'Venice had parted with her old nobility of soul and enjoyment had become the only aim of life. . . . She had become the city of pleasure . . . the convents boasted their *salons*, where nuns in low dresses, with pearls in their hair, received the advances of nobles and gallant abbés. . . .' 'There is no hour of the twenty-four in which the town seems perfectly still and quiet', writes Mrs Piozzi, for market produce arrived from 3 to 6 a.m. and gondoliers were rowing their employers home from 6 to 8. She ends with: '. . . this gay and gallant city, so often described, so certainly admired—seen with rapture, quitted with regret. Seat of enchantment! headquarters of pleasure, farewell!' And Monnier describes '*la population de fête: poètes et parasites, perruquiers et usuriers, virtuoses, filles galantes, ballerines, comédiennes, croupiers de banque,*★ *courtiers d'amour, tout ce qui vit du plaisir ou l'alimente*'. Or again: 'One works when spare time allows it, in the empty hours, between diversions, among noise and crowds, in a little café facing San Giorgio Maggiore, in the wings of a theatre, where one dips one's pen in an old rouge pot, or between a bottle of Tokay and a packet of Spanish tobacco, like da Ponte, who in this way produced three opera libretti in sixty-three days. . . .' Behind all this we can still perceive

---

★ Somewhat suspicious. Patricians alone were allowed to undertake this task in the *Ridotto* and could never have been identified in the street. A.L.

another topsy-turvy world, that of a bombastic pride,* of patricians walking the Broglio, that third of the Piazzetta nearest the Doge's Palace, while suppliants kiss their sleeves (hence *imbroglio* from the intrigues that started in this way). We read accounts of patricians who supplement their income by smuggling (Montesquieu) and yet give punctual and unremitting attention to the affairs of state (Piozzi), and of patricians who leave the council chamber with one arm already out of their toga, the more quickly to don mask and domino.

The carnival was the quintessence of all that was light-hearted, frivolous, carefree and vicious. We can understand the confusion in the mind of a Turkish sailor who had seen it end on Ash Wednesday. 'The poor Christians', he said, 'are crazy and almost actually mad till they find a grey powder which they put on their heads to restore their senses.'[3]

The *cavaliere servente* represents a strange episode in Italian manners and customs. It is not essentially Venetian, as claimed by Bailly; in fact the cult (for that is what it was) came to Italy through the Spanish possessions, Naples and Milan, and seems to stem from the exaggerated courtesy that Cervantes satirized, among other affectations. The cicisbeo, as he came to be called (though less in Venice than elsewhere) was a man, usually young, who attends to a married woman not his wife, and is treated like a tame, and usually doctored, cat. La Lande thought that the custom safeguarded the virtue of the woman; others only go so far as to say that it allowed her to be unfaithful to two men. He is usually pictured as a scented dandy, content to be at his mistress's beck and call and busy with every activity from exercising her lap dog to lacing her stays. He might be petted or even kissed, much as a woman may pet and kiss a tame cat, but there familiarity usually ended. When de Brosses enquired in 1739 he was told that only about fifty cicisbei had relations with their lady; as a matter of fact it was far more usual for him to seduce the lady's maid, while the lady consoled herself with the hairdresser.[4] Casanova[5] had a fellow prisoner in the 'leads' who was a hairdresser; he was imprisoned for seducing the daughter of a great noble.

Lady Mary Wortley Montagu, however, wrote, 'The lady grants what one naturally thinks he asks for, and the occasion presents itself very frequently; for the husband dare not show the slightest suspicion of jealousy.' More likely, the husband was acting as *cavaliere servente* to another's wife. Jonard is probably right when he points out that marriages had been arranged between a young man and a convent-bred girl. Love played no

* In the print room of the Ca' Rezzonico in Venice is an illuminated book of this period, dedicated to the *Serenissimo Principe*, the Doge, and containing such sentences as '. . . that the near and remote nations, even if not included in your wide dominion over earth and sea, are nevertheless turned to the Veneration of your Majesty'.

part in a business contract of this kind and it was only right that a young woman should have a man to fetch and carry, to escort her out-of-doors and to be seen with her at the café or theatre. In Goldoni's *Il cavaliere e la dama* she even says, 'It isn't done to ride in a carriage without a gentleman to escort one', and when the servant comes and is told that she didn't summon him, he announces a visitor. 'Who?' 'Don Alonso would like to present his respects.' 'Idiot! The *cavaliere servente* has no need to be announced.' And so she is served, from her rising at noon to the brink of bed—but usually no further—early next morning. Goldoni himself may have had a bad memory, for in *La casa nova* he makes the old man say, 'Respectable married women don't go about without their husbands', but when he got to Paris he seemed astonished that husbands and wives went out together. Goldoni's rival, Carlo Gozzi, on the other hand,[6] makes it clear that a jealous and loving husband would never be a party to *serventismo* and Diehl then counters by maintaining that a husband would have been ridiculed if he appeared in public with his own wife. It seems that the custom may have been limited to a small part of the upper class and would-be upper class, but where it obtained it became an official arrangement and Constantini[7] quotes a marriage contract in which the lady is entitled to the services of four cicisbei.

Dr Sharp would have none of these fanciful accounts of the innocent nature of *serventismo*. His robust British common sense made him most suspicious of the custom and he guessed that many became *cavalieri serventi* because it was cheaper than visiting the diminishing number of prostitutes. O excellent Dr Sharp! Indeed, to the pure all things are impure. It was on this very question that La Lande took issue with Dr Sharp, whose criticisms (I may be misunderstood if I call them strictures) he attributed to black bile, jealousy and insularity. Cicisbeism was for the sake of decency out of doors and the woman often has little taste for her cicisbeo, who takes no liberties. He sometimes even complains to the husband of the wife's indifference. Surely this last conflicts with La Lande's argument? This will serve to warn the reader that much which is untrue has been written about eighteenth-century Venice.

It has, for instance, been thought that ladies found their confessor a convenient antidote to the charms of their cicisbeo and this brings us to the licentiousness that has been attributed to the Venetian clergy of the time. There is no doubt that they were a strange assortment, but so they were elsewhere; we have no reason to suppose that living in Venice made them less virtuous, only more obvious. Molmenti's examples range from family chaplains employed as domestic servants to tonsured dandies; perhaps this is why marriages were commonly performed (at least in Goldoni's plays) by the couple holding hands in the presence of witnesses, the priest being an afterthought. Among the *Barnabotti*, where there were several brothers it was usual for only one to marry, to avoid dispersing the little patrimony that was left. That all the brothers might share the wife is understandable for in this way family succession was assured; but that the youngest should normally be the bridegroom is explicable only by the primitive rite of ultimogeniture.[8]

Of women's morals there is much to be repeated and some to be believed. Our authorities lick their lips and plunge into an account of sexual morals, forgetting that immorality includes such transgressions as slander and cheating at cards. Apart from these authors' neglect of all classes except the froth, they tell us too little about women's places in government and society; that they were not behind their menfolk in sampling extra-marital pleasures may be taken for granted. Have they ever been? Monnier recounts how women used to spy on every activity, from the Senate down to the freemasons' lodges, and used their knowledge to influence magistrates and become intriguers. At the café, in bed, at their *casini*,* even on the bidet,[9] so it is said, they exercised their influence in every sphere, from government edicts to university appointments. Their defence was that they had a passionate desire to learn, and certainly women in the eighteenth century everywhere played a leading part in encouraging knowledge. Goldoni, that most acute observer, remarks in his memoirs that women, who had formerly read little, had a liking for *The Spectator* and were beginning to become philosophers. Whether the politically inquisitive were the same patrician women as those whose sexual morals are so often impugned is another matter; certainly Molmenti, champion of Venetian society, states that few of the patrician women were dissolute and among the latter does not include any of the 'bluestockings'. Of the few whose *casini* were closed by the State Inquisitors for loose conduct, none figure as *letterate*.

The eighteenth century saw women enjoying a freedom that their mothers had never known and Mrs Piozzi mentions their immunity from household drudgery and their sweet manner in such a way that one feels that she connects the two. Instead of strict surveillance at home and the wearing of high pattens (*zoccoli*) out-of-doors, necessitating a supporter on either side, they wore the more convenient ('much too convenient' commented one suspicious nobleman) low shoes. The mask and domino guaranteed anonymity for half the year and a gondola with the *felse* coupé-top saw to the rest. Perhaps jealous of the fame of the courtesans and the respect often accorded them, some wives of patricians plunged into licence with all the enthusiasm of a duckling having its first swim.

* Two- or three-roomed apartments near the cafés of the Piazza, where receptions and conversaziones were held. When gambling halls were closed play continued at the *casini*. They seem to have taken the place of the salon and might have been designed to avoid having to ask people into one's home—a signal mark of honour in Mediterranean countries. They were also used, it is scarcely necessary to add, for assignations.[10]

Accounts do not suggest that they felt any guilt, any more than did their menfolk for reciprocal activities; in fact they treated both life and its creation as a series of frivolous episodes.

Scandal after scandal disfigures the records of the State Inquisitors, who were charged with the maintenance of order and decency, but there is no record of warnings or confinement to home having any effect. On the contrary, as the century grew older the women grew bolder: 'The blonde patrician beauty, Angela [usually spelled Angiola] Tiepolo, the mistress of da Ponte, was attractive, impish, petulant and unfaithful in character', wrote Molmenti.[11] Cecilia Zeno Tron, according to the same author, seemed 'ever gay and ignorant of all that is bitter and harsh in life'; popular amusement at the ladies' goings-on seems to have made use of an obscene word to end a stanza; so, when Cecilia sold her theatre box at San Benedetto, a wit composed a rhymed epigram that left only one word to the imagination: 'Clever La Trona sells her box for more than her . . . .', to which she replied, 'You're quite right, for sometimes I make a present of the latter.' In diaries and letters, over and over again, we read of these light-hearted, kind-hearted ladies, avid of pleasure into their old age—La Trona, Lucieta, La Benzona for whom the vastly popular air '*La biondina in gondoleta*' was composed, and many more. 'Fine porcelain' the Prince of Denmark called them. De Bernis, the French ambassador, had a high opinion of the witty Caterina Barbarigo, whom he had met only twice; on his departure she told him, 'Be assured, Ambassador, that I shall remain ever constant to you and never faithful.'*

The professionals were also changing, possibly as a result of amateur competition. Though a few of the more expensive continued to ply their trade, there are few reports of their owning palaces as in the previous century. But as their numbers and social standing fell, so their fame attracted ever more visitors, even including foreign princes; as late as the beginning of the eighteenth century, though, a few courtesans held salons where wit and conversation provided them with an agreeable break in their working hours, and there are mentions of some attending church, or simply strolling in the most sumptuous dress. Others would wear their finest raiment and jewellery to lean out of the window and attract custom. One such, who found the opposite balcony conveniently near, kept up a merry conversation with the priest who occupied it, tapping his nose with her fan from time to time to emphasize a point, in full view of four thousand people. De Brosses, who tells this story, seems to have had the true scientific spirit of enquiry, for he adds that this girl had a dagger in her bag; one of Rousseau's finds kept a pair of pistols in case a customer should be lacking in proper respect. But in spite of their decline, most

---

* The date agrees with Casanova's account of a de Bernis, French ambassador, a *voyeur* with whom he shared a nun as mistress.

chroniclers—or at least most honest ones—found the girls charming and even adorable. Rousseau was very ashamed of himself when, visiting the beautiful Zulietta, he recoiled on observing that one of her nipples was inverted. After a pause and looking out of the window without the slightest sign of annoyance, she simply said, 'Zanetto, leave women alone and study mathematics.'

By 1728, according to Montesquieu, the number of prostitutes had fallen to 10,000, though at one time there had been up to 25,000. He attributed this to a drop in visitors, from 35,000 to 150, a figure that is not borne out by other observers. But de Brosses confirmed that the girls were few, except during carnival, when they called up the reserves and under the arcades of the Piazza di San Marco 'one may see as many on their backs as on their feet'. In addition, he said, there were upwards of five hundred 'commissioners of love' in the Piazza, who invited the passer-by to visit the wife of Senator X or patrician Y; and had even heard of husbands being offered a visit to their own wives. Among the cream of the harlots de Brosses professed the greatest regard for Ancilla who was also, he said, a favourite of the King of Naples. From Casanova, himself an appreciative customer, we learn that Ancilla became mistress of the British resident, John Murray, Joseph Smith's brother-in-law by his second marriage. Ancilla is described as dying of syphilis (though the symptoms suggest consumption with tuberculous laryngitis and possibly tuberculosis of the skin) and asking Murray to make love to her within a quarter of an hour of her death. The dauntless Briton not only complied, but did so in Casanova's presence.[12] Thus died the most elegant and beautiful of Venice's courtesans.

La Lande thought the lower types hideous and warned that female dancers, though debauched and cheap, were dangerous. It is interesting to read that actresses were usually respectable, being often married women and in any case earning enough on the legitimate stage.

The convents were a convenient target for every callow visitor who thought it strange that nuns should wear well-cut clothes, jewellery and even cosmetics. That they had a parlour in which they could talk to visitors from behind a grille was still stranger, as was the possibility of attending receptions there, hearing opera or just watching a Punch-and-Judy show. Some are pictured with short but well-dressed hair; there are also reports of hair that had been allowed to grow to normal length.[13]

Let us study a few facts: first, that Italian allegations of loose conduct in convents were few; secondly, that foreigners who saw them as haunts of vice were sometimes guilty of other anti-Catholic sentiments; thirdly, that only half of the thirty-four or -five convents in Venice were open to visitors; fourthly, that many convents sheltered a number of débutantes whose parents were unable to find the money necessary to marry them off into a good family and provide for the sons as well, and who therefore had no sense of vocation, only of deprivation;* and lastly, that convent life was not necessarily a penitential one. We think of Spain, where the nuns of Las Huelgas entertained distinguished visitors in the fourteenth century with singing and dancing, and even of St Teresa who set the nuns dancing with castanets on feast days. Before her reforms the Carmelite nuns of Spain used to entertain friends in their parlours, give concerts and wear jewellery. Of course, in Venice there was loose conduct too and recounting it may have helped to sell books. Casanova, expert though unreliable witness, said that one could have any nun in Venice for the right sum and told of his love affair with the nun who was the mistress of the French ambassador, probably embellishing the story of Maria da Riva,[14] who did run away, first with a French ambassador and later with an Italian colonel. There is no denying that some nuns were known to have had lovers whom they saw frequently, and that they habitually left their convents in disguise and attended carnival jollities masked. It is most unlikely, however, that the spiritual authorities were parties to such behaviour and de Brosses' tale of the three convents who disputed the privilege of providing a mistress for the papal nuncio is too typical of a witty Frenchman of the Age of Enlightenment to be taken seriously. I can only add that, if the story is true, the nuncio must have been an austere one to be content with one mistress when he could have had three.

---

* The case of Arcangela Tarabotti, who was forced to enter a convent in 1616 at the age of eleven, is often quoted. Of her writings, the earlier show how frustrating the life was for the unwilling bride of Christ; the later date from the days when she had become religious and could extend some consolation to other unhappy maidens.

4

A Diversity of People

Details of social life can be ascertained with a fair degree of accuracy. We know that the wealthiest families lived in 'palaces' even though only a portion of the huge building may have been occupied, except for receptions; others used only a single floor. Going round the corner to the post office to see if there were any letters was apparently a part of daily life, or at least seems so in Goldoni's plays, and there were various depots for posting home and foreign mail. Transport inside the city was by gondola, private in the case of the wealthy. Severe sumptuary laws curtailed the use of colour and decoration, so that by the eighteenth century the gondola had assumed the sombre appearance that we see in the view painters' pictures—and up to this day.

For travellers, inns in Venetian territory, as elsewhere in Europe, could be good in cities and were usually bad elsewhere. Bread and wine, even though the former was made of fine, white flour, was 'detestable', or at least not to the taste of de Brosses, but French cooking had been adopted in the previous century, in spite of the usual protests from conservatives who held that people could be masked but not food. Mrs Piozzi gives us more detail, from the sale of ducks and chickens by public auction, the availability of sturgeon (though it seems likely that she confused this with tunny fish) and turbot, to the fried liver, 'sad stuff in Venice', she says, though it is usually thought delicious today. Eating and drinking habits have, however, changed considerably and today we should be astonished to hear a Frenchman commend the Canary wine after the soup and the Burgundy with his dessert.

Coffee played a great part in the social life of the time. Trease reminds us that the Venetians had pioneered its use in Europe a century earlier and that coffee houses were established as early as 1640; this was hardly in advance of England, for coffee was imported direct by the East India Company and in Queen Anne's reign there were over five hundred coffee houses in London. In Venice, as in England, they became the haunt of gamblers and the century achieves a certain renown from the opening of the two which every tourist knows today—Florian's (1720) and the Quadri (1775), both in St Mark's Square. Giorgio Quadri, though a late arrival, at least had the distinction of first serving genuine Turkish coffee, whose preparation he had probably learned in his native Corfu. It was customary for the ladies with their cicisbei to assemble for morning chocolate after midday, until, that is, they were forbidden by law; but by 1786 the regulation had become so unpopular that women were once more allowed to enter coffee houses. Here they could join in conversation with the wittiest and most learned of their fellow citizens or listen to the latest sensation, such as the frenzy which accompanied the squabbles of Goldoni, Carlo Gozzi and Chiari. Official closing hours were introduced in 1777 so that others might meet in taverns and discuss current problems over glasses of Malmsey* and the more learned might meet in a book shop or pharmacy, in which latter they might renew the family stock of theriac. A favourite household remedy in Italy, *triaca* might be made or imported in Venice or, as some preferred, be brought from Orvieto.†

The calendar was crowded with entertainment. Carnival, Ascension Day, the Fair; opportunities for distraction followed each other from October till May. Then, on 12 June, to allow a day for travelling to Padua to attend the celebrations for St Anthony's day, or, as others say, because the canals began to stink, the great exodus began. The *villeggia-tura*, or summer holiday, was passed by the rich in their country villas, of which about 130 were in use. Many of them are still open for our admiration and we can see how their owners encouraged the arts of architecture, sculpture, horticulture and topiary. Part of their pleasure was the trip up the Brenta Canal and River, whose banks are still lined with sumptuous dwellings, or beyond, where the vines were trained like creepers up and along the trees of orchards. Life at the villa was an extension of the carnival, except that masks were not worn. All night parties were common, guests could drop in without warning and even adventurers were welcome if they had an idea of the social graces and especially if they were amusing. Fifty guests at 'pot luck' were not unusual and a curious custom arose of serving dinner on three separate tables, soup and entrée on the first, main dishes on the second, fruit and sweetmeats on the third.

In holiday time there was no longer any attempt at disguise: life was for gaiety and amusement, music and gambling, dancing and love-making. Bread and wine were distributed to the poor who patiently waited outside, attracted by the sounds of revelry, and in many cases money was

---

* Malvasia, a sweet wine exported from one of Venice's last possessions in Greece, Monemvasia.

† Mithridates VI, King of Pontus, gradually accustomed his system to numerous poisons and their antidotes, so that finally he was taking a compound of more than sixty ingredients every day. This 'treacle' became a household remedy (Culpepper in 1653 called 'treacle mustard' by the alternative name, 'Mithridate mustard'). Treacle is simply the English rendering of *triaca*; we can now understand why it was given as a medicine, along with brimstone (sulphur). The Orvieto brand of *triaca* was sold in the streets of Venice and referred to by French writers as '*orviétan*'.

thrown among them. Mazzotti[1] tells us how an operetta by Ginnasio Gavardo Vacalerio illustrates the frivolity of the holiday season. Its title was *L'Arcadia in Brenta, ovvera la melinconia sbandita* (Arcady in Brenta, or Melancholy banished) and the characters are sailing, or being towed up the Brenta in the *burchiello*, a craft that used to ply between Fusani and Padua; it has recently been revived, with canned music and built-in horsepower, for summer visitors. Though many patricians preferred to go by coach, the *burchiello* protected one from sun, dust and bumping over pot-holes, and offered the additional comforts of tapestries, pictures, mirrors and closets; many well-known foreigners found the *burchiello* pleasant and convenient, and some Italians too, among them Goldoni and Casanova. The operetta had no need to exaggerate, for it was usual for the passengers to render impromptu concerts on the cabin roof at night. Fortunate people, born too late for Venice's wars and too early for mechanical noise, gliding over the silent water with food, wine and music to sustain them, while villa after villa swam into view with windows emitting the lights of candelabra and strains of dance music to alternate with their own. So popular was the time and place, in fact, that the French ambassador was persuaded to pay twice the normal rent for a villa on the Brenta; 'swindled', Rousseau called it.

Apparently, stink or no, many returned to the city for August and September, resuming the *villeggiatura* from the fourth of October until the middle of November, by which time carnival had already started. This was the season for shooting and Venice was again emptied of its patricians. So much so, in fact, that when the poet Angelo Maria Labia was asked at what period Venice had been best governed, he replied 'during the *villeggiatura*'.

The common people of course greatly outnumbered the patricians and their families and, though we learn little about them from travellers' diaries, we may fill the gap in our knowledge by studying official edicts, genre paintings and contemporary plays. They too enjoyed their country holidays, shorter it is true, and cheaper, but apparently far more to our taste. Picnics and excursions for some; country villas, though modest ones, for the merchant class who, once a year and away from the city, allowed themselves to ape the manners of the patricians. Goldoni's *Le smania per la villeggiatura* shows up their snobbishness. Here the lady whose servant advises abandoning the *villeggiatura* as a measure of economy replies, 'It's easy to see that you are a nobody' and makes fun of those who sell cloth or cheese over the counter for most of the year and then blossom out in the country as vulgar imitators of the patricians, with the same flirting, dancing, story-telling and gambling. So much for Goldoni, but we must remember that the bourgeois despised the tradesman (as happened in Britain well into this century) and that his remarks illuminate his own snobbery more than theirs. But for the rest of the year they lived quietly at home, keeping their families from mixing outside their class.

A step down the social scale and we are among the artisans, sailors, gondoliers and small shopkeepers. Mrs Miller[2] was most impressed by the milliners and grocers. Nevertheless, in this rigid society we can detect the universal desire to improve status. 'He has a little money of his own—enough to buy himself a position' says one of Goldoni's characters; titles of honour gradually depreciated, as has done our 'Esquire', and shopkeepers called themselves '*Illustrissimo*' and bought titles when they had saved enough money.

Molmenti[3] gives us a pen picture of what must have enthralled the foreigner on his first tour of the city. 'The air was full of strange tongues, and above all rose the harmonious dialect of Venice. The doctor hurrying to the bedside of a patient, the artisan on his way to the arsenal or the workshop, the gondolier making for his traghetto, passed in the crowd the Armenian selling galengale roots [*bagigi*], the Turk with a huge turban, the Albanian in baggy breeches, the Jew in his long gaberdine. The noble, on his way to the Council chamber, replied by a wave of the hand and an "*adio caro vechio*" to the respectful salute of the *tabarro* [citizen] hurrying by about his business.' Foreigners noticed that the streets, though paved, were dirty and that the crowds were perpetually on the move, chaffering, singing, gambling, swearing, buying, selling and talking, talking, talking. A whiff of garlic as you pass an Albanian who chews it as you would a sweet, or of Turkish tobacco from a sailor's pipe, completes the scene.

St Mark's Square was always full and colourful, with the variously hued togas of the officials and the capes of the Turks, Greeks and Dalmatians. A hectic feeling was in the air, even outside the six months of carnival. Artisans took pride in their homes, which offered modest comfort and clean linen. Their families, too, were respectable, more so indeed than those of many patricians; their dialect took the place of slang and they had their own jokes, of which a fair example was to tell a man he was cuckolded by saying 'you belong to the Ca' Corner' (*corna* = horns). The Ca' or Palazzo Corner is now the Ca' Grande, the Prefettura, or Police headquarters. We can see why Voltaire and others called the Venetians 'the most amiable and pleasing people in the world'. Few others would wrap up their vulgarity so attractively.

As usual where foreigners congregate, Venice became a favourite haunt of those who live by their wits as well as a refuge for such as find it convenient to change their abode. Cagliostro belonged to both groups and not surprisingly made Venice his home for a time, sold his elixir of life and moved on. The fortune-teller, on a humbler level, was a familiar sight in the streets and squares; in the Venice Accademia the genre painter Pietro Longhi portrays one, whispering his prognostications into the customer's ear through a long tube, and Piazzetta's '*L'Indovina*' in the same gallery shows a young female practising the same art. Visits of famous charlatans made news: such a one was Giovanni Greci, called 'The Cosmopolitan', who came to Venice in January 1759 with a retinue of pages in picturesque dress and, among other rarities, twelve horses. A super-specialist, he proclaimed that he could cure any disease on earth: 'I am a doctor of great worth, who restores their health to all', are the words Goldoni puts in his mouth.* He did in fact 'cure' a friar of an illness that the best known doctors of the time pronounced incurable. Two weeks later the friar shook off all his troubles by departing for the next world, whereupon Greci left Venice in a hurry.

Another whose career was more colourful than most was 'Princess' Tarakanova. Young and beautiful (like all females who make the headlines) she claimed that she was the result of a secret marriage between the Empress Elizabeth of Russia and Prince Alexis Razumowski, and therefore a more legitimate claimant to the throne of Russia than the present incumbent, Catherine the Great. Supported by Prince Radziwill, who saw in her a hope of liberating his native Poland after its first partition, Irene Tarakanova made a triumphal tour through Italy. According to Antoinette Drago, she was received by officials of La Serenissima as royalty and escorted to the French embassy, where she stayed for several weeks, attending the glittering receptions that Venice always staged for visiting royalty. Though she was soon revealed as an impostor, she clung to her pretensions until she died in a Russian prison soon after her Venetian adventure.

In contrast to isolated instances of swindling on a princely scale, Molmenti[4] enumerates many, genial or morose, whose ambitions were more modest. The mild treatment handed out to them is surprising; perhaps this had something to do with the noble Venetians' custom of contracting debts during their travels abroad and later neglecting to pay them. Rousseau, who makes this allegation, also tells of Venetian actors who accepted an advance from the French and, instead of departing for Paris to fulfil their contracts, continued to work in Venice. Whatever the cause of this type of crime, the mildness of punishments is, as usual, blamed; pickpockets were let off lightly and, according to Morris, even allowed to keep a portion of their loot if they surrendered to the city guards. Galley slaves and volunteer rowers were indulged, to the extent of having their petty crimes completely overlooked, says Casanova.[5] It seems only suitable that Venice's own fall should be part of an international confidence trick. But bad language was punished severely, one offender being stood in the pillory and having his tongue cut out; the sentence seems still more

---

* *Io sono medico di gran valore*
  Che a tutti reca la sanità.

brutal since sudden quarrels, usually accompanied (as everywhere) by some profanity, were speedily patched up among these peaceable folk.

Casanova of course remains the archetype of adventurers, not only for his amatory exploits, or such as really happened, but for the fact that at various times he followed the professions of card-sharper, actor, fortune-teller, violinist, pimp, spy and man of the world. There must have been few who, like Casanova, could claim to have had several conversations with Voltaire as well as sharing, with a French ambassador, a nun as mistress. Perhaps Venice, with her adventurous history, was especially suitable for the production and refuge of those who lived by their wits, legitimately or otherwise. One of the former category was Goldoni, who knew nothing pleasanter than to travel with actors, partaking of their trials and pleasures and helping with their productions. In this way Fate arranged his meeting with Casanova: travelling with Imer's troupe he met the comedienne selected for musical *intermezzi*, the widow Maria Giovanna Farusso (or Farusi), also known as '*Là Buranella*' and as Zanetta Casanova.* Her eldest child was Giacomo Girolamo Casanova.

Another subject that drew much comment was dress—not the everyday costume of the rich Venetians, which was essentially that of France, but carnival wear. Official dress was also striking, and was obligatory for patricians; the toga, as it was called, was an example of the Venetian desire to claim descent from Imperial Rome, though she had less preten-sion to this than any other Italian community; symptomatic were the numerous fanciful derivations of patrician families from Roman consuls.[6] The Doge's dress was distinctive, one could even say gaudy, from the peaked bonnet, or *corno* down; like so much else connected with cere-mony, it was of Byzantine origin. The Civic (Correr) Museum displays an everyday bonnet; a special one was used for the coronation and called the *zoia*; it was state property and kept in St Mark's. His toga was of gold fabric and his various ministers wore scarlet, violet, blue, red or gold, according to their rank. Still in the Correr Museum, some of these togas may be examined; it will be noted that they have little in common with the parent garment of Rome, for these hook up at the neck and have a broad fillet thrown forward over the left shoulder.

The uniform, for that is what it amounted to, was compulsory wear for patricians, but as the century wore on they adopted the habit of wearing it only in the Council Chamber and at public functions, or to enter cafés, so that a *procuratore* is described as dancing in red toga and full-bottomed wig at a state ball. Doctors and lawyers gradually abandoned the prescribed wear, but among the patricians it was of some use; for instance, the width of the sleeve showed the wearer's rank, the Doge's golden ones being the

* Zanetta is Venetian for the diminutive Giovanetta. '*Buranella*' implies that she came from Burano.

widest; de Brosses remarked that a boon was sought by kissing the sleeve of the prospective benefactor.

In the Querini-Stampalia Gallery, among Bella's numerous genre paintings, is one of the Hall of the Council of Ten, which pictures a session of eighteen patricians. The Doge is easily distinguished by his bonnet and of the others six wear red robes, and eleven black. The former would have belonged to the Doge's Council, the latter to the Council of Ten. All, by the way, wear the full-bottomed wig, a most important part of the patrician's costume, though somewhat new-fangled. It had been introduced from France in about 1665 by Count Vinciguerra of Collalto and at first met considerable opposition; indeed, it was not until 1758 that the last patrician opponent of the perruque died at the age of eighty-four—Antonio Corner, who kept a full head of his own hair to the end.

Many contemporary paintings show that powdering of the wigs was not uncommon and the fashion also entailed being clean-shaven. This, and the requirements of the ladies, for whom they often acted as go-betweens (in more than one sense), increased the number of barbers. Apart from obligatory uniform, there was a tendency for wealthier men to wear foppish clothes, lace ruffles, brocade and velvet coats and waistcoats, shoes with buckles of gold, silver and precious stones, embroidered sashes round the waist 'and braces to keep up their breeches', concludes Arcangela Tarabotti, who may have been gifted with second sight. A contemporary document[7] ironically lists the outfit needed for a visit to Padua, the thirteenth and last item being 'a box containing Asafoetida which will do for a lady suffering from Hysterical Complaints, which are mostly fostered by pleasant smells'. Anyone who has smelled asafoetida will agree that it should keep hysteria away, as well as the gallant who carries it.

The lower orders were far more soberly dressed, with pantaloons instead of the recently imported French or Spanish *culottes*, or knee-breeches, and until the middle of the century wore white, black or blue cloaks instead of the patrician scarlet; but they even adopted the last when it seemed safe to do so, as well as wearing a sword. Gondoliers are pictured with a cap of the 'Phrygian' shape, and dull clothes except during festivals, when those working for private families wore silk jackets and stockings, white shoes and red sashes and caps, or even hats with plumes. None of the view painters show gondoliers wearing the round straw hat (though Longhi has black felt ones) with red ribbon which has recently become the badge of the not-so-grand tour. On gala days state gondoliers were dressed in red velvet capes, braided with gold, and wore large Albanian bonnets; we are not surprised to read that they preferred to be towed on such occasions. Many travellers commented on[8] the gondoliers' habit of changing their shirts in public when damp, though, as one remarks, 'damp sheets are universal in Italy'.

Women's dress, as noted by Goldoni, was a sure way of distinguishing class. La Lande, describing women of the upper class, says 'they often wear their hair tied up with a ribbon, or even in a plait, rarely a bonnet; one often sees them in curl papers, their heads a sight, even in the theatre box; they never wear a scarf round the neck and they wear drawers during the winter.' Like Tarabotti a century earlier, the astronomer seems to have had his own sources of information. Of the bourgeoisie, he says 'they dress very much like the French; when they go out they cover the head with a coif, which may be crossed over the chest and tied behind and which they call *zendalino* [Casanova and other Venetians called it the *zendà*]; they usually plait the hair and may then secure it on the crown with silver pins, and they wear large, pendant earrings. Peasant girls wear big straw hats and have the pleasant custom of wearing a rose or other flower over the ear.' Others remark on the exaggerated effects achieved, in contrast, by the dress of upper-class females, the huge panniers and crinolines, the audacious combinations of colours and the bold *décolleté*. As Loredano[9] remarked, 'The woman herself was the smallest part of the show.'

But for describing women's dress we must surely use the aid of a woman; Mrs Piozzi describes the *zendà* or *zendaletto*, as 'black like the gondola, but wholly calculated like that for the purposes of refined gallantry'. Later she says that 'it is worn in the morning by every Venetian lady' and here she shows some confusion, for she describes it as 'a full, black silk petticoat, sloped just to train a little on the ground and flounced with gauze of the same colour. A skeleton wire upon the head, such as we use to make up hats, throwing loosely over it a large piece of black mode or persian [a type of thin silk used for linings], so as to shade the face like a curtain, the front being trimmed with a very deep, black lace or souflet gauze, infinitely becoming. The thin silk that remains to be disposed of they roll back so as to discover the bosom, fasten it with a puff before at the top of their stomacher and, once more rolling it back from the shape, tie it up gracefully behind, and let it hang in two long ends.' This, of course, was the *zendà*, not the petticoat she first mentions. Without quoting more and wearier detail, I shall simply remark that the wealthy had dresses made to ape every new foreign fashion and follow every Venetian innovation.

Women's accessories are more interesting. Hats were either the three-cornered type⋆ worn by men and a part of carnival wear, or became so heaped up with flowers that it was said they carried trays of produce on their heads, like market women. Professor Toaldo, the Paduan meteorologist, jokingly suggested that they be fitted with lightning conductors.

⋆ Women inevitably made a functionless miniature of it. A good example can be seen in Antoine Watteau's 'Italian comedians' in the National Gallery of Art, Washington, D.C.

Patches are seen in women's portraits of the age from all European countries. Their situation was supposed to convey a special meaning, among the Venetians.[10] '*Appassionata*' at the outer corner of the eye, '*assassina*' at the corner of the mouth, 'bold' at the base of the nose and, I suppose, just pimples on the chin. Jewels were allowed to be worn only in the first year after marriage, but special permission could be obtained for exceptions from the Sumptuary Board; mostly, however, women simply ignored the restriction.

Perfume was the rule and for cosmetics white or brown face powder* was regularly used, in addition to a trace of rouge. In 1759 a new fashion for furs arose, possibly in an attempt to circumvent the sumptuary laws. Shop windows in St Mark's Square looked like menageries; furs and stuffed animals were displayed everywhere, sables, foxes, martens, ermines, leopards and tigers. Muffs were expensive but women, and even men, were not satisfied unless they had at least a dozen. In the Longhi room of the Pinacoteca Querini-Stampalia there are two versions of masked women in a gambling hall, their hands concealed in muffs and the Guardi '*Ridotto*' shows an old man using one.

Another event was the introduction of wigs for women. In August 1725 two Englishwomen were admiring the paintings in the Scuola di San Rocco when they in turn became the object of interest, for their hair was cut short and each wore an attractive wig. In a few days the Venetian ladies' hair also fell under the hairdressers' scissors and the fashion for wigs spread rapidly. Fans were a regular part of summer wear and stimulated artistic ingenuity in ivory carving, lace and miniature painting. Fine examples may still be seen in museums.

The strangest anecdote about women's clothing brings us back to Mrs Piozzi. She went across to the island of San Giorgio Maggiore one day to see Veronese's 'Wedding at Cana' in the monastery, but was refused admission as she was a female. Later, however, she was told that it was her own fault, for she should have gone in men's clothes and would certainly have been admitted, even if the imposture was obvious.

Transvestism was also one of the ways of 'dressing up' during carnival. It did not, however, extend to the other occasions on which citizens were allowed to go masked. Concealing the features was a privilege; permission was in fact read out at a public ceremony and greeted with applause every year, though everyone knew the precise dates on which masking would be allowed. Basically, carnival extended from 26 December to Shrove Tuesday; later, masks were allowed to be worn, in the evening only, from

* Called *cipria* as allegedly coming from Cyprus. A special licence was needed to make it and on one occasion (1763) a certain Giovanni Lucatello produced an 'infallible' method of detecting wrong preparation of *cipria*. That in general use consisted of chalk, lime, beans and 'other additions harmful to health', according to the same Lucatello.[11]

5 October to 16 December and on numerous special and recurring holidays. So important were these festivities, possibly because of tourists, that the death of Doge Paolo Renier on 18 February 1789 was not made public until the beginning of Lent twelve days later; hence there was no interruption of the carnival. Here indeed was a sign of decadence; let those who wish to moralize do so now.

The origin of the custom of masking is not known: my impression is that it derived from the Byzantine prohibition of going out-of-doors without a veil, applicable to all women.[12] When the veil became a mask women could say (as in one of Goldoni's plays), 'no lady would be seen in the street without one'. The attraction of masks was undoubtedly the anonymity they conferred.* Respectable women felt free to behave in a manner anything but respectable. Anonymity must have seemed desirable to the authorities too, for masks were compulsory in the *Ridotto*, or official gaming rooms, for all but a few patricians, and when the Doge gave his routine banquet on Ascension Day the general public was allowed to come in and see the first part—provided they were masked.[13] Anonymity also meant that the classes could mingle without embarrassment or detection and no introduction, other than *Sior* (or *Siora*) *Maschera* was used. Accounts of secret and unexpected meetings are many; a whisper, a tap on the sleeve and an intrigue might begin. 'I have no doubt' wrote Addison, 'that the love adventures of a carnival of Venice would make very diverting novels.' It was even said to have been common for a casual acquaintance not to know whether his partner in the gondola was a patrician or a harlot, until it was time to settle up, that is. It was all a normal part of the feverish life of Venice, more suited to a Mediterranean people than to those of a more restrained temperament; we could not imagine a Venetian woman in the part of Fielding's Amelia, the patient and obedient wife who defers to her husband in everything except going to a masquerade.

Normal masked wear for both sexes, apart, that is, from carnival fancy dress, consisted of the *bauta*, a piece of black lace or silk that covered the head and shoulders and was drawn across the lower jaw. It rested on the *tabarro* or domino, a long, dark cloak that hung half way down the calf. Under the *bauta* was worn the mask, commonly a white velvet one of grotesque shape called *larva*—and a beaky ghost is what it made the wearer resemble—which came down as far as the upper lip. If a black velvet mask, or *moretta*, was worn by a woman it might be with a white equivalent of the *bauta*. Above all was the three-cornered hat, worn by either sex, as shown in Guardi's '*Ridotto*'. So normal were masks in their proper season that they were worn during visits to convent parlours;

* But Montesquieu tells of a kneeling man stopping the masked Papal Nuncio to ask for his blessing.

parish priests would have been criticized by their flock and archbishops by their clergy if they had walked down the street without them, at least, says Diehl, in their hand. Children wore them, and so did servants going to market, but a commentator possibly exaggerated when he spoke of a masked mother suckling a masked infant. Mask and *bauta*, the Venetian *maschera*, was almost a uniform, then, and far more commonly worn in carnival time than Harlequin, Pulcinella or other forms of fancy dress.[14] So it is not surprising that mask manufacturers, who had their own section of the painters' guild, became numerous and prosperous in the eighteenth century. At sixpence a time, which Lady Mary Wortley Montagu paid, they should indeed have done well.

5

Some Entertainments

It would be a mistake to believe that the entertainments I shall mention here were signs of a luxurious civilization sinking to its end; I have dealt with the fallacy that the Roman example of *panem et circenses* necessarily had any fateful consequences. Venetian love of display and joy in the parading of its wealth go back to the Middle Ages and there is scarcely a ceremony that I shall describe which did not have its origin centuries before. Custom forced the Doge and *Signoria*, or Council, to make frequent public appearances and the display of priceless robes and jewels flattered the populace, who saw in it the splendour of their own state and hence their own grandeur. Making new laws, which were largely ignored, appears to us a secondary activity.

State processions began on the first of January when, with silk-clad escort and the blare of trumpets, the Doge went to St Mark's to worship the Holy Sacrament. Two days later another procession, this time with an accompaniment of silver trumpets and with the golden umbrella unfurled,[1] paraded in the Piazza. Nor were other religious festivals neglected: Epiphany, anniversaries of patron saints (and Venice showed its gratitude for the intercessions of more than one) and of the theft, or 'translation' of the body of St Mark, Annunciation, the cloud of pigeons released on Palm Sunday—these are but a sample. One climax came at Easter, another on Corpus Christi, and a year of ostentation came to an end with the musical accompaniment to High Mass, in the Doge's presence, in the Basilica di San Marco on 31 December.

Between state–religious ceremonies frequent visits to parish anniversaries were made, especially to the *sagre*, the annual celebrations of local patrons in the six districts of Venice; here popular enthusiasm was boundless, the richness of the Doge's retinue inflating parochial pride. One of the most picturesque of such semi-religious processions commemorated the obsolete 'Feast of the Marys': on one first of February it is said, Istrian pirates raided the lagoon and kidnapped a shipload of maidens on their way to be married, dressed in their wedding gowns and gilt diadems. The parishioners of Santa Maria Formosa sallied forth, overtook the pirates, killed them and rescued the brides. Even when the full thanksgiving cere-

mony lapsed, in about 1380, the Doge and Council continued to celebrate
the anniversary by attending Mass at the Basilica and going in solemn
procession to the Church of Santa Maria Formosa, where they were
entertained with malmsey wine; with this, the parish priest gave his distinguished guests gilt straw hats to commemorate the damsels' headgear.[2]
You will realize how frequently an excuse was found for official celebrations, when I mention G. B. Brustolon's etchings of a series of Canaletto's paintings entitled 'The Twelve Dogal Solemnities'. And these were
only the most important.

The election of a new Doge called for more festivities, as did the visit
of any distinguished stranger, or even a Venetian hero. When Morosini,
for example, returned from directing Venice's last victories over the
Turks in 1687, there was a procession of state officials which took them on
foot to a fountain of Neptune and attendant dolphins, spouting wine. The
Doge's coronation and, more rarely, that of his wife, the Dogaressa, were
other excuses for display. And in case a dull week should intervene, celebrations might be decreed for new cardinals, patriarchs, *procuratori* and
ambassadors. Then there were the sumptuous feasts given by patricians to
celebrate anything from a new job to a wedding; these, inspired more by
the desire to score off their peers than to enhance the glory of the Serenissima, were sometimes more elaborate than the official functions.

All in all, the moths had little opportunity of making their homes in the
robes of the nobility. Among the foreigners for whom special shows were
staged in this century were the King of Denmark and Norway, the Duke
of York, Prince Frederick Christian, son of the King of Poland, the Elector
and Archbishop of Cologne, the Duke of Württemberg, King Gustavus
III of Sweden and Pope Pius VI, to take a few names at random. Whether
or not they travelled *incogniti*, reception arrangements, public and private,
reached the peak of splendour. Instead of press photographers, painters of
views and genre left us their impressions of these and other celebrations
and carry us back to scenes so splendid as to put mere vulgarity in the
shade.

As befitted an amphibious city, aquatic displays played a great part.
The *freschi*, processions of open gondolas on the Grand Canal, began on
Easter Monday and continued on every Sunday and holiday till September. There was racing by women and by the young, a display of gorgeous
clothing by both sexes and the passing and repassing with smiles and bows
that recalled the *liston*, or evening promenade in the Piazza di San Marco.
On such occasions the patricians made use of their *bissone*, ceremonial boats
with decorated hulls, the prows often adorned with plumes, palm fronds
or, by inference from contemporary paintings, fringed decorations of
ornamental glass. 'A procession in gondolas' wrote the impressionable de
Brosses, 'is to my way of thinking a divine sight, all the more as then [on

state occasions] they are not ordinary gondolas, but those of the Republic, superbly carved and gilded, accompanied by those of the ambassadors, still richer and more gay.' Picture the effect, especially when the craft were manned by the state gondoliers in their red velvet capes trimmed with gold and their large Albanian caps. What matter that their costume was too heavy to permit them to row? There was always the musicians' skiff to tow them.

The first view painter of note in Venice, Luca Carlevaris of Udine, was especially fond of picturing regattas and processions, a lucrative exercise; his etchings were widely disseminated and did much to attract visitors; it is noteworthy that his aquatic studies give more satisfaction than his views of buildings. It is sometimes stated that regattas were staged only for crowned heads, and this may be true of the more sumptuous spectacles, for Lady Mary Wortley Montagu writes of one that was intended for 1740, 'the last one being given thirty years ago'. But it is quite probable that more modest displays were common. Thus we read of a comic regatta for bakers in July and open events, in which the consolation prize for fourth place was a live pig.[3] Much detail, some of it in verse, and of little interest to this age, may be found in the pages of a strange book by an anonymous 'Philosopher'. It at least demonstrates the importance of water sports to a nation whose maritime prowess had once raised it to world power.

But the climax of ostentatious parade came with the Feast of Ascension (Sensa), especially treasured by the Venetians as a reminder of the imperial glory that once was theirs. Solemn festivals accompanied the annual *Sposalizio*, or 'Wedding of the Sea', the 'Rule, Britannia' of an enfeebled state. The ducal barge was only the stepping stone for boarding the wondrous *Bucintoro*, a glittering galley that was often painted by Canaletto and other artists of the day. A hundred feet long, it was built with two decks, the lower for the rowers at the twenty-six pairs of oars, the upper decorated like the interior of a palace, with statues, a throne, ornate furniture, priceless hangings and, in fact, everything calculated to make the craft top-heavy. That the danger of capsizing was a real one is shown by the fact that the admiral in charge was responsible with his head for the Doge's safe return from the ceremony; consequently he was apt to exercise a caution with which we can sympathize and postpone the event until the lagoon was calm and the winds no more than moderate. Such postponements were regarded as a sign of bad luck by the superstitious; perhaps persisting with the ceremony would have been still less lucky for some.

The stupendous spectacle stirred the patriotic hearts of the populace; never had there been a more ornate *Bucintoro* than the last one, launched in 1728; never had the gilt, carved panels sparkled more opulently or the

crimson awnings with more majestic splendour; never did the great gold
and scarlet banner of St Mark flutter more bravely. At least, so it seemed
each year. Then, amidst fanfares, rolling of drums and the salvoes of
saluting cannon, the great unwieldy vessel left the basin of St Mark and
made its ponderous way across the lagoon to the point of the Lido, where
stands the Church of St Nicholas. But not alone. As many as four thousand
smaller vessels had been known to accompany the *Bucintoro*, the gilt *pajots*
of the ambassadors, the state-owned, gaudy gondolas, the musicians'
barge (for a less impressive aquatic progress on the Thames Handel had
composed his 'Water Music'), the patricians' *bissone* and every other
lighter skiff or gondola that could be propelled. Then came the wedding
ceremony, said to date from the eleventh century, followed by Mass at
St Nicholas and the slow progress home, where the most sumptuous
banquet of all awaited the Doge and his guests, who exchanged the satins
and velvets of the *Bucintoro* for those of the ducal palace. What matter that
the ceremony had lost its meaning? All Venice was gay, bubbling over
with pride in their city that could stage such a tremendous spectacle. Only
a few foreigners gave a pitying smile, when they thought how the Turk
now ruled the waves and occasionally allowed La Serenissima to trade with
what had once been her own possessions. Well could Bellay write cynic-
ally of Venice as the cuckold husband and the sea as the Turkish lover.*

Ascension Day was also the signal for the opening of the annual *Fiera*,
the great trade fair which still showed the world that Venetian art and
craftsmanship were not yet dead. Booths went up in every part of the
great Piazza, until in 1776 Bernadino Maccaruzzi designed a temporary
oval, wood and canvas structure to occupy a part of the open square
every year. Here shops and artists were able to display their wares, and it
is said that Canova first exhibited here; the more expensive shops were
inside the oval, others on the periphery, while carnival rule revived for the
fortnight that the fair lasted. A laughing, jostling crowd filled the square,
some waiting for the hour to strike so that they could see the procession of
the angel and three Magi pass the Madonna's throne on the *Torre dell'oro-
logio*; clowns and harlequins engaged in mock battles, jugglers and charlatans entertained the idle, quacks and itinerant dentists paraded their skill,
the latter with a whole armament of cauldrons to be beaten, thus drowning
the patient's cries, while 'painless' extraction was performed. Cosmoramas,

* *Il fait bon voir, Magny, ces coïons magnifiques,*
  Leur superbe arsenal, leurs vaisseaux, leur abord,
  Leur Saint-Marc, leur palais, leur Realté, leur port,
  Leur change, leurs profits, leur banque et leurs trafiques,
  Mais ce que l'on doit le meilleur estimer,
  C'est quand ces vieux cocus vont épouser la mer,
  Dont ils sont les maris et le Turc l'adultère.
                    Joachim du Bellay, *Les Regrets*, Sonnet 133.

acrobats and rope walkers contributed their share, and one of the last would slide down a rope from the campanile to the Doge's courtyard, to present the Most Serene with a bunch of flowers.

The recreations of the populace were on the whole more interesting than the contrived revelry of the nobility. All the fun of the fair was by no means restricted to the fortnight after Ascension. Maundy Thursday was the occasion for a real frolic, understandably for those who had passed a whole thirty-nine days of deprivation. Out came the fancy dress; fireworks consumed more powder in a day than the armed forces in a year; bull-baiting, as pictured by Zuccarelli,[4] could be seen in the courtyard of the ducal palace and on the slope of the Rialto Bridge, where Gabriele Bella captured an exciting moment for his series of genre paintings in the Querini-Stampalia Gallery. A bull was decapitated in the Piazza with a single sword stroke by a champion of the smiths' guild; *Forze d'Ercole*, or human pyramids, made by each row standing on staves laid across the shoulders of two men in the tier below, were noted at the beginning of the century by Addison; organized fist fights between parishes were staged on the bridges which, innocent of balustrades, allowed losers to tumble into the canal. Modern games, too, were represented: Jonard mentions baseball, alleging (my apologies to the United States) that it came from England; a form of tennis is pictured by Bella, perhaps an indoor court of a game like racquets, in which squares on the wall behind the player are variously numbered; football was an absorbing passion and enthusiasts will be interested to read in Marangoni[5] that in 1753 'Carlo Guerra, one of the most popular footballers of the time, died in Venice. Though he was a native of Udine a local team had paid a large transfer fee for him. In Venice football had by now become a game which charges spectators an entrance fee, the delight and chagrin of thousands of fans. *Pirie*, or public wagers, had been introduced, a kind of ancestor of the modern football pool.' As with most popular pastimes and activities, a game of football can be seen depicted by Bella, along with his other glimpses of Venetian life.

But the usually grave Venetians could be animated by less organized shows: during the second half of the century wheelbarrow races became popular and in many parishes mid-Lent was celebrated by burning the dummy figure of an old woman. The burning of straw men and women is a common practice in and after Lent throughout Europe and the 'burning of the old woman' was still practised in the Val di Ledro, in the Tyrol, until quite recently.

Along with pagan customs and light-hearted scrimmages the common folk of Venice preserved, if not a measure of artistic sensibility, a marked enthusiasm for their own artists. When Tiepolo's 'Virgin of Carmel appearing to St Simon Stock', on the ceiling of the Scuola dei Carmini, was unveiled in 1743, the whole parish made a holiday of it. As on *sagre*, the parish square (*campo*) was splendid with flags and rugs hung out of the windows all round, stalls displayed their wares and young men and women, in their best clothes, danced in traditional style while their tuneful songs echoed over the quiet canals. A change from the gondoliers singing alternate verses of Tasso with an old-time and rather mournful melody; popular holidays of this kind were so spontaneous and joyful that the laughing, chattering populace had little envy of the bourgeoisie and none of the patricians.

Gambling was the universal vice. Not an unexpected one in a community of merchants, and maritime ones at that. Sea insurance was invented in Holland, among another set of maritime merchants; it moved rapidly to England and Venice too did its share of business. Only towards the end of the seventeenth century, we learn from Bragadin,[6] did the insurance companies of Venice refuse cover to ships passing through corsair-infested waters, and allowed the business to go to Dutch and French companies. Now the insurance business is essentially a form of gambling: to the merchant who approaches them the insurance company and underwriters say, in effect, 'We will wager £50,000 against your £100 that your ship and cargo come home safely.' When gambling of this kind lapsed it was only to be expected that some other outlet would be found.

By 1638 official permission had been given to a patrician, Marco Dandolo, to open the *Ridotto*, a public gambling hall, in his palace near the Church of San Moisè. There is still a street here called the Calle del Ridotto and a Ridotto cinema, which is closed, presumably having had a run of bad luck. Maccaruzzi, who designed the oval structure housing the *Fiera*, enlarged and adapted the premises in 1768, so that there were a luxurious entrance hall, refreshment rooms (one of which can be seen in the background of the Guardi '*Ridotto*') and ten rooms for the card games which extracted the clients' money. There was an outcry from the public, for the government had carelessly paid for the improvements with money obtained by the sale of ecclesiastical benefices; but thinking it over, one can only call the public illogical, for the Church followed One who advised the wealthy to give away their money, an object which the *Ridotto* was promoting. But there were more direct aims in the mind of the authorities; private *ridotti* had sprung up, haunts of card-sharpers, confidence tricksters, prostitutes and others who separated men from their money in less orthodox ways.

Contemporary articles and paintings have made us familiar with the *Ridotto*. All but the patricians or their womenfolk were obliged to wear masks, presumably even outside the official masking seasons. Bankers had to be patricians who attended, each behind his table piled high with sequins and ducats, wearing full-bottomed wig and toga and without masks, ready to take on all comers. This was one way by which the *Barnabotti* could augment their government pension. Those who were not thus employed came as punters with what they could beg or borrow, sometimes returning home naked under a borrowed cloak, for there seem to have been facilities for pawning one's clothes. There are no reports of women doing so, for the proceedings were conducted in a quiet and austere *ambiance*; but all are agreed that those of them who lost heavily might sell their hidden assets for enough to enable them to continue gambling, and that the transaction was made with a scandalous lack of concealment.

A few fortunes were won and many lost. Some of Venice's oldest families retired into obscurity, having sold all they possessed, and public opinion forced the government to debate closing the *Ridotto* in 1774. The voting in the Grand Council showed 720 in favour of closing and 21 against. Casanova hinted[7] that the voting, or the counting was 'rigged', as three-quarters of the Council were for keeping the *Ridotto* open and, of course, many of the Council depended on it for their living. Certainly there were loud and frequent complaints, some facetiously claiming that the hands of the *Barnabotti* dealers would atrophy from disuse, others later affirming that the financial consequences were disastrous. Gouver,[8] for instance, showed that the measure led to 30,000 fewer *baute* being sold in the next two years, which meant that 600,000 lire had gone out of circulation.* Thirty producers of luxury articles shut up shop and inability to gamble led to a startling reduction in the sale of foodstuffs, for enjoyment was said to increase the appetite—'*Dalla danza si passa alla pancia*'. Cardinal Flangini was no doubt pleased, for he was the leader of the 'abolitionists', as we might call them, but there were as many long faces in the Piazza as contented ones. Goldoni, who thought unrestrained gambling a bad thing, produced his *Il Giuocatore* (The Gambler), one of his few failures.

In the end things went on as before, except that the government lost the money it had made from the *Ridotto*. Smaller *ridotti* opened and were closed. Private *casini* and many cafés came to serve the same purpose and Venice, like so many governments before and after, discovered that there was no way of stopping people from throwing away their money, and others' too, if they could get their hands on it. One small triumph followed the introduction of the *lotto*, or public lottery, which was formally established in 1715 and again, after a temporary suspension, in 1734. The *tombola*, on the other hand, was declared 'dangerous' in 1789. According to one cynic, the whores and Dr Parola were the only ones to benefit by the closing of the *Ridotto*; the former because so many men had so little

---

* The conclusion seems a bold one; the money could have been spent on other, perhaps preferable articles.

to do in the evenings, the latter because he specialized in what were then known charitably as 'diseases of gallantry'.

For the lagoon-dwelling Venetians, exotic and not-so-exotic animals were a rare treat. The rhinoceros that arrived for the carnival of 1751 was so popular that several artists painted its portrait, notably Pietro Longhi,[9] who is known to have produced two versions, and members of his school who may have painted several more. A strange detail is provided by the showman, who waves the amputated rhinoceros horn in his right hand; it is easy enough to suggest that it was removed for the safety of visitors, but I came across what may be of significance a short time ago. James Morris mentions that the well which used to give fresh water to the Arsenal was always pure because two rhinoceros horns had been thrown in it. This is only one of the horn's supposed functions; it fetches huge prices in the East as a sovereign remedy for impotence and it is likely enough that the showman had his own plans for the disposal of the horn. This rhinoceros was honoured, not only by being painted, but by having a commemorative medal struck, so that forty years later the Philosopher reported, 'a citizen of quality said one evening that among his medals he kept one struck on the occasion of the arrival of a rhinoceros in Venice'.[10]

A tame lion was also shown once and fearlessly painted by Pietro Longhi during the carnival of 1762; the picture hangs in the Querini-Stampalia Gallery. A few years later an elephant—the first ever to be seen in Venice—enthralled the populace. But surely the strangest show was that which astonished Mrs Piozzi, when she saw 'poor people paying a penny a-piece for the sight of a stuffed horse'.

In April 1784, less than a year after the first successful balloon ascent by a human, a crowd watched Count Giovanni Zambeccari make an ascent from the Grand Canal opposite the Piazzetta, outside the Doge's Palace. Enthusiasm was tremendous and poems were written, medals struck and paintings executed by Guardi and Bella.

Another whiff of the atmosphere of La Serenissima in the eighteenth century is conveyed by Offenbach's *Tales of Hoffman*, based on E. T. A. Hoffman's stories. They are all there—Spallanzani the mad scientist, the courtesans, the charlatans, the demon fiddler and, of course, the gondolas and the now hackneyed 'Barcarolle', And, so typically in the tinkling melody of a doll, the lilting refrains and *coloratura* exercises, there is not one breath of sentiment or sincerity; it is a true reflection of the tourist's Venice.

For the Venetians, festival nights in any parish were ablaze with fireworks, torches and lights of gondolas, but on others the solitary walker had to rely on a link-boy or *codega* (possibly from the Greek *hodegos* through Venice's Byzantine past) where the shops were closed. For in about 1719 some shopkeepers in the area including San Marco and the

Rialto Bridge began hanging out lights. When Goldoni left to see Paris for the first time there was no other illumination; when he returned in 1737 he wrote: 'I had not yet seen Paris and I arrived there from a city where at night one had to walk through the shadows. Now see how the lights of Venice made a useful and pleasing decoration, all the more so because they were not the responsibility of private individuals. Independent of the street lighting was that of the shops, the majority of which did not close until midnight while others never closed at all. At midnight one could see, as clearly as at noon, every kind of foodstuff attractively displayed, the restaurant doors wide open, hotels and inns ready to serve dinner, the Piazza and neighbouring streets crowded, cafés thronged with *beau monde* and men and women of every type. There was singing in the streets, in the squares, along the canals. Shopkeepers sang while displaying their merchandise; workmen sang on their way home; gondoliers sang while waiting for their passengers. Gaiety was the essence of the nation, just as humour was the quintessence of its speech.'

Here were the haughty patricians, the merchants, the tailors, the barbers, the servants, the strolling idlers, the vagabonds, the laughing, scolding, swearing, singing, chattering crowd round the stalls of the *campielli* or leaning out of the windows to have the last word. These were the people he knew best and liked best, the characters he would make immortal. This was home.

Part Two

INTELLECTUAL
ACHIEVEMENTS

6

The Spirit

It was only right that honour should be accorded to literature and scholarship in the century of the encyclopaedists. Even Casanova, as carnal a scoundrel as ever lived, declared on his death-bed: 'I have lived a philosopher and I die a Christian.' La Lande, himself a noted astronomer, observed that Venice contained many celebrated, erudite men of letters, including Greek and Latin scholars, and singled out Count Gaspare Gozzi for special mention in the domain of poetry and literature. La Lande found everywhere an active and widespread participation in the Age of Enlightenment and noted particularly that a wealth of medieval Greek manuscripts was being translated and published. Although La Lande was disappointed to find few mathematicians in Venice, more could be met in Padua and we must remember that the civilization of La Serenissima embraced that of the *terraferma*, an integral part of the Republic.

The Gozzi family belonged to the new poor among the Venetian nobility and their ramshackle palace became known as 'The Hospital of the Poets'. Gaspare himself was a strange character, a walking skeleton, absent-minded, whimsical and melancholic in turn. Married 'inadvertently', to use his own word, early in his twenties to Luisa Bergalli the poetess, ten years his senior, he dedicated to her a sonnet in the style of Petrarch, wherein he called her 'amorous lily'. The lily responded by presenting him with a child every year. Discomforts were unnoticed, while his head was full of the poetry that sought the light of day. And not poetry alone, but its sublimation into visions, daydreams and fantasies as quaint and attractive as the *capricci* of the contemporary painters. Monnier[1] gives us the liveliest account of the family at home, the frenzied activity of the search for a rhyme, the shifts to which they were reduced: once they solved their problem by selling their furniture and taking a lodger who brought her own. Too soon came the inevitable quarrel and she left—with her furniture. '*Non si sapeva*', wrote one of Gaspare's sons later, '*dove posar le natiche*'—'We didn't know where to rest our bottoms.'

The amorous lily wrote, a bedspread over her shoulders, her husband's wig keeping her head warm; Giacomo, Francesco, Carlo, Marina, Girolamo, all wrote. While the old house decayed, doors sagging, floors

sinking, spiders' webs in every corner, while children yelled and adults squabbled, Gaspare worked on among the ink splashes. 'I only remind you', he wrote 'that the best ground I own is the sand in my hour glass.'*
Not quite true, but effective; they still had a country house, in which they could pass the summer at less expense. With a thousand distractions he never stopped writing, about everything or nothing, poetry or prose, speeches, reports, news items, essays, outlines of plays, jocular verses, satiric verses, love sonnets; has anyone worked harder or been more versatile? In the Age of Enlightenment it was easy to see that he had no new, trenchant ideas about the destiny of man; but reading between the lines one could discern the life of hardship and an ill-concealed bitterness.[2]

Short stories and translations from Greek, Latin, French, English and German flowed from his quill and the best survive in his three journals. For those were most important productions. Broadsheets existed, purveying the latest murder or scandal, and, as today, the crowd jostled each other to buy them; but Gaspare Gozzi was ambitious for improvement and enlightenment. So his *Gazzetta*† listed a lost and found section, goods for sale or hire, prices and exchange rates, all interspersed with articles that give us a better idea of life in Venice than do a dozen grand tourists. The inauguration of a church or a *procuratore*, a new book or Goldoni play, a mathematics coach looking for pupils or a young widow wanting to try a second run, all appear in the yellowed pages.

News items there were too, but of a novel kind: an old wife's tale of her strange chicken, which had not laid an egg for a year and was now little more than skin and bone and, of course, feathers; of a modern Diogenes who undressed down to his shirt in the Piazzetta and slept till the following dawn on his piled-up clothes. Scraps of conversation overheard in busy streets, dreams, restaurant menus, complaints and questions. Can scientists be held in the toils of Love? What are the characteristics of Petrarchian poetry? Why do poets and painters always represent Love as a child? 'A pretty question from an unknown: he knows that women's inconstancy exasperates me; one of them has jilted him and he would like me to prove that she was wrong.' Here is day to day life in Venice, the best journalism, and if you don't agree, go back to your 'Father of ten slays eleven' and your 'Woman with three husbands. (Exclusive)'. And if you maintain that a journal should instruct as well as entertain I answer that the very first number of the *Gazzetta* included a description of the thirteen movements to be used by the well bred in taking snuff. In more serious vein, he had a leading article on the 'Consolations of Philosophy' by Boethius and a review of 'The Life and Adventures of a Lap-

* '*Sol ti ricordo che il miglior terreno*
   Ch'io m'abbia al mondo è un oriuol d'arena.'
† From its price of a *gazzo*, a small Venetian coin; some say five *gazzi*.

dog'. This had been published in Italian by Zatta, who had made a reputation with his editions of Petrarch and Dante; the original, which he did not try to conceal, was 'The History of Pompey the Little', a satire by Francis Coventry (1751). His views on art do not show him as knowledgeable, but he declares himself in favour of it 'as it causes money to circulate';[3] it would also be useful, he thought, if it publicized the piety and sacrifices of the patricians.

Of poets there was almost a surfeit in the *settecento*,[*] many of them combining their gift for versifying with other attainments; Scipione Maffei of Verona and, of course, Gaspare Gozzi are two who readily come to mind. Two more are still spoken of: the elegiac poet Pindemonte with his pre-Romantic melancholy, literally *fin-de-siècle* (he was born in 1753) and known as the 'Tibullus of Italy'—not Venice alone, you will observe—and Cesarotti of Padua. The former was a friend of Foscolo and Alfieri, who used to ask him 'please to run through my doggerel', a compliment indeed. Among his more enduring works was the sonorous translation into Tuscan Italian of Homer's *Odyssey*. Cesarotti not only taught Greek and Hebrew literature at the University of Padua, but translated into Italian the collected poems of Ossian, as rendered in English by James Macpherson. Among his friends he too counted Alfieri and Ugo Foscolo; Napoleon, a great admirer of the bombastic, probably derived his enthusiasm for the Gaelic poems from Cesarotti's Italian version, for he honoured him in his old age.

The exchange of knowledge and opinions is admittedly a civilizing factor and Italy, especially Venice, was not far behind the rest of Europe in this respect. In 1710 Apostolo Zeno inaugurated a journal for men of letters and edited it until 1718, when he left for Vienna, where he was appointed court poet; the journal had a record life of twenty-two years. Others followed, but it was left for Gaspare Gozzi to emulate English practice and issue a journal on the lines of *The Spectator*. The *Gazzetta* began publication in 1760 and survived for a year. It was followed by the *Mondo Morale* and this again by the *Osservatore*, Italian for 'Spectator'. Even in their ephemeral existence they imitated the English model, the last one coming to an end late in the second year. *The Spectator* had about the same life span in its first existence, but lasted less than three months on revival. In 1763 Giuseppe Baretti, under the *nom de guerre* Aristarco Scannabue, began a highly contentious and critical review called *Frusta Letteraria*. Baretti had lived in London, where he belonged to Dr Johnson's circle, and we get a refreshing echo of that great man's forceful and direct methods.

In 1785 another journal appeared with the avowed aim of advertising

---

[*] The Italians count centuries very simply and 'the 700' is more easily appreciated than 'the eighteenth century'. The *seicento* is 'the 600' i.e. the seventeenth century.

sales, bargains, exchanges and so on; alas, even with its third number, short stories began to fill the gaps and soon the paper was a collection of novelettes, with one sole commercial advertisement at its last appearance. Two years later there was issued the first number of the *Gazzetta urbana*, self-styled successor to Gozzi's reviews and with no better fortune. Following the history of these and many other imitators of *The Spectator* and the French *Journal des Savants* we find that none survived for more than a year or so, chiefly through lack of interest or money in the reading public. In 1765 La Lande wrote that there had been five weekly papers in Venice (an understatement) and now there were but two, one of them a medical monthly.

Perhaps better business management might have helped; perhaps there was too much competition; perhaps chance plays too big a part in this enterprise. We ourselves have seen journals rise and fall, without discerning a reason for either. One activity, however, persisted. Venice, one of the first and best centres of the publishing trade, continued to produce books. A random count of publishers in business in 1750 reveals twenty-eight, and there were others in Padua, Verona, Bassano and elsewhere. With printing and publishing went libraries and these were many and fine, whether belonging to private families, monasteries, universities or the public; and indeed the excellence of letter-press and engravings deserved the homage which Venice had always paid the printed word. To ensure against its debasement, the printing and publishing trade was in 1780 subjected to regulations regarding typography and copyright.

Journalism, the hobby of the *letterati*, could be combined with other pursuits. The three examples of 'all-rounders' I have in mind were patricians, possibly the only class that had time for a wide range of interests. The Doge Marco Foscarini had been a child prodigy, having held his own in a philosophical argument with a Professor of Bologna University at the age of eleven; he had written poetry and treatises on politics and Venetian literature. His library, where he often entertained his friend Gaspare Gozzi, who called him '*il gran Cagnesco*' ('the great surly one', or, as we might say, 'The Great Bear') was famous and, after his death in 1763, was sold for the ludicrous sum, even for those days, of 5000 lire to the Vienna Library. His was the inspiration for the geographical Sala dello Scudo in the Doge's Palace, globes and maps recalling the long passage in the Vatican Museum, and decorated by a pupil of Tiepolo.

The Marchese Francesco Scipione Maffei was another prodigy, a great scholar, writer, poet, dramatist, historian, art critic, antiquarian and journalist. This last activity was given its opportunity when he collaborated with Zeno in the *Giornale de' Letterati* (an obvious analogue of the *Journal des Savants*); but his greatest achievement was the painstaking collection and cataloguing of his Lapidary Museum in Verona, where you

1 *Il Parlatorio* (The Convent Parlour). Francesco or Gian Antonio Guardi (or both).
In the Sala del Ridotto of the Ca' Rezzonico, Venice

2 *La Sala del Ridotto* (The Gambling Room). Francesco or Gian Antonio Guardi.
This hangs in the room of the same name in the Ca' Rezzonico; in fact this painting
gave its name to the room

4 The Campanile of San Marco, after being struck
by lightning on 23 April 1745. Pen and wash by
A. Canaletto

3 The Bucintoro. The ceremonial barge about to convey the Doge to the Lido for
the ritual of Venice espousing the Sea. A. Canaletto

5 The Church of the Gesuati, a masterpiece by Giorgio Massari who completed the Ca' Rezzonico. The proportions embody all the ideals of the Palladian school

6 Façade of the Church of the Scalzi, by G. Sardi. Here the attempt at creating something less ponderous has failed. Overloading and decoration of the Classical proportions have resulted in more heaviness

7 Façade of San Stae, by D. Rossi, nephew of G. Sardi who built the Scalzi. Improving on his uncle's methods he has succeeded in lightening the effect of Baroque interpretation of a Classical front

8 An engraving by A. Sandi from a painting by F. Guardi showing a temporary wooden stall in the Piazza di San Marco erected for the annual Ascension Day fair

9 Ballroom of the Ca' Rezzonico. Here the visitor gets an impressive view of the best of Venetian Rococo: a building by B. Longhena and G. Massari, a ceiling painted by G. B. Tiepolo, furniture by A. Brustolon and glass from Murano

can see the overflow of exhibits in the courtyard if you peer between the bars of the padlocked gate. But the road to the alleged tomb of Juliet (who never existed) in the same city is well worn by the feet of mawkish visitors. As a dramatist he earned the respect of Voltaire who, needing no reflected glory, dedicated his own drama 'Mérope' to Maffei, whose version had priority. Verona decided that flattery could not soothe the dull, cold ear of death and that their honoured fellow-citizen should live to see his own statue. I cannot find where it stands.

My third example was also a friend of Voltaire. Count Francesco Algarotti was of course many-sided, otherwise he would not be mentioned here. But he differed from the others in being cherished as well as honoured by the intellectual and elegant world.[4] He was a little less precocious than Marco Foscarini, for his interest in science and letters remained dormant until he was in Bologna at the age of fourteen. Luckily his special field in physics was Optics and, as Newton was regarded in Bologna as Galileo's successor, so Algarotti became Newton's. His fame in this subject, however, was based solely on the papers he wrote to confute a certain G. Rizetti, who had displayed anti-Newtonian beliefs in his *De luminis affectionibus,* and a popular work on the same subject, condescendingly made easy enough for the female reader, *Eccovi il Neutonianismo per le dame.*

At twenty Algarotti went to Paris and met Voltaire, who was much impressed. Only three years later he was invited to Cirey—possibly by Voltaire's mistress, Gabrielle Émilie, Marquise Du Châtelet-Lomont—and the three searchers after truth, Émilie, Voltaire and his '*cher cygne de Padoue*', got down to some serious thinking. This interlude may have been of first importance in Algarotti's education. Next year he went to England and made numerous friends, including Lord Hervey, Philip Dormer Stanhope, fourth Earl of Chesterfield (to whom he brought a letter of introduction from Voltaire), David Hume and David Garrick. It was now that Lady Mary Wortley Montagu had the misfortune to meet him.

In 1740 he was invited by Frederick the Great to visit him at Potsdam, at the same time as Voltaire; he quickly climbed into favour and remained there off and on for twenty-five years. He found time to write poetry and articles on art, music, Rome, the Incas, Horace, the *Periodicity of Genius,* the *Académie française* and many other subjects. He also found time to visit Russia, where he was enchanted with everything in the court of the Czarina, and spent three years with the Elector Frederick Augustus III of Saxony, later King of Poland and one of the greatest art patrons of an art-conscious century. For him Algarotti travelled back to his home in order to buy works of art; these were to swell the collection of the Elector's father which eventually became the nucleus of Dresden's famous Gemäldegalerie. Himself an amateur draughtsman, his taste in art was sound on the whole, and today's estimate of Venetian artists of the *sette-cento* is largely that of Algarotti. He was instrumental in securing commissions for more than one painter, including his close friend Tiepolo. Imbued with the classics and unconsciously heralding the taste of the century's end, he insisted on correctness (as he understood it) in classical history painting and liked to discuss details of the composition with his artists; it must be, and freely is admitted that his suggestions on Tiepolo's 'Cleopatra's Banquet' led to its improvement.

We know little of his personality from descriptions of contemporaries; he was said to be handsome and women adored him ('Lady Oxford', wrote Voltaire, 'asks after you continually and, like all fine souls, is in love with you'). Opinions are still divided as to whether Frederick the Great could be called a 'fine soul' in view of what follows. Among Algarotti's mass of writing an operetta stands out for sheer stupidity: in *Il congresso di Citera* he imagines a council of nations meeting to discuss the right way to make love.[5] The theme was the superiority of hedonism, which may have been Algarotti's idea but not that of some of the women he met. He has been described as a homosexual, but perhaps this was no more than the corollary to Frederick the Great's friendship. When he died at Pisa in 1764, at the age of fifty-two, a royal tombstone was placed over his grave in the Camposanto. On it was engraved:

ALGAROTTO OVIDII AEMULO, NEUTONI DISCIPULO
FREDERICUS REX

Opinions about him today vary and he is called everything from *uomo universale* to busybody. But his influence in fostering the arts of Venice was a good one; I have even wondered whether his interest in optics had anything to do with Canaletto's use of the camera obscura.

The eighteenth century in Europe might well have been called the Age of Academies, for as man drifted away from revealed religion he needed to satisfy his curiosity, the first crime in the history of man (and woman). Curiosity thrives on company and bands of truth-seekers dated back to the previous century; most of them were essentially open-minded, and the Royal Society in London was broad-minded too, for even royalty was admitted to their deliberations. The movement was nowhere more active than in France, where every town soon had its *Académie*—an unfortunate choice of a title, for the great model of all academies, over which Plato presided, set out to solve the problems of the universe by inductive reasoning; experiment, which became the stand-by of the Age of Enlightenment, had no place in Athens. France showed the way but Venice emulated her in the foundation of academies that had, by the end of the seventeenth century, degenerated into mutual admiration societies, whose sole function was to enable members to listen to each others' poems and essays.

Along with the borrowing and perversion of the French academic idea came the slavish translation of French literature, and its circulation, to the detriment of the local product. Even the Italian language became bastardized and (just as in Spain) gallicisms became ever more current. Thus Algarotti's prose was criticized by Baretti as 'a jargon of badly Italianized Venetian and badly understood French', while one of Casanova's earlier lights of love thought that habitually speaking French gave her an air of refinement.

But the name 'Academy' was also applied to museums and art galleries —the celebrated Accademia of Venice and the Carrara at Bergamo worthily sustain its prestige—that played their part in the Venetian enlightenment; Beckford, for instance, was greatly edified by the Venetian Museum of Antiquities. The Abbé Farsetti performed a service by founding a museum of casts for the study of sculpture, architecture and copies of celebrated paintings. Among those who took advantage of these facilities was the young Canova. The Civic Museum of Venice also owes its inception to private enterprise, by the patrician Correr, and private libraries, such as that of the Pisani family, were thrown open to the public for reading on certain days of the week.

During the eighteenth century we find much of the rubbish swept away; academies became sober, industrious societies for the acquisition and propagation of knowledge. Part of the disappearance of thirty or forty academies of windbags must be put to the credit of ridicule. Obscenity had become common in satirical poetry, so what follows must be read with this in mind. A party of the younger intellectuals, sated with the mushroom academies that were springing up, was out walking one afternoon in 1747 when they dropped in on the Monastery of St Dominic, whose inmates had their own Academy of Poetry, dedicated to St Vincent Ferrer. There they heard a priest, Giuseppe Sacchellari, 'with the voice of a mosquito and the hands of a spider',[6] reciting a worthless poem. Daniele Farsetti, the brilliant ringleader of the party, relates how they approached Sacchellari, begged him to take the post of patron of their academy and to accept the titles of *Arcigranellone, Testiculorum Princeps* and *Coleorum Princeps.**

Thus the ingenuous and unsuspecting priest became the head of the Academy of the Granelleschi, which met in the various members' houses, in cafés or in the open air. We may read in the works of both Gozzi brothers, leading spirits in the jape, how the *Arcigranellone* was persuaded that an uncomfortable chair placed on a table, his throne, was that of the great Dardi Bembo, the Platonist; how a wreath of radishes, lettuce, beetroot and green plums was set on his brow and a medal weighing a

* The Italian words *colleone* (Fr. *couillon*)—a favourite of Napoleon's, by the way—and *granello* have the same anatomical meaning and are also used to signify a blockhead.

pound hung round his neck; how they welcomed him with a fanfare on wooden trumpets and gave him further titles, such as 'Granelleschi the Grand Turk', and made the King of Prussia an honorary member, later withdrawing his nomination as he was not a Catholic.

With all its burlesque, the new 'Academy' succeeded in two objects, to provide an outlet for wit and to make fun of the majority of Venetian and Paduan academies. They gave each other comic names too and chose a motto for the 'Academy': '*Testes plures certe sunt quam homines*',* all without arousing the suspicion of their artless chairman. There was a blending of wit and wisdom at their meetings: a new sonnet in the style of Petrarch could be followed by Gaspare Gozzi's paper on children's toys, on wigs or enemas, or his fellow-member Seghezzi's on the cough, or on melancholy. It was a sign of the times, not only in Venice but throughout Italy; natural gaiety burst the bounds of sobriety and sometimes of good taste, culminating in the peculiar flamboyance of the Italian Rococo.

We cannot know precisely how much women contributed to the intellectual life of Venice. We read of Cecilia Conti, niece of a Doge, whom Montesquieu thought worthy of the title of philosopher, remarking also that she was learning algebra; of Cornelia Gritti, the poetess; of Cecilia Grimani Corner with her wide knowledge of letters and science; of Giustina Renier Michiel, beauty, patriot and writer; and of the celebrated literary 'salon' of Silvia Curtoni Verza.[7] But too often we find a 'salon' presided over by beauty or gaiety, as with Lucrezia Basadonna (often called *La Mocenigo delle Perle*, from her jewels) the attractive; or Caterina Sagredo Barbarigo, who was so witty, they say, that the Emperor Joseph II spent five hours talking to her during an evening's reception; or we read of the sparkling meetings in the *casini* of Marina Quirini Benzon or Cecilia Zeno Tron. The sister-in-law of the last-named, Caterina Dolfin Tron, a poetess and accomplished letter writer, probably came nearest to achieving the heights to which French 'salons' had attained, but all are agreed that even so she could not be compared with the Marquise du Deffand, or her pupil and imitator Mlle de Lespinasse.

If Goldoni or Gaspare Gozzi regularly attended the soirées of Caterina Dolfin Tron, Maria Sagredo Pisani, Cecilia Quirini Zorzi, Cornelia Barbaro Gritti or Faustina Rezzonico, it might have been no more than the attraction of their personal charm, the dullness of their competitors or, in the case of Gozzi, a change from the poetess at home. We suspect, however, that Caterina Dolfin took an active interest in the works of Voltaire and the encyclopaedists; a bookseller called Lucatello, knowing that the State Inquisitors punished anyone who harboured the works of those 'who entertained erroneous and dangerous doctrines and sentiments contrary

---

* The pun is as old as the Roman playwright Terence; see his *Heautontimorumenos*. The word '*testes*' also means 'witnesses' in Latin.

to . . . our Catholic religion', had stored his dangerous stock in the house of a woman friend. The government, acting on information received, instituted a search in the house of Caterina Dolfin (before she married the *procuratore* Andrea Tron) and searched very carefully under the maid Lucietta's bed. There the books were found but no one knew which of the women was the chatterbox, nor even which was the bookseller's friend. Nor do we know what happened to the maid or the bookseller; but the informers were duly rewarded.

The government showed a revival of interest in education throughout the century. Commerce, agriculture and engineering, with their ancillary sciences, all received encouragement and, though the first was dwindling fast there was a university chair of pure and applied mathematics in connection with ship-building and navigation. In Padua a chair of agriculture was founded in 1765, along with a model farm, and a veterinary school in 1772; we need hardly take Montesquieu's observation seriously, that the standard in Padua had fallen because there were so many other universities and because degrees could be obtained with greater ease in Venice. One result of awakened interest was the introduction of the mulberry into Friuli, a necessity for the survival of the silk industry after the loss of the Morea. It is unfortunate, but consistent with the spirit of the times, that free education for the poor was confined to patricians' children; another irrational event was the printing and emendation in Padua of the great French Encyclopaedia, although works by individual contributors had been subject to suppression by the State Inquisitors.

Elementary education, which had been largely in the hands of the Jesuits, came under the government when these were expelled in 1773; unlike higher education, it was not limited to the nobility, though the preamble to the Education Act did mention '. . . the better discipline of a sound literary education, especially among the young nobility'. Gaspare Gozzi was entrusted with the educational programme in the primary schools of both Venice and the *terraferma* and the salaries and allowances were his first step towards solvency. Thereafter his fortunes brightened in the strangest way: while in Padua he became ill and, in his delirium, threw himself out of the window into the river. Rescued and brought home he was cared for with all the tenderness and liberality that were so prominent in the nature of Caterina Dolfin Tron, and remained her protégé thereafter.

There was no branch of science in which Venetians were not distinguished. Father Vincenzo Coronelli, who died in 1718, had published extensively and was one of the leading cartographers of the day. Twenty-five years after his death his great project for building a breakwater south of the Lido was begun; the *murazzi*, as they are called, have stood up to wind, water and time ever since and ensured Venice's continued existence as a seaport. The naturalist Giuseppe Olivi of Padua is remembered as the first marine biologist, having catalogued the fauna of the Adriatic and, in particular, the Lagoon of Venice. Even meteorology had its exponents, of whom the Abbé Giuseppe Toaldo, professor of astronomy, was foremost. I mentioned earlier that he joked about women's hair styles, suggesting that they be fitted with lightning conductors. Later, the joke was on him: one day the *procuratore* Andrea Tron was planning an excursion and asked Toaldo what the weather would be like. 'Your Excellency', replied the expert, 'it will stay fine all day.' It rained and spoiled the outing and Tron, meeting the meteorologist again, asked him brusquely, 'Tell me, who is the softest saint in Paradise?' and, on Toaldo replying that he did not know, 'I'll tell you: it's St Mark [i.e. the State] who pays you professors your salary.'

Venice contributed to the advance of physiology in the *settecento*, for Spallanzani, though he worked in Modena and Pavia, published his results in Venice and through this channel achieved world fame. He almost became an honorary Venetian for he appears as a Venetian in *Tales of Hoffmann*. He had the gift of directing his interest to problems that would later become of first importance, spontaneous generation, exchange of oxygen and carbon dioxide in the body, and the sixth sense that bats possess, now known to be Nature's radar.

With the scientific background established by Spallanzani and his pupils it is not surprising that Medicine at last began to make progress. The 'immortal', as Molmenti calls him, Morgagni directed the course of European Medicine from his chair at Padua University for three-quarters of a century. He combined careful review of symptoms and signs in the living with the post-mortem appearance of their organs, both by naked-eye and microscopic examination; in this way he was able to connect certain types of illness with disease in corresponding organs. He is re-membered today for, among other achievements, his lucid description of acute yellow atrophy of the liver, the lungs in pneumonia, tuberculosis of the kidney and aortic aneurysm. Like his brilliant pupil Scarpa, his name is commemorated in parts of the human body or their infirmities, a certain way of achieving immortality; but he deserves to be the eponym of more than two structures, one of them a part of the rectum at that.

Morgagni was only the brightest star in a galaxy, but in a superficial review it is impossible to mention all whose genius and industry deserve acknowledgment. Like most prodigies, Morgagni could not have existed in a vacuum, and there had to be workers before, as well as after him. Santorini made important discoveries in anatomy a year before Morgagni took the chair in Padua and in the opinion of many Vallisneri displaces Morgagni as the first pathologist. To those who have seen Medicine develop during this century it is astonishing that Venice should have had special wards for tuberculosis patients as early as 1735; it is gratifying that she should have had rules for a home for the aged sick; and that her quarantine regulations should have been adopted throughout Europe is not surprising in view of her long and unhappy experience with plague imported from the Near East.[8]

As plague never died out in the Ottoman Empire it was essential that every person or object arriving thence should be subjected to the strictest control. Although it was not then known that plague is spread by rat fleas, great importance was attached to the fumigation of cargoes and the use of tarred ropes in towing. Both fairly efficient anti-rat precautions, these measures stand out from among the mass of useless but time-honoured ones. There were, of course, quarantine stations in every harbour and on every road, and ugly stories got about that they were an excuse for measures other than the preservation of health: de Brosses thought of them as delaying the delivery of textiles from the East, in order to favour home industries, and Casanova attributed the quarantine between Venice and the Papal States to pure pique, each party wishing to save face by compelling the other to relax its control first. Apart from anti-plague measures, public health was closely supervised, first by the old ordinance against filth in the streets (often, unfortunately, defied), then by the segregation of noxious industries, the provision of ample, clean drinking water and the regular scouring of canals, an activity which is maintained to this day in its established rota.

As implied by de Brosses, trade still played a large part in the life of La Serenissima. In 1715 Niccolò Tron, the Venetian ambassador, returned from the court of George I* with information about British industrial methods, among them wool processing. With the help of Italian capitalists he founded a flourishing wool industry at Schio. About ten years later the new venture was brought up to date, when the Boschetti brothers submitted to the Ministry of Trade fifteen specimens of a new fabric, called 'London seconds', in the style of a French product; the new material was exported and succeeded in replacing the French product. The lace industry of Chioggia, the product hand-made by the women, brought considerable sums to that city and the eight thousand workers thus helped in the support of their families and contributed to their daughters' dowries, and here I may mention a tough material, similar to the *rassa* used for roofing gondolas, which found a new use in the eighteenth century, for strips were strung together to make the first Venetian blinds.

Although no regular fire brigade was announced until 1777, fire fighting must have had some kind of organization, for in 1737 cobblers were ordered to attend all fires in their district, in order to repair leaky leather hosepipes should the necessity arise. Another activity was the prevention

* Marangoni says George II, so he has mistaken either the date or the number.

of damage by lightning in this city of tall bell towers. The campanile of St Mark's was praised for its stability, but was repeatedly struck by lightning; one of Canaletto's pen-and-wash sketches shows the progress of repairs to a damaged corner.

In 1786 the marine engineers of Venice had a chance of showing their skill. The 74-gun *Fenice* had sunk in one of the main channels of entry to the lagoon three years before. The patrician Giovanni Zusto undertook the removal of this danger to navigation, brought her to the surface with floats and kept the waterlogged wreck afloat while she was towed away. But the most ambitious project of the century was undoubtedly the building of the *murazzi*. The idea was Vincenzo Maria Coronelli's; it was Bernardino Zendrino who put it into effect. State mathematician and water conservator, he saw the project begun in 1744 but did not live to see it finished seven years later. The dyke is made of huge blocks of Istrian stone, for the nearer mainland has nothing of enduring quality, and its two sections together measure over three miles. Yes, measure: present tense, for the *murazzi* stand as sturdily as ever, the truly Roman labour of a dying state. But, once more, how does a state know it is dying when its dissolution is fifty years away?

7

Viva Goldoni!

There was no shortage of theatrical entertainment in Venice. Both in drama and opera there were splendid performances with every known kind of stage machinery. Hence the need for realistic scenery and the employment of artists who, in this way, obtained a good grounding in perspective and *trompe-l'œil*, which they later put to even better use else-where. Opera could be with or without ballet;* there was drama, in which at the time the Abbé Chiari was the leading author in the depart-ment of melodrama; in Naples and Rome, but rarely in the North, there was comic opera; and lastly there was comedy, to which Venice was such a great contributor. Drama and comedy had their origins in ancient days; most cultured men had read or at least were acquainted with the Greek dramas of Aeschylus, Euripides and Sophocles. In Athens the comic counterparts of the drama were written by many authors, from among whom only Aristophanes has come down to us. Plautus and Terence took over his very necessary function in pre-Christian Rome and have also survived, witness the first production in Venice of *Miles gloriosus* (The boasting soldier) by Plautus, on 19 February 1515.

But over the years a new, impromptu form of comedy had developed in Italy. No parts were written and the author simply pinned up an out-line of the story; the actors were adept at improvising and a certain amount of slapstick and off-colour humour was expected; the latter was not for the fastidious and Addison wrote that 'the Italian comic writers† fall into the most filthy double Meanings imaginable, when they have a mind to make their audiences merry'. Old sobersides seems to have over-looked the essence of the *Commedia dell'Arte*, as it was called, which was to make the audience merry. Dr Burney[1] saw the *Commedia dell'Arte* given in Verona—Montesquieu mentioned earlier that the amphitheatre was still in use for plays—'in true Italian purity'. Perhaps his Italian was not as good as Addison's.

* Goldoni (*Mémoires*) recounts that his friend Imer wanted to introduce musical inter-ludes into comedy, as had at one time been done in grand opera; but that they were later suppressed to make way for ballet. In the usual cycle of taste ballet later made way for musical interludes, for instance, in the best known operas of Mascagni and Leoncavallo.

† As stated above, the dialogue was spontaneous, not written, but see later. A.L.

The characters were traditional and their number varied; basically, there were two old men, the futile, later genial, Pantalone and the pompous Doctor, and two servants, Arlecchino and Brighella; these last were also known as the '*zanni*', another link with the classics for a buffoon in Latin was '*sannio*'. Brighella was the direct descendant of the clever servant in Greek and Roman comedies in which, by the way, he was represented with red hair; he also survived, or was reincarnated, as Figaro. The last reminder of antiquity was the mask worn by each of the above four actors, but not by the others, who usually conformed to set types: Pulcinella the clown, Tartaglia who alternated cunning with Brighella if both appeared, and two pairs of young lovers. Many of their names were carried over into Goldoni's comedies, used in this way by the very man whose mission it was to bring the Enlightenment to the theatre. The troupe of actors with whom Goldoni ran away as a boy of thirteen or so numbered twenty and included some characters that I have not mentioned, of whom one was Scaramouche,* a boastful poltroon. Perhaps we should not take too seriously the statement that only a rough scenario was drafted: Goldoni's greatest opponent, Carlo Gozzi, the supporter of the old, 'wrote' *commedie* and La Lande informs us that Molière had borrowed whole scenes from the *Commedia dell'Arte*. The nearest to it that we have seen are the 'custard pie' comedy and Fred Karno's sequences.

This Gozzi was the younger brother of Gaspare and therefore, according to continental custom, also a count, and he too was something of a poet. But he interests us here for the important part he was to play in the development of the Venetian theatre of the *settecento*. When he was nine an acquaintance, the midwife Angela Armano, wanted to console a friend in Padua who had lost her dog, by sending her own bitch with a poem. Carlo Gozzi volunteered to produce the latter, his first sonnet as it chanced. The sentiments are adult,[2] as 'Whoever is born, dies', but there is a breath of adult humour in 'I am sending Delina, who can make you a dozen dogs.' His early youth was spent sharing the family's frenzy for versifying and by sixteen he had written four long, and innumerable short poems. He joined a company of *Commedia dell'Arte* (or, as he called it, *commedia improvvisa*) players and went with them to Dalmatia. He tells us that the company was an all-male one and the youngest were called on to take female parts; his was that of a servant and he made a success of it by cleverly combining the Venetian and Dalmatian dialects. He reminds us that it was customary for families of every class to invite actors and actresses to dinner; he later belonged to the company of the Great Sacchi, the most successful actor-manager of the day, whom even Goldoni compared with David Garrick, and who was always addressed as 'Signor Conte'.

The morals of the players were above reproach and probably better

* From the Italian *scaramuccia*, our 'skirmish'.

than those of the aristocracy; looseness of conduct among females seems to have been mainly that of ballet dancers. Carlo Gozzi was of a quarrelsome nature and vindictive when he felt injured; he was the *cavaliere servente* to the comedienne Teodora Ricci, and was so jealous of her that he caricatured her lover, the Secretary to the Senate, leading to a long, acrimonious and pointless correspondence about the imputation that he had stolen his play *Le Droghe d'Amore* from the Spanish. His behaviour to Goldoni, which we shall consider later, was equally spiteful. But of his ability there can be no doubt; his fairy-tale plays, *Le Fiabe teatrali*, even though prompted by a squabble with Chiari, are enchanting. They are largely in verse and the parts, including those for Pantalone, Brighella and other stock characters, are fully written in most of them. The first one was performed in 1761 and their importance lies in showing that the most ardent supporter of the *Commedia dell'Arte* was not above writing a full text.

The *Fiabe* were a great success; witty and poetic, they caught the imagination and have such sound construction and atmosphere that two of them have been adapted to opera; they are *Gli Amore delle tre melarance* and *Turandot*; even in the latter Gozzi wrote parts for his stock characters under their traditional names. But though Carlo Gozzi scored over Goldoni his fame did not last; Goldoni had the heart of the public, perhaps through his use of the Venetian dialect in his plays, whereas Gozzi, a member of the Granelleschi Academy,* tried to introduce the pure Tuscan; as well present the Uncle Remus stories in Boston English.

At one time during the century there were fourteen theatres in Venice, nearly all privately owned by patrician families. One group was reserved for opera, another for drama and the third for comedy. Reformation of opera had come just in time; Zeno and then Metastasio replaced uninspired libretti to such good purpose that many of the latter's could be produced successfully without music. Tragedy was not to the taste of the Venetian public and the occasional interlude of buffoonery was greeted with applause; one such example, mentioned by Goldoni, was Harlequin defending Roland's castle by throwing pots and kettles at Charlemagne's troops. Drama came to rely chiefly on revivals: Tasso was still performed and Maffei of Verona was one of those who made a compilation of old, but good Italian tragedies. In spite of their relative unpopularity they were good enough to pack houses, and it was said that during the evening in Venice half the homes were empty and all the theatres full. Theatres were usually known by the name of the parish in which they stood and in Goldoni's day only two were regularly used for comedy, San Luca and Sant'Angelo. Late in the century, when a new theatre was beyond the means of a single patrician family, a combine was formed and the *Fenice*

---

* In some respects he might well have been elected 'Testiculorum Princeps'.

represents such a joint enterprise. It was not opened until 1792, when the great days were over, but no one would think so from seeing it today. It is a genuine and well-preserved example of Rococo interior decoration, including clusters of candle-holders round the five tiers of boxes, the frescoed ceiling with its huge candelabrum of Murano glass and the curtain painted to represent Morosini's triumphal return.

Audiences behaved abominably. When Goldoni attended the first performance of his *Pamela nubile* in Rome, there was a continuous sound of interjections and calls for Pulcinella, whom the Romans liked to see early on; jokes, whistles and howls, until the poor author was quite reconciled to witnessing one of his rare failures. At the end of the act someone mentioned that Goldoni was in one of the boxes; heads turned, conversation became applause, then cheers and cries of *'Viva Goldoni!'*, while even the actors, grouped in front of the curtain, clapped. But behaviour in Venice was even worse, in spite of writers' complaints. There was applause and hissing, depending on which faction prevailed,* bursts of immoderate laughter, rough voices and sharp voices, cock crows, cat calls, cackling, sneezes, forced coughs, yawns. . . . Meanwhile the gilded youth of Venice, leaning out of their boxes with their female companions, occupied themselves throwing candle ends on the audience below or even spitting on them. 'God pardon them', commented Gaspare Gozzi, he of the *Gazzetta*, 'They'll catch cold.'†

The noise was not always hostile and a decree was promulgated in 1793 ordering moderation of enthusiasm. And indeed, when a favourite actress made her entrance there might be cries of *'Oh cara! Oh bella! Viva, viva! Siestu benedeta!'*; poems were declaimed in her honour and from the balconies came showers of sweets, flowers and white doves. The climax was reached during a benefit performance for Grisellini, called *La Farinella*. From the topmost tier there rained partridges, pheasants and wild duck and the performance was suspended during the ensuing hunt.

Patrician women's dress had become so daring by 1776 that the Council of Ten decreed its regulation, possibly bearing in mind that masking and the opening of the theatres began on the same day, and that the former could help combine concealment of the features with over-exposure of the body. The consequence was that the display became routine and masking often dispensed with. The new law was designed to combat 'the advanced degree of licence shown by patrician ladies and even those of other respectable civic status, dressed with the maximum of indecency and fancifully adorned' and insisted that women should either wear mask and domino, or dress soberly. A few ladies of the nobility ignored the

* At one time Casanova turned an honest penny in the claque of a theatre.
† A phrase that could also imply that they would pick up a different kind of infection, from their companions.

decree and were seen at the theatre in sumptuous dresses and the *bauta* thrown back on their shoulders. Their punishment was to stay at home for three weeks.

In the same year the Council of Ten, whose functions included those of theatre censorship, prohibited the ballet of *Coriolanus*, in case its drama might inspire feelings of revolt. But all their vigilance could not suppress the tumultuous life of the theatre and the quick tempers of the Venetians, easy-going though they were as a rule. Greeks were vituperated at the performance of one historical play, French at another, and even Carlo Gozzi's squabble over Teodora Ricci was the excuse for what is called today 'audience participation'. During his short term of acting as a government spy, Casanova had to report on the political implication of plays and it was he who had warned the Inquisitors against *Coriolanus*. But there was another, more humorous side to the by-play; when the Angelus sounded, audience and actors went down on their knees, facing East, and de Brosses was only one who remarked that an actress, lying on the boards and supposedly in a faint, got to her knees when the viaticum was carried past, and then calmly resumed her insensibility.

Goldoni was the perfect playwright. He had theatre in his blood and because he loved people and studied them he became the greatest portrayer of all classes of Venetians that has ever lived. He was kind and impartial, a good family man who never passed through such crises as Carlo Gozzi experienced, because his nature was benign and understanding. Himself thoroughly honest, he could appreciate fair dealing in others and commended the Grand Council when, keen gamblers that most of them were, they voted for closing the *Ridotto* in the public interest. But we must not let our liking for this paragon cloud our judgment of facts; he was certainly the first and best Italian comic playwright but he was not, as is often claimed, an innovator. Molière was his model and example of perfection and, possibly mindful of the Restoration plays, though too early for Goldsmith and Sheridan, he frequently expressed the desire to copy English ways. It is best to think of him, then, as a reformer, whose ambition it was to raise the Italian stage to the level of the French and English.

A man of the world in the best sense, he stressed our equality in the eyes of Nature before Rousseau did so; but it would be asking too much to expect profundity or philosophy as offerings to such audiences as I have described. Pietro Longhi the artist and Goldoni regarded each other as fellows in the quest for reality and as mirrors of their generation; Goldoni's reflection seems to give less distortion. Even reading his plays brings his Venice before us; not the Venice of mysterious canals, gleaming domes and dreaming palaces, but the Venice of the ordinary man and woman. 'Did you pull the cord to open the door?' asks one sister of the other, when a visitor is waiting below; and at once we are transported to the second or third floor of one of those gloomy *palazzi* that line the smaller *calli*.

Carlo Goldoni was born in 1707 and his entry into the world was typical of his later behaviour. His *Mémoires* begin: 'My mother brought me into the world with little pain, and this increased her love for me. My first appearance was not, as is usual, announced by cries; and this gentleness seemed then an indication of the pacific character which from that day forward I have ever preserved.' Pacific, yes; but not devoid of enterprise. At eight he wrote his first play. At thirteen he ran away from his tutor at Rimini and joined a boat hired by a company of players and passed the three-day journey to Chioggia in their company.

His mother forgave him and, when he received the news, so did his father, who was practising medicine in Perugia. This city being in the Papal States, women were not allowed on the stage and young Goldoni, now staying with his father, was chosen for a female part, just as his rival Gozzi had been in Dalmatia. He tells us that he was unable to finish his speech for the shower of *confetti* (sugared almonds) that were the usual form of applause. He was next sent to an ecclesiastical college which failed to appreciate the satirical play he wrote about it, and his father begged him to make Medicine his career. But at fourteen he had found records of the theatre in England, France and Spain; only Italy since the Renaissance was not represented. Dissatisfied, he roamed and dreamed; later he did some serious work for a law degree at Venice and obtained it when he was twenty-five. But getting clients was another matter; perhaps his jovial face and genial manners frightened customers who wanted to confide their affairs to someone responsible and solemn.

He wrote plays: *Amalasinta*, which was rejected because of its cumbersome title; *Belisario*, which was produced in Venice's San Samuele theatre in 1734 and ran for three weeks, something of a record for those days. But tragedy was a dying form of entertainment and, although he composed a successful libretto for an Ascension Day musical drama, Goldoni realized that this would not be his forte. From 1734 to 1736 he again wandered through Northern Italy, with a company of actors. He carried his impetuosity into private life. In Genoa he saw a girl on a balcony and within twenty-four hours had her father's consent, and hers too. They married shortly after and his 'good Nicoletta' was to share his triumphs and disappointments for the next fifty-seven years. Back they went to Venice, after a quick visit to Paris, and in the too frequent intervals in his legal practice he wrote scenarios for Imer's company of *Commedia dell'Arte* players.

In 1740 he wrote his first attempt at a comedy in the style he had read as a boy, that of the revered Molière, and, with the help of actors from Imer's company, produced *Momolo Cortesan* (Gentleman Jerome); even this had to be a compromise, with a written part only for the protagonist and the retention of all the stock characters of the *Commedia dell'Arte*. Goldoni wrote that he was satisfied with the play's reception but we are entitled to doubt whether he regarded it as more than the first rung in the ladder of reform. For his ambition was to make a radical change in Italian comedy. Plays should be written, if possible with the stage sense and wit that Molière had used, and the day of slapstick and 'gags' was over. Then, and for no reason that we know, he abandoned all thought of the theatre as a profession and took Nicoletta to live in Pisa, where he could practise as a lawyer and perfect himself in Tuscan, then as now the purest form of Italian.

Four years later a stranger came to his office, as though to consult him. You must read Goldoni's *Mémoires* to get the full flavour of this huge man, Cesare d'Arbes, Pantalone and pantomimic extraordinary in the Medebac company in Venice. The scene must have been worthy of the pen of Goldoni himself; Cesare pleading that the lawyer throw up his practice and write plays for the company; Goldoni refusing, laughing at the big man's pantomime, his shrugs and his rueful countenance, but still refusing. Then Cesare was shrewd enough to mention how successful one of Goldoni's plays had been, the first one in which he had written the complete dialogue for all the actors. Which of us is immune from subtle flattery? Goldoni weakened; and when the flattery became less subtle he yielded.

His first play on his return to Venice, *La Vedova scalta* (The shrewd widow), was an enormous success, with packed houses for thirty nights; but to detract from it his enemies—for by now the orthodox were fighting for their obsolescent *Commedia dell'Arte*—staged a play in which the Venetian 'heroine' was devoid of all intelligence. Goldoni countered with *La Putta onorata* (The honest maiden), where the girl is the sturdy daughter of a family of gondoliers and in which the gondoliers themselves were included in several scenes, with all the art that observation and genius could bring to the task.

Gondoliers had the privilege of free admission to Venetian theatres, and those who had brought their employers to the play naturally made use of it. As Goldoni explained to their deputation, which had come to congratulate and thank him, he could not contemplate being unpopular among the gondoliers; henceforth he was their friend. But with others he was less benevolent. The cicisbei came in for some delicate satire and this may have been one of the reasons why Carlo Gozzi, himself *cavaliere servente* to Teresa Ricci, became offensive over what should have been an academic problem. Another play showed up the absurdity of duelling, snobs were derided in *Le Femmine Puntigliose* (The punctilious women), and the proud noble fallen on evil days (another smack at Count Carlo Gozzi?) in *I Pettegolezzi delle Donne* (Women's gossip).

His character was largely moulded by his early life, and that again by his kindly and inquisitive nature, too kindly ever to put a villain on the stage, but delicately making fun of fools and coxcombs. He began as he continued, a happy man and a good one, a rare combination. When young he roistered with the rest, but only up to a point; taken one night to a brothel he found the solution to his embarrassment by jumping out of a window. But he was simple too; though he could portray petty rogues for the stage he could never detect them in the flesh. He was often victimized by women, for he could think no evil of them, and once a trickster disguised as a monk sold him a lace from the Blessed Virgin's corset.

This is how he discovered about the people he was to present on the stage, by rubbing shoulders with them; nobody was too high for his satire, none too low for his sympathy. '*Homo sum, nihil humanum alienum a me puto*' could have been his motto two thousand years after Terence put it in the mouth of one of his characters. I called him happy, and like most happy men he was blessed with eternal optimism. On his wedding night he fell ill with smallpox; 'Patience,' he wrote later. 'Luckily it was not dangerous and I was left no uglier than before.' But there was another side to the picture. Attacks of melancholy, dating back to childhood, would sometimes plague him and render him unfit for work or amusement while they lasted; his worst came on after a superhuman effort, entirely his own doing. This in turn was the result of one of his acts of impulsiveness that we meet again and again in his story. On the eve of Lent the audience hissed one of his plays. Goldoni showed no sign of anger or regret; he sent the leading actress before the curtain to promise the audience that there would be sixteen new plays in the ensuing year. Some say he wrote seventeen, but the sixteen are listed. It may have been during the subsequent depression that Doctor Baroni told him, 'Look on your illness as a child attacking you with a sword in his hand; if you look out he won't hurt you. But if you bare your breast to him he'll kill you.' The advice is said to have produced a permanent cure.

Goldoni was not devoid of diplomacy. When d'Arbes refused to abandon the traditional mask, the stronghold of the *Commedia* that Goldoni was fighting, he wrote *I due Gemelli Veneziani* (The Venetian twins), in which there is a glorious part for an actor as the identical twins who, of course, are never on the stage together. A mask would have ruined the play; this time d'Arbes succumbed. Mainly, however, Goldoni's plays deal with real people of every class. Their actions reveal their character and the scenes he gives us were the familiar ones of everyday life in Venice. Women talk about their housemaids as they always have done: 'As soon as we are in bed', says one, 'she fills the kitchen with a whole crowd; once I found four of them round the dish'; 'Exactly like mine.

When I gave her notice and went through her things I found all sorts in them, even raisins.'

But two old men, holding their own meeting, have a different story to tell. 'Mine is a treasure. . . . Hardly does the sun show but she's up and about. She lights the fire and looks into my room. If I'm awake she opens the window, puts my stockings to warm . . . Ah! one doesn't find girls like that today. In the evening there are just the two of us by the fire; we tell each other stories or play some game or other. She roasts chestnuts; you should see those chestnuts, tender as butter; you'd think they were made of marzipan.'

And so the scenes follow each other, every event and character so true to life that you could swear it happened in your street yesterday. No wonder he was the darling of the audiences; who does not like to see himself portrayed, provided it is without malice? Goethe, who saw *Le Baruffe Chiozzotte* (The squabbles of Chioggia)* years after Goldoni had left Venice, wrote 'At last I can say that I have seen a play. Every type has its counterpart in real life.'

Goldoni's secret was a simple one: 'Every man' said a thinker once, 'is three people. The man as he sees himself; the man as others see him; and the man as he really is.' Goldoni put the last on the stage. Anything pompous and affected was loathsome to him and, child of the *settecento* that he was, Classical drama was a favourite target for his wit. In *L'Antiquario* Brighella sells the slipper which Nero wore when he kicked Poppaea, and the lock of Lucrece's hair that was torn out by 'false Sextus'.

Perhaps it was this contemptuous attitude to serious drama that made Chiari attack him with a vulgar parody at the height of his fame. The quarrel began in 1748 and went on for six years; Gaspare Gozzi supported Goldoni and then his brother Carlo joined in, making the contest a three-cornered one. Carlo Gozzi put on *Gli Amore delle tre melarance* (The love of three oranges) to show how naively Venetian audiences had accepted the plots of the disputants. More of his fables followed and he became popular, though Goldoni lost no ground. When in 1760, however, Voltaire wrote in praise of Goldoni, the fight became acrimonious; Goldoni, tired of spiteful intrusions into his happy nature, jumped at a royal invitation from Paris, also inspired by Voltaire, it is said. You would have thought that a major calamity had befallen Venice at the last performance. 'Good-bye, dear Goldoni! Come back soon!' They clapped and they stamped and they cried. But he never came back. Chiari retired to Brescia.

Gozzi followed up his success with four more fables, containing much sound verse, but a bare three years after his rivals' departure the sixth of

---

* And remarked, incidentally, that it 'is one of the few plays of Goldoni which is still performed'.

the *Fiabe* was such a failure that it forever ended his career as a playwright. Goldoni came to Paris to write for the Italian company that had been a permanent attraction for over two centuries;* his old ambition was fulfilled, too, for after a while he saw one of his plays produced at the *Comédie Française*, the very theatre that had seen Molière's triumphs. He had successes and failures but he never felt the urge to return to his beloved Venice and those dear Venetians he immortalized. Instead, there came a summons from the King and Goldoni had to travel to Versailles one evening in order to produce his *Burbero benefico* (The kindly boor), after its Parisian success, in the royal palace. There he was as popular as always and was given the post of Italian tutor to the royal children.

But his life outside Venice hardly concerns us. He lived on a royal pension and, when that was annulled by the Revolution, he went on living in abject poverty. The poet Marie-Joseph de Chénier, a member of the National Convention, succeeded in having his pension restored. But it was too late: they learned that he had died the previous day, and so voted a reduced one for his widow. So the good Nicoletta, who had taken the bulky *Mémoires* at his dictation, was able to survive for a few more years. His autobiography, the rather inaccurate memories of an old, hungry man, are so full of kindness and good humour that we must love him for that alone. His reputation has outlasted his rivals' and anyone who wanders into the Square of San Bartolomè in Venice can see the bronze statue of the man who wrote two hundred plays and

> Who saw life clearly and saw it whole,
> The mellow glory of the Attic stage.

*   *   *

Perhaps the *Commedia dell'Arte* wins after all. Venice the discerning has greeted the greatest pantomime actor of our century with the enthusiasm formerly reserved for kings and princes. In the Fenice Theatre Charles Spencer Chaplin, who embodies the gifts of Sacchi, Gozzi and Goldoni, was presented with a golden Lion of St Mark, a ceremony which confers as much honour on the donor as on the recipient.

---

* The Italians had their own theatre, where the Boulevard des Italiens commemorates them. They performed chiefly *Commedia dell'Arte*.

8

Evvivan i Sassoni!

' "Just look at those gondoliers!" said Candide, "Do they ever stop singing?" '

' "You don't see them at home with their wives and their little brats", said Martin. "The Doge has his troubles and the gondoliers have theirs." '

So Voltaire, the incorrigible debunker, showed up the gaiety of Venice that laughed and sang and feasted but could not conceal its underlying melancholy. That, at least, is how Valeri[1] puts it; no other traveller seems to have detected the underlying sadness. For the Venetians of the *settecento*, and here I refer to the majority and not the chosen few for whom the way was smoothed by money and servants, were a merry crowd. Grosley,[2] with a Frenchman's eye for essentials, tells how spontaneous singing would begin in the Piazza di San Marco: 'A labourer or a shoemaker or a smith, dressed in his working clothes, begins to sing a tune and other workmen join in, supporting or harmonizing in part-song, keeping an intonation, precision and taste which, in northern countries could be essayed only by persons of education.'*

Pleasure in music was one feature of the Venetian character which Goldoni presented so shrewdly and which gave rise to a flood of musical plays in other countries, all different except that they agreed in using 'The Carnival of Venice' in their titles. When Goldoni returned from Paris in 1737 he enjoyed the almost universal singing; the subject seemed of less importance than the melody, city factions insulted each other in sweet song, chants that had formerly welcomed back La Serenissima's victorious galleys were dying out, but very slowly. Love was the common theme, then as now; only then it was sung, and melodiously at that.

Dr Charles Burney,[3] a professional musician and a member of the circle that included Johnson, Garrick, Reynolds and Burke, gives us the most realistic of all accounts of popular music. 'The people here, at this season, seem to begin to live only at midnight. . . . If two of the common people walk together arm in arm, they seem to converse in song. A mere melody, unaccompanied with a second part, is not to be heard in this city: all the ballads in the streets are sung in duo.' And later, 'The first music I heard

* Grosley had apparently not been to Wales.

here was in the street ... performed by an itinerant band of two fiddlers, a violoncello and a voice, who, though as unnoticed here as a small coal-man or oyster-woman in England, performed so well that in any other country of Europe they would not only have excited attention but have acquired applause, which they justly merited.'

Home concerts seem also to have been common, as they were in England in Pepys' day. Casanova[4] takes his Henriette to one where she, the only woman, surprises everyone by performing on the violoncello. At the Goldoni house there is a painting, allegedly by Pietro Longhi, of an indoor party with the *cimbalo*, or harpsichord, lying along the table, at whose sides sit fiddlers and other musicians with their music sheets on long rests. Thus even the upper classes could provide their own music if they didn't want to go to the theatre or Conservatory.

In fact there is scarcely an English traveller who did the Grand Tour who has not something to say about the music of the people. Addison, at the very beginning of the century, remarked that it was customary for ten or twelve of the common people to sing stanzas out of Tasso in turn, 'to a pretty solemn tune'. Of these *canzonette* Cicogna[5] collected 180, some of them duets, some for soprano with *basso continuo* (extemporized, figured bass). The gondoliers would sing verses from the Classics. Goethe hired a two-oared vessel to take him out on the lagoon, one singer forward, the other in the usual place aft. The piece was sung in alternate parts and stirred him to tears; the words were by Tasso to a tune which, he says, 'we know through Rousseau', something between a choral and a recitative. He mentions 'almost forgotten, legendary folk music' and describes how the song is taken up from afar, 'like a lament without its sadness'. Tasso's *Gerusalemme Liberata* was the usual poem (Goethe also mentions Ariosto's verses, but Della Corte remarks that these were not sung) and Goldoni[6] wrote, 'The gondoleer [sic] took to his oar again and turned the prow of the gondola towards the city, singing all the way the twenty-sixth strophe of the sixteenth canto of the Jerusalem Delivered.'

'I had brought with me from Paris,' wrote Rousseau, 'the usual Parisian prejudice against Italian music* but behold, when I listened to the boat-men I realized that I had never heard singing until that moment; and pretty soon I became so enthusiastic for the opera that I left the company I was with and, alone in my box, gave myself up to enjoying myself there, in spite of the length of the show, right to the end.'

Venice was indeed the city of music *par excellence* and the opera ranked highest in popular esteem. Casanova rented a box and took the same

---

* This was in about 1742. He was still pro-Italian in 1753; but during and after 1773 he took an active part in the dissension that split Paris, between the Italian Niccolò Piccini and Christoph Gluck, a fringe Frenchman. Perhaps as the result of flattery, Rousseau allied himself with the Gluckites.

Henriette there twenty times and, on the first night, praised the music of Galuppi in an *opera buffa*. A hundred years before, Monteverdi had improved opera by suiting the music to the theme and by improving the musical accompaniment to the recitative; Antonio Lotti subsequently carried this further and, with increased attention to libretti, one could now rarely say, with Addison, 'The poetry of them is generally as exquisitely ill, as the Musick is good'. Unfortunately we are not in a position to offer intelligent comment, for operas were rarely printed. Burney explained this by reminding us that there was so much music, and most of it ephemeral, that it would not repay a printer's trouble; a few arias were all that one could find.

There was exaggerated enthusiasm for singers: each new favourite was the greatest in Italy, especially if female and passably attractive. The Portuguese Todi aroused such idolatry that her portrait was reproduced on a medal with the caption, 'Venice: the Year of Todi' just as, two centuries before, the victory of Lepanto had been commemorated. Faustina Bordoni was one of the favourites, perhaps partly because she was the wife of the German musician Hasse. De Brosses remarked, with his usual suavity, 'She is the pleasantest and best woman in the world, but not the best singer.'

The *castrati* are blamed for the decline of Venetian opera, later in the century; they too could have phenomenal triumphs, but reacted badly, their bearing being at once feminine and aggressive, though one might not think so from their portraits. The *castrato* Farinelli was a friend of the painter Amigoni, whose portrait of him hardly prepares one for the accounts of the vocal acrobatics of this soprano. When he appeared in a duet with a female soprano he had the unpleasant habit of pinching her bottom to make her utter a false note at a crucial point, and himself come in for all the credit. It is instructive to read of this old Italian sport in the province of the *castrati*; foreign visitors, take heed! As regards their vocal activities, opinions varied. For certain types of performance they were regarded as essential; they had been included in the Papal choir since 1601 and in the drawing room they are said to have given much satisfaction. De Brosses admired their voices; Rousseau thought they sang without warmth or passion. All agreed that they were bad actors.

Concerts were popular, especially those of the four Conservatories, which attracted the grand tourist and gave him an unforgettable experience. Other public concerts were given in theatres, especially that of San Samuele; in the Villa Pisani at Strà is a painting of a performance given in that theatre by a women's orchestra of about eighty performers, seated in three rows; the theatre had its regular orchestra too, and for a time Casanova fiddled there.

But the serious musical life of Venice centred round the Conservatories, four charitable foundations for the education of girls without dowries, which they later received from the Republic, in addition to a small monthly stipend. Concerts were given either in a special hall of the institution or in the church to which it was affiliated, in which case the girls were concealed by a grille. Otherwise they roamed about among the audience during the intervals, possibly their only taste of social life.

The famous four were the *Pietà*, very near St Mark's Square, the *Derelitti* (more commonly called *Ospitaletti*), the *Incurabili* and the *Mendicanti*. The first was reserved for illegitimate girls and had the best reputation for instrumental music; the *Mendicanti* was equally famous for voices; but it is likely that such minor differences varied through the century. La Lande heard one of the choirs in church and remarked that the music was so gay it was almost like dance music. But he, like all who heard them, was bewitched. Rousseau wrote that he had never heard anything so voluptuous or touching as that music and that the oldest of the performers was under twenty; he adds, however, that on close inspection the girls were frightfully ugly, even one-eyed. Others, however, were less critical and gladly attended concerts in the Conservatories where the choir could mingle with the audience. Burney reported on the *Incurabili*, that he could not say which was more charming, the composition or the execution and tried vainly to introduce the same system into England. Goethe heard an oratorio called *Saul* at the *Mendicanti*; a contralto took the name part and he wrote that he had never heard a voice like hers, which was stupendous and, in some passages, infinitely beautiful.

But de Brosses goes into most detail; after a concert at the *Pietà* he wrote to his friend de Blancey, 'They are educated and maintained at the expense of the State and their sole training is to excel in music. They sing like angels and play the violin, flute, organ, oboe, violoncello and bassoon—in fact there is no instrument big enough to intimidate them. They are cloistered like nuns. They perform without outside help and at each concert forty girls take part. I swear to you there is nothing more entertaining than to see a young and beautiful nun in her white habit, with a spray of pomegranate flowers* over her ear, conduct the orchestra, beating time with all the grace and precision imaginable.' He loved the four Conservatories and was equally enthusiastic about their instrumental performances. 'Chiaretta of the *Pieta*', he wrote, 'would be the first violin of Europe were it not for Anna-Maria of the '*Hospitalistas*' [*Ospitaletti*]'; even then he added that he preferred Margarita of the *Mendicanti*. He did not know that his lady of the pomegranate posy had a European reputation as a choirmistress; and 'Greghetta and Anzoletta', said Casotti,[7] 'did not chant but enchant.'

* Not from coquettishness, but because the pomegranate was the emblem of the *Pietà*. A.L.

But all this talent would have lain fallow had it not been for the succession of great musicians who came to Venice, or were born there and spent their days composing. The first, and possibly the greatest, was Handel, whose first visit in 1707–8 was after a stay at the Court of Tuscany; he had been to Rome, where he met Domenico Scarlatti; the two youths had competed under the auspices of Cardinal Ottoboni, a patron of the arts. After honours had been declared even, the two became firm friends. His second visit to Venice a year later was with a letter of introduction from the Viceroy at Naples to Cardinal Vicenzo Grimani. As the Grimani family were the proprietors of the theatres of San Giovanni Crisostomo and San Samuele, Handel was given every facility that a musician needs. His success was phenomenal; his opera *Agrippina* ran for twenty-seven performances and his fortune was made; he obeyed a summons to the Court of Hanover and later went to England, whither his recent employer the Elector would follow, as George I, in a few years.

The story that the Earl of Manchester, English ambassador in Venice, persuaded him to go to England, must therefore be discounted; it is probably derived from the Earl's part in persuading two Venetian painters to make the journey. But Venice did not let him go too easily; his *Agrippina* had been presented with a superb cast and its success was unprecedented. The performance used to end in an uproar of applause—surely enough to tempt him to stay—'Bravo! *Viva il caro Sassone!*' and that the dear Saxon should give credit where due, '*Viva tua madre, che t'ha fatto così!*' (Long live your mother, who made you like this!)

Handel was only one example. With the exception of the Bach family, there was scarcely a musician of note who did not come to Venice and use his time of residence to produce some of his most alluring music. There was Domenico Scarlatti, the most accomplished harpsichord player of the time; Porpora of Naples, whose tuition was essential for all practitioners of *bel canto*; Jommelli, Sacchini, Gluck, Piccini and Paisiello. Cimarosa died there and Mozart passed through in Carnival time, while being dragged round Europe as the infant prodigy; he was fifteen and left us the mention of negotiations for the production of an opera of his at San Benedetto and the remark 'I like Venice'. From his father Leopold's notebook we learn that they stayed in the 'Cavaletti' House at the 'Bridge of the Barcaroli' on the Rio San Fantino. It does not need too bold an imagination to make this the Cavaletto Inn, one of the best known hotels then and now, which looks over a backwater where the gondoliers (*barcaroli*) park their vessels at night and wake the guest at an unearthly hour with their chatter. And the Church of San Fantino is only a hundred yards away. (Foreigners readily changed Italian terminations from '-o' to '-i' as in the case of Canaletto.)

Perhaps the most influential foreigner was Johann Adolf Hasse, born near Hamburg in 1699. He was a student of Porpora in Naples and in 1727 was invited to direct the choir of the *Incurabili*; he soon followed Lotti as chief organist at San Marco and, apparently deciding that his future, music-ally and matrimonially, lay in Venice, he became a Roman Catholic; where Henri IV thought Paris worth a mass, Hasse thought the same of San Marco and Faustina Bordoni, with whom de Brosses (and unkind people said many others more successful) was so enchanted. She must have had some vocal skill, for all the Frenchman's judgment, for she was known as the first who could crowd sixteen notes into a bar, a notable feat of *rubato*. She loved her '*caro Sassone*', for Handel's pet name had apparently devolved on Hasse,★ and they lived in intermittent harmony for many years near the Church of San Marcuola, where they are buried.

Hasse did much for music in Venice and the world, and to him we owe the popularization, if not the introduction of the *recitativo accompagnato* in place of the *recitativo secco* (it is more usual, however, to point out that the invention was used by J. S. Bach in his Passions and Cantatas). Today Hasse is remembered as much for his more intimate works and church music as for his hundred operas; his *Miserere* in C minor for two sopranos, two contraltos, strings and organ deserves immortality. His fame had crossed the Atlantic by 1765, when one or more of his compositions were performed at a concert in Charleston, South Carolina. We can be sure that Hasse's continued popularity in Venice was enhanced by his frequent invitations to perform in foreign countries, whither he regularly travelled with his Faustina, to return as punctiliously. His concerts must have been major events, for Grosley wrote that 'four hundred singers and instrumen-talists picked from among the *virtuosi* of Italy, filled the orchestra, which was conducted by the famous Saxon, composer of the music ... the charming nuns came and went to two grilles which divided them from the altar, made conversation and distributed refreshments to gentlemen and clergy [no joke apparently intended] who were all, fan in hand, gathered round one or other grating.'[8]

There were enough Venetians to balance the foreigners in music. What Monteverdi had begun, Lotti, Caldara and Vivaldi carried to perfection; Corelli, though not a Venetian, had such an influence on the structure of musical composition that he must be mentioned; he was a violinist and, in spite of this, took the honours away from the soloist in a concerto and divided them among a group of instruments. Vivaldi and others followed and the climax of these *concerti grossi*, as Corelli called them, was reached by J. S. Bach in his six Brandenburg concertos. That they were still strange

★ As a son of Hamburg, he could hardly be called a Saxon, though the province of Niedersachsen was near enough to Hamburg and his fair hair could have been partly responsible. In any case, the Venetians might have called any German a *Sassone*.

in 1739 may be deduced from a passage in de Brosses' correspondence: 'They have a sort of music here that we don't know in France and which would be most suitable for the Bourbon Gardens. They are big concertos without a principal violin.'

But music had not become a science devoid of emotional overtones. Vivaldi, 'the Red Priest', so-called because of his red hair, was hauled up before the Inquisition for leaving Mass at the supreme moment in order to rush to the sacristy and jot down a phrase that had just occurred to him; he was exonerated.* Faustina Bordoni's marriage was the result of an impulse; when she heard Hasse accompany his own singing on the clavichord, she swore she would have no other husband than this *caro Sassone* with the fair hair. And her teacher Benedetto Marcello,† sitting at his window one night, heard a gondola pass, its girl passengers singing, one of them outstanding for her voice, 'as brilliant as a pearl' he said and might have added, 'pouring forth thy soul abroad, in such an ecstasy'. He took no chance of doing without it and married her.

The whole atmosphere of Venice made these adventures seem rational. The singer Guadagni was made a Knight of St Mark, and Cimarosa was escorted home with a torchlight procession after his *Convitato di Pietra*.‡ The opera has a history. Molière called his version of the play 'The Feast of Stone'; later authors, including Goldoni, omitted the statue and called the play 'Don Juan Tenorio'; but the statue came back in opera and several were written with titles identical with, or similar to that of Cimarosa. Giuseppe Gazzaniga produced his version in 1787 and introduced his famous catalogue of conquests—one refrain now very familiar is '*Ma in Spagna vi sono mill tre*' which da Ponte stole and offered to Mozart for his *Don Giovanni*.

Antonio Vivaldi shared with Lotti the admiration of and affection for Venice. He was not only a prolific composer but a noted violinist. Opera was the best source of a composer's income, so Vivaldi began composing operas when he was thirty-five and was soon affluent; forty-eight, almost a half, of his operas survive, which is remarkable when we remember Dr Burney's remarks about printed music. He composed six hundred concertos and not, as Stravinsky sneered, 'one concerto six hundred times'. He made full use of the *concerto grosso* form and from him it passed to J. S. Bach, who also arranged nine of Vivaldi's works for the harpsichord and

* In fact he had a heart complaint and was excused from celebrating Mass. Perhaps this is the truth behind the story of the Inquisitors.

† Sometimes confused with his elder brother Alessandro, whose mistress Faustina had been.

‡ The original of what we now call *Don Juan* was a play by Tirso de Molina about an imaginary Don Juan Tenorio. The title was *El Burlador de Sevilla, y Convidado de Piedra* (The joker of Seville and the stone guest). The title refers to the tomb-statue of one of Juan's dead enemies, which he has jokingly invited to supper and which finishes by clasping him in its stony grip and sinking with him to the underworld.

four for the organ. The master's implicit approval should surely be enough for us. Perhaps Vivaldi's greatest attraction was his preference for polyphonic music, and his counterpoint exercised the same influence on Bach as did the Italian painters of the Renaissance on Albrecht Dürer.

Vivaldi is mentioned frequently in connection with his post of director at the Conservatory of the *Pietà*, where de Brosses must have seen him, and we already know that his girls were thought the best of the four Conservatories by some listeners. Unfortunately we do not know what happened to the affluence that opera brought him; he resigned from his post at the *Pietà* in 1740—another mystery—and is said to have died in Vienna a year later, being buried in a pauper's grave. He thus set the fashion for other great musicians, notably Mozart and Schubert, and finds himself in worthy, if needy, company. Like Tiepolo, Vivaldi could produce a work of art in record time; in fact he boasted that he could compose a concerto with full score in less time than it took a clerk to write it down.

In the second half of the century there was no falling off in musical talent. Antonio Sacchini the composer stayed in Venice in about 1770, so there is some evidence that the old tradition was maintained and that musicians came to Venice to acquire polish. Antonio Salieri, who was born in Verona in 1750, went to Vienna while still in his twenties; a conductor and composer, he won fame by teaching Beethoven and Schubert and became the friend and adviser of the former. My only criticism is that he disliked Mozart.

But the great figure in the musical world of Venice was Baldassare Galuppi (1706–85) who, having been born on the Island of Burano in the lagoon, was naturally called '*Il Buranello*'. He seems to have matured late, or perhaps he was overshadowed by Vivaldi in his earlier years; at all events his genius appears at a time when he and Goldoni were both famous and united by friendship. There was nothing vague about his music, nor his character; in opera and in church or chamber music his touch was sure and craftsmanship was never sacrificed to sentiment. A true artist, his temperament forbade the plunge into sensuousness. 'His artistic spirit', says Della Corte, remains among the examples of the *settecento*. With his subtle wit and discriminating tenderness, he seems the most Venetian of them all.' Through him Goldoni's common sense came to rescue opera libretti from absurdity; Galuppi was, in fact, Goldoni's counterpart in the province of music. Browning, himself no mean musician, did the same for English poetry; of a *Buranello* toccata he wrote:

Brave Galuppi! That was music! Good alike at grave and gay.
I can always leave off talking when I hear a master play.

If Browning's verbal output was as generous as his written, this would have been praise indeed; we must remember, too, that Galuppi died seventeen years before Browning was born. Incidentally, the Roman audience to whom Goldoni presented his *Pamela nubile* was not enthusiastic about *Il Buranello*'s incidental music. His later life was spent abroad, first in London, then in St Petersburg and in both he composed and produced operas; a true son of Venice, he returned there to die.

There are few records of virtuosi, for the composers themselves were, without exception, masters of one or more instruments. Thus Pietro Antonio Locatelli of Bergamo, some of whose works are still in the concert repertoire, was a famous violinist; Lotti and Handel were accomplished organists, Vivaldi was noted as a violinist and Hasse, Domenico Scarlatti and Galuppi were all outstanding performers on the harpsichord. But there is one who shone as an instrumentalist and is mentioned only parenthetically as a composer; Giuseppe Tartini, whom de Brosses heard in Padua, is still known for 'The Devil's Trill'; Tartini claimed to have dreamed of the Devil playing a sonata which he could only afterwards vaguely remember. On waking, however, he composed and played 'The Devil's Trill'.

Libretto has been mentioned more than once and it is only fitting that the home of opera, Italy, should have produced the first poetical librettists. Of them Goldoni[9] wrote: 'These two illustrious authors effected the reform of Italian opera. Before them nothing but gods, devils, machines and wonders were to be found in these harmonious entertainments. Zeno was the first who conceived the possibility of representing tragedy in lyrical verse without degradation, and singing it without producing exhaustion. He executed the project in a manner most satisfactory to the public, reflecting the greatest glory on himself and his nation.'

First Apostolo Zeno, then Pietro Metastasio (whose real name was Trapassi) inaugurated and sustained the doctrine that the poetry of an opera is as important as the music. Thanks to them Italian posters announce an opera performance:

OTELLO
by
ARRIGO BOITO
Music by Giuseppe Verdi

Lorenzo da Ponte remains the most famous of all librettists. Born of Jewish parents in 1749 and converted early, he became a Catholic priest with every advantage except a sense of vocation. He went to Venice, where he led a dissipated life as far as poverty permitted. He was, in fact, a friend of Casanova. An interval in Treviso, as teacher in the seminary, was ended by a difference on a point of dogma. In 1779 his conduct became so flagrant that he had to flee Venice, leaving behind his patrician mistress Angiolina (or Angela) Tiepolo. He was welcomed in Vienna by the enlightened Joseph II and wrote libretti, among which the best re-membered are those for Mozart, who composed the music for *Don Giovanni* and *The Marriage of Figaro*. In the latter da Ponte took care to leave out much of the political satire of the original play by Beaumarchais, partly because the Emperor Joseph had forbidden the staging of its revolutionary sentiments. When Joseph died da Ponte was superseded at court and went to Trieste and from there to London. He married an Englishwoman and sent Mozart an invitation to join him in London, but Mozart knew that death was reaching out for him and refused. Da Ponte and his wife went to America; he became a storekeeper in Elizabethtown, New Jersey, then a distiller in Sunbury, Pennsylvania and finally a teacher of Italian in New York City. With a sudden return of enthusiasm he staged Italian opera performances there in 1832, introduced an Italian company and instigated the building of an opera house. Though it was soon turned over to less melodious purposes, da Ponte had succeeded in making the New York public aware of Italian opera; he thus sustained Venice's reputation for not only producing the ornaments of civilization, but for disseminating them throughout the civilized world.

Part Three

FINE ARTS

9

Architecture

In assessing any period of art, your own taste should have priority. Avoid, therefore, the temptation of thinking, 'I don't know anything about art, but I know what the art critic of the "Weakly Acetic" likes.' The seductive doctrine of blindly following the expert had its repercussions in the architecture of Venice and the *terraferma* and from there spread to distant lands, especially Britain; not, let me add, that this was necessarily bad. It all began with the Roman Marcus Vitruvius Pollio, who studied Greek and Roman buildings in the first century B.C. and wrote down his conclusions. He found certain proportions between the diameters of columns and their heights, and that spacing was likewise governed by arithmetical rules, if it was to be elegant; when all that was Classical, Greek or Roman, became automatically the best, the Renaissance had, by definition, arrived and the canons of Vitruvius, having come to light, were destined to be dictator. It was Andrea di Pietro who went to Rome in 1540 to study the principles of Vitruvius in the Roman buildings that survived; and it was his book, *I Quattro Libri dell'Architettura*, that influenced his contemporaries and successors. While still young he showed such grace and wisdom that he was nicknamed 'Palladio' after the goddess of wisdom, an indication, if one were needed, of the homage then paid to the Classics.

For a time the cold, Classical proportions of Palladio ruled a world that had tired of the flamboyant Gothic. Then Baroque stepped in; the reaction against Classicism took the form of emphasizing light and movement and of concealing, as far as possible, the linear and rectangular features of the Classical temple. But once more tastes changed: with the discovery of the treasures of Pompeii and Herculaneum a second wave of enthusiasm for the Classical swept Europe. Antiquarians of the eighteenth century, culminating in Winkelmann, set the stage for what became almost a second Renaissance. Thus de Brosses could deplore the Byzantine and Romanesque glories of St Mark in Venice and San Zeno in Verona, Goethe 'offer up a grateful prayer' at the grave of Consul Smith, to whom he owed his copy of Palladio, and Rousseau praise the choirs of the orphanages and write not a word about Venice's amazing buildings.

Knowledge of architecture, in fact, seems scanty in the memoirs of most travellers who give us, perhaps fortunately, far more detailed accounts of manners, customs, music and other impermanent elements of Venice.

Among the many wise sayings of Mr George Mikes is this: 'It is not so much the few great artists as the many minor ones that make a period of art really outstanding.' Compare this with the Durants': 'It was in the little things of life that the eighteenth century displayed its most careless wealth and most careful art.'

The art of eighteenth-century Venice, as we shall examine it, and especially its architecture, might have been devised to illustrate these truths. There is no great name; there is no novel style. But we stop again and again, after a surfeit of Gothic and Renaissance palaces and churches, to admire the triumphs of an exquisite decorative taste rather than a new basic structure. Take as examples the unfinished façade of San Marcuola, ponderous and threatening; then compare it with the fronts of two completed churches by the same architect Giorgio Massari—those of the Pietà and the Gesuati (see plate 5); note how Paladian proportions can be combined with light-hearted decoration, how the churches, probably weighing as much as San Marcuola, seem ready to float away, while avoiding the fussiness of pure Baroque, which seems only to add weight to the structure. The Church of the Scalzi by Giuseppe Sardi is a good example of such misplaced zeal, of the attempt to put all the goods in the shop window (see plate 6). And lest you should believe that Massari was an exception, look at the façades of San Stae (now but a hollow shell) by Domenico Rossi, nephew of Sardi, or San Rocco by Bernardino Maccaruzzi (see plate 7).

The last was mentioned earlier as the designer of the oval, temporary fair stall that was put up for two weeks every year in the Piazza di San Marco, which Guardi thought worth painting, whence an engraving by A. Sandi. For architecture is not to be judged by church façades alone; it is true that the exteriors of palaces of this period are not as attractive as those of churches, but their interiors, and especially their staircases, are often masterpieces. An illustration readily comes to mind: the Ca' Rezzonico, that great palace on the Grand Canal that now houses the Museum of the Art of the *settecento*, was begun by Baldassare Longhena in the seventeenth century and completed by Massari nearly a hundred years later. The upper floors of the exterior are as much Longhena's Baroque as the sombre ground floor, but the interior gives you an idea of what Rococo architecture could do with an imposing staircase or a ballroom. One of the airiest and most delicate interiors in Venice is in the Ghetto synagogue, where an anonymous architect of the eighteenth century added an oval women's gallery with the lightest of light wrought-iron screens.

10   Venice: the Ghetto. A glimpse of the sombre results of segregation and overcrowding. The streets are exceptionally narrow and the houses high

11   The *Portici* of Monte Berico, Vicenza. This enormous gallery, over a mile long, allows worshippers to walk up to the Basilica of the Madonna del Monte under shelter. Many chapels are incorporated. It was designed by Francesco, son of Antonio Muttoni in the first half of the eighteenth century

12   An arch in the grounds of the Villa Pisani at Strà

13. Stables at the Villa Pisani. This beautifully decorated building has been allowed to decay while more flamboyant, some would say vulgar, parts of the palace are kept spick and span for the tourists' delight. Georgina Masson took this fine photograph

14 One of the main entrances and delicate wrought-iron gates at the Villa Manin at Passeriana, near Udine

15 Gates of the Villa Manin. Venetian wrought-iron work was especially attractive during the *settecento*

16   The Villa Lattes, Giorgio Massari's earliest work. A jewel of *settecento* architecture

17   The public park of Prà della Valle, Padua. A seventeenth-century solution to the problem of swamps

19 Antonio Corradini: Apollo flaying Marsyas. An
example of the heights to which garden statuary
rose in the hands of this Venetian master. He was
noted for his light treatment of drapery

18 The mask over entrance to the campanile of Santa Maria Formosa in Venice.
Though Ruskin assumed that it represented the spirit of evil, it is an example of an
inborn malady, neurofibromatosis. It was probably intended to be apotropaic

20 Bronze half-gate of the Loggietta, Campanile of San Marco, by Antonio Gai.
For all its over-decoration it still impresses me as elegant, if not actually frivolous

But you must not think that all was gaiety and lightness. The Gozzi house in the San Barnabà parish is a picture of gloom, naturally enough in the heart of the *Barnabotti* district; and in the Ghetto, where no expansion was allowed, floor was piled on floor, with no thought beyond supplying shelter for a growing population.

To me one of the surprising facts about eighteenth-century architecture in Venice is the quantity that was built. There was not only a new lightness of style but an astonishing output, so remarkable that it is difficult to reconcile it with the economic state of La Serenissima as outlined authoritatively by Fanfani.[1] On Monte Berico, for example, outside Vicenza, over a mile of solid stone arcade allows the worshipper to walk up to the Basilica of the Madonna del Monte. It was designed by the younger Muttoni at the close of his career in 1746 and the huge expenses were met by the voluntary contributions of the pious, who could thus go to church dryshod and take a rest in the numerous chapels that are built into the *Portici*.

Very occasionally one reads of the surprise felt at the amount of money spent on decorating a bankrupt city. Such was the case with the lavish reconstruction of the side wall and high altar of San Geremia in 1760. The cost was met by the parish priest himself, a poor man called Giovanni Zaniol. Questioned by the authorities, he stated that the source of the money was a secret he could not reveal. Later,[2] it was alleged that he had found gold and silver in a tomb in the church and had used it to beautify the building. Here the matter rests, except for an inscription we shall find later (see page 98).

Another aspect of architecture is the accessories; you may not like the bombastic façade, so typical of Jesuit churches, of the Gesuiti* in Venice, but you will be impressed with its bronze doors. The materials are important too, but not often mentioned: marble and Istrian stone, this also sometimes called marble, form the main blocks, but some large buildings simply have a marble or stucco facing over brick as may be deduced from the unfinished front of San Marcuola by Massari. Floors in private palaces are often of parquet and in such cases the pattern may vary from room to room; otherwise they could be made of the conglomerate of marble chips and coloured cement that La Lande was so delighted to discover in its best form, Venetian *terrazzo*, far superior to the recent French attempts at imitation; Addison, too, had admired 'ground brick, worked into mortar, laid as a red floor and rubbed with oil', making a beautiful surface.

One of Venice's most famous buildings is the great seventeenth-century Church of the Salute, Longhena's Baroque masterpiece. In an age when Baroque ornament was running riot it serves to remind us of the sober

* Not to be confused with the Gesuati, a branch of the Dominicans.

taste of Venice, whose buildings were not overloaded with broken pediments, functionless scrolls and excessive sculpture. I have mentioned this in order to point out that a reaction set in and there was a general desire to return to the dignified (apparent) simplicity of Palladio. Of this, Venice's best example is the Church of San Giorgio Maggiore; you will observe, not only the Classical style of the façade of a church built in the sixteenth century, but the faithful imitation of the bell tower of St Mark, built in the eighteenth. The huge, barrack-like Palazzo Pisani, not far from San Moisè, combines a sober, Neo-Classical façade with the tall window arches of Byzantine buildings and with forty-two sculptured marble heads over them. Austere, but not forbidding. The purist reaction against Baroque excesses swept over Europe in the eighteenth century, and it is a question whether the revival of Palladian architecture that was thus born began in Palladio's country or elsewhere, quite possibly in England. Towards the end of the century it is said to have changed into a 'cold and tedious classicism',[3] but I suggest it would take an expert to determine where this took over from the purist reaction.

A strange fact about Venetian architects is that so many came from the mountains. Italian Switzerland was foremost and at least four of the best known—Longhena, Sardi, Rossi and Muttoni—came from Lugano. Many started life as masons, often following a family trade; many combined their architectural with other gifts. So the great Sansovino was a sculptor; Piranesi became famous through his engravings though he did actually design one church in Rome and always signed himself 'architetto Veneziano'; Maccaruzzi was an engineer; Rossi and Cominelli were sculptors and Visentini a painter and engraver. Nearly all showed good taste and moderation. We are grateful when we consider what could have been done with the bell tower of San Giorgio Maggiore, especially in comparison with the tasteless one that was added to Verona Cathedral, and see the one that was actually built.

Reading technical writing makes architectural appreciation in Venice a hazardous experience and strengthens me in recommending the individual's taste. Says Valeri,[4] 'the prevalent pictorial or scenographic tendency, which from the beginning has characterized Venetian architecture, triumphs resolutely in the more bold and free inventions of Baroque fantasy or allows itself to be recognized, as a Rococo grace-note, within the neo-classical plans of Palladian influence.' I submit that all that is meant is that the elegance of the Palladian Classical style benefits from a touch of frivolity. We shall meet the same effect in some of Tiepolo's paintings.

So let us leave the world of theory and definitions, the ponderous palaces and the churches with their athetotic marble saints on the pediment, and follow the nobles of Venice to the *villeggiatura*, where frivolity was the aim.

We can today accompany the greater part of the Brenta Canal by road, on the small but pleasant highway between Venice and Padua. On either side are the patrician villas, most of them bearing the stamp of neglect, but here and there we find one that has become a show place and is to some extent preserved. Such a one is the Villa Pisani at Strà, built by Frigimelica and Preti* when Alvise Pisani was elected Doge in 1735; here is the climax of the Palladian, the imposing centre with its eight engaged Corinthian columns (the back has a portico even more like a Greek temple, with six free columns), the Classical pediment, the wings whose windows have alternative triangular and curved pediments and whose roof line is broken by urns and statuary. All this, you may feel, is too solemn for a country house and indeed there is little of the frivolity of the *villeggiatura* about it, perhaps because of the owner's rank. But the garden, even in its present state—and the upkeep of so many acres is practically impossible today—has those elements which delighted the eighteenth century. There is a maze which eventually leads to a gazebo, from whose roof you see what were once lawns, copses and superb outbuildings among the venerable trees. Bisecting the gardens and therefore at right angles to the main block is an ornamental pond so long that Georgina Masson calls it a canal. Along it runs a low wall, supporting more symbolic statuary, and at the foot, a good quarter of a mile from the villa, are the Palladian stables, whose interior, to this visitor at least, is more interesting than showpieces such as reception rooms, Napoleon's bedroom or the bed of his stepson Eugène de Beauharnais. But what a shock on looking through the broken windows and seeing the state to which the once proud stalls have fallen! You will realize, at least, how dignified was the Doge's frivolity and sympathize with him.

The interior of the main block is all in keeping with the spirit of the Rococo. The vast ballroom has a ceiling whose centre-piece by G. B. Tiepolo is almost spoiled by its over-ornate setting; a sunken marble bath is fed through huge, copper taps which, in this home of elegant over-ornamentation, look as though they had been borrowed from a marine engine room.

The other large, in fact the largest Venetian villa is that of the Manin family and is at Passeriano, near Udine. So huge is it that one becomes quite confused as to which is villa and which stables and farm buildings. For no sooner have you decided that this or that group must be the villa itself than you turn round to see another gleaming mass of marble on the

* Venetian architects designed many villas: Francesco Antonio Muttoni built La Favorita at Monticelli di Fara, Lonigo in about 1710; Giambattista Pozzo, the Palazzo Pompei at Ilasi; and Alessandro Tremignon, many villas in the style of Longhena, his inspiration.

other side of the main road, which runs through the grounds. Perhaps its wrought-iron gates are its most artistic feature.

Now for one of the smaller villas, where you can easily imagine a modest Venetian family enjoying a light-hearted holiday: the villa—a little gem with a ponderous name—Tamagnino-Negri-Lattes, near Treviso, was Giorgio Massari's earliest work, completed in 1715, whereas his period of activity is usually given as 1726 to 1743. It is enjoyable because it is small, because its proportions are harmonious and because its garden, at least in front, is kept in good shape; in short it is a country house in which anyone of taste would like to spend a holiday, which is more than could be said of the other villas I discuss. Note how low the wings are and yet how everything is in proportion: the balustrades are shorter, the urns smaller than usual and the statues are those of children. Elena Bassi[5] draws attention to one feature which is a sort of compliment to Palladio, the two *oculi*, one on either side of the top floor windows. This villa, in fact, is one of the earliest demonstrations of how the *settecento* copied Palladio, whereas the *seicento* had only paid him lip service.

It also reminds us, with its name, of details in the life and background of Massari. His uncle, Paolo Tamagnino, was also his first client and commissioned this villa; Massari married Countess Maria Negri of nearby Bassano di Grappa. I could not discover where the name Lattes came from; I suspect that it belonged to subsequent owners. There is a portrait of Giorgio Massari in the villa, by Rosalba Carriera; very handsome he looks too, but Rosalba was the kindest of creatures.

Some villas, like the Pisani and Manin, are memorable for their grandeur; others like the Villa Capra (La Rotunda) at Vicenza, for their exquisite proportions; and still others for their interiors. I am not referring to villas with famous murals, such as those of the Tiepolos at Villa Valmarana ai Nani, or the Villa Barbaro with its Veronese frescoes. At the Lattes there is the furniture that was in everyday use; not the over-decorated pieces that were kept, like the main floor, for special occasions; simple, tasteful, often beautiful examples of the cabinet-maker's art, or a white porcelain group from Capodimonte, or even the collection of musical boxes upstairs which, no doubt, caused roars of laughter, for a tune tinkles forth as you sit down, another when you pull out a drawer, or take a drink, or even when the clock marks the hour.

But these are only a small sample from the many villas that still dot the Veneto, most of them half-forgotten, some half-remembered, usually neglected or converted to base uses. The Villa Negri at Piovene near Bassano di Grappa is fairly well kept, and the garden of the Villa Rizzardi near the Valpolicella (Verona) is still a masterpiece; but the Villa Dolfin at Rosà is the ghost of splendour standing in a tangled wood. Others, when you approach them, give you the feeling of *déjà vu* and you know that they are familiar; you may imagine that you have seen them photographed in a travel article or a tourist poster, but all that has happened is that you have seen an imitation in the English countryside.

For Ackerman has called England 'the most enthusiastic and influential of Palladian nations'. It began with Inigo Jones who visited Venice and presumably Vicenza, where he must have seen many examples of Palladio's style, for back in England he earned the title of 'the English Palladio'. Christopher Wren followed on and inspired Restoration architecture. At heart a Palladian, he had much to contend with: popular taste wanted Baroque fripperies to break up the very lines he prized so highly, or confused Palladian with papist and insisted, as in St Paul's, on having a Gothic interior as an antidote to the Classical façade. Michel is not quite correct in saying that Vanbrugh and Hawksmoor propagated his style; they favoured the Baroque with their own modifications, as can be seen in the former's Blenheim Palace. By the time they had completed their span the usual reaction set in, just as in Italy.

The second 'Renaissance' came in the first quarter of the eighteenth century: Richard Boyle, third Earl of Burlington and fourth Earl of Cork (1695–1753) was an enthusiastic patron of the arts. In 1716, with all the fire of youth, he had a sumptuous edition of Palladio's *Quattro Libri* printed and at about the same time came across a new English work, the *Vitruvius Britannicus* of Colen Campbell. Burlington, having done the Grand Tour, put his aspirations into practice; he brought back from Rome a young English painter and architect, William Kent, and remained his patron for many years. The flood of books on the 'new' architecture was exceeded only by the new buildings themselves. Burlington House in Piccadilly, where Kent was a permanent guest, was remodelled to the Palladian pattern and Burlington himself continued to promote the cause of Palladianism. He was thwarted once: when he submitted Kent's plan for a new Mansion House, he had it turned down because Palladio had been a papist; but with the new finds at Herculaneum and Pompeii, enthusiasm for pagan architecture overlooked its Popish intermediary.

Burlington had a country house built at Chiswick, as nearly as possible a copy of Palladio and Scamozzi's Villa Capra (La Rotonda), outside Vicenza; the same design was used by Colen Campbell for Mereworth Castle in Kent. Alas, their passion for Palladio made them forget the nature of the English climate and that a refreshing breeze in Italy is a nasty draught in England. In the fourth epistle of his *Moral Essays* Pope drew attention to this very defect in the villa at Chiswick, with its four Classical porticoes:

Then clap four slices of pilaster on't,
That, lac'd with bits of rustic, makes a front:
Shall call the winds through long arcades to roar,
Proud to catch cold at a Venetian door;
Conscious they act a true Palladian part,
And if they starve, they starve by rules of art.

Had Pope heard the story that Palladio introduced his style in revenge, to impoverish the nobles who had treated him with contempt? It would be tedious, and is certainly unnecessary to list Britain's Palladian buildings, from Burlington House, itself now the headquarters of Art, through the Horse Guards and Kedleston Hall, Derbyshire, to St Martin-in-the-Fields. It suffices to remember that the Grand Tour of the Englishman brought home a revival of Palladio, and that this then spread to the remotest parts of Europe, perhaps even back to Italy.

I have mentioned gardens, an integral part of country houses in any land. The so-called Italianate or formal garden had a firm hold in England at the time of the Palladian revival and it was William Kent, strangely enough, who was among the first to favour the 'natural' garden, which reached its zenith in the landscape gardening of England under Lancelot ('Capability') Brown, in the second half of the century. But in the *terra-ferma* you can still see the wrecks of many formal gardens; the box or myrtle hedges now riot extravagantly, the balustrades look different but no worse for having one side green with moss; ornamental pools are either dry or scummy and one author's photograph shows a priceless Corradini statue standing in a field of maize. For garden statuary became a department of sculpture and gardens had the additional task of giving the architect scope for designing follies, gazebos and ornamental gateways with their display of wrought iron. We still see traces too of a strange eighteenth-century tendency in and around Venice, that of transforming gardens into paved *cortili*, where statues and exotic pot plants took the place of lawns and borders. Nor must we forget that it was through Venice that many eastern flowers came to Europe: the oriental hyacinth, the garden ranunculus and probably the tulip and mimosa.

In the democratic days of the Veneto even the humble citizens had access to gardens, some of them prepared and maintained at great cost. Thus at Padua the great circular area which was once a Roman theatre and later a swamp was drained by the City Council and the Venetian *procuratore* Andrea Memmo became responsible for reclaiming it. He employed the architect and engineer Domenico Cerato and by 1776 a new park was open to the public. It consists of a central, circular island, surrounded by a moat and occupied by tall plane trees. At the four cardinal points bridges cross the moat and their paths continue, to intersect at a central fountain.

Everything recalls the elegance of the Rococo; the balustrades of the bridges, the coping of the moat and the eighty-seven statues that surmount it on either side. Not that they are great works of art—the only one by Canova is now housed in the Civic Museum—but they commemorate the glorious past, from Livy to Morgagni; there are popes, cardinals and monks, artists and philosophers, scientists and senators, all standing with their backs to the moat, half of them looking outward over the encircling meadow, the rest inward. There is nothing studied about the placing of the statues; indeed the Parks Committee missed the opportunity of hinting at the mutual dislike between the Florentine Guicciardini and one of his teachers at the University of Padua. With eighty-seven famous people to use as pawns, something more apposite could surely have been attempted.

10

Sculpture and Minor Arts

If the sculpture of eighteenth-century Venice rarely reaches the heights, as does painting, at least it is not as uniformly boring as the preceding wave of Baroque which had replaced Mannerism. In neither style was there room for humour and precious little for accuracy either. It is my belief—a purely personal one—that the arts of eighteenth-century Venice tried to embody both, depending, of course, on whether the artist had a sense of humour.* My hypothesis may earn a moment's reflection in the light of what I have written about daily life in Venice. The Age of Enlightenment saw the awakening of Science which, in its turn, depends on accurate observation. Hence the view painters and hence, of course, the realism of sculpture, culminating in Canova, who finally discarded all idea of the portrayal of majestic power and rugged symbolism and substituted sensuous grace and beauty; you might call him the Praxiteles of the West. The century that went out with Canova began with the second greatest, Corradini. The rest was filled with competent second-raters, some of them spare-time architects, for Bernini had stated a profound truth when he said that architecture and sculpture were complementary.[1]

The accuracy I mentioned is shown not only by a reversion to realism, though this plays the greatest part. The best example I can produce is the grotesque head over the entrance to the bell tower of Santa Maria Formosa. Of this hideous mask Ruskin wrote, 'In that head is embodied the type of the evil spirit to which Venice was abandoned in the fourth period of her decline, and it is well that we should see and feel the full horror of it in this spot and know what pestilence it was that came and breathed upon her beauty until it melted away'; and Molmenti[2] adds, 'rightly did Ruskin declare that human fancy could fall no lower'. But this is simply an example of ignorance cloaked under fine writing. The mask is not fanciful and it has a function. It is a widespread belief that the Evil Eye can enter a building through the doorway and that an amulet should be placed there. Hence the Jewish *mezuzah*, the henna painted on the jambs and lintels of oriental houses, the amuletic hand as a

---

* It may be worth considering whether the Enlightenment was intimately bound up with the rise of a modern sense of humour.

94

door-knocker and the devil mask seen in many western countries; the last is on the same principle as the Medusa head which has for millennia been used in Greece and Southern Italy as a protection. The more hideous it is, the more efficiently it will act. And now for the second fact: the head over the *campanile* entrance is not the product of a debased imagination or diseased fancy. It is the accurate representation of a diseased model, one who suffered from neurofibromatosis, or von Recklinghausen's disease, a rare, inborn malady. Molmenti says that Charcot, the great French neurologist, recognized in it 'the study of obscure problems'; he had probably seen a similar case and since his day every medical student is expected to recognize it. So here we have, not 'the evil spirit to which Venice was abandoned', but a poor, deformed model and an example of the accuracy of representation to which Venice had risen.

The previous century had produced no Venetian sculpture of note; in fact, the most famous sculptors were from Bologna and Genoa, or Flemings and Germans. The first Venetian to demand our attention is the little-known Orazio Marinali (1643–1720), whose busts of Cardinal Querini are in the Querini-Stampalia Collection in Venice. Here, for the first time since Bernini, marble takes on an appearance of life. Marinali produced much garden statuary and it is quite likely that the two weather-beaten Caesars behind the Villa Tamagnino-Negri-Lattes are by his hand; in keeping with the unpretentious nature of the villa, the statues are in Istrian stone, not marble. He also made the fine statue of St Bassano, in the main square of the town that bears the same name, and most of the statues and bas-reliefs of the great church on Monte Berico, Vicenza, that are reached through the mile-long arcade.

Antonio Corradini (1668–1752) was the first of the famous Venetian sculptors after the Renaissance. His merit derives more from his technique than from originality and his 'speciality' was the portrayal of veiled women in solid marble; his personal mannerisms, in fact, are chiefly directed towards drapery which, in the case of 'Apollo and Marsyas', as well as 'Zephyrus and Flora', make a graceful addition to cumbersome compositions. Apart from this idiosyncrasy, and the swags and bouquets of which he was so fond, he stands out as a milestone rather more than half way between Bernini and Canova. We can recognize both in some of his works, but there is no suspicion of plagiarism, either on his part or Canova's.

Corradini's statuary can be found in places widely separated for, like other leading Venetian artists, he was often called away; some of his figures are in Corfu, others in Carinthia, Naples, Rome, Lisbon and Germany. It is interesting to read[3] that in 1743, while he was working in Rome, his studio was visited by the Old Pretender and his two sons, the elder still Bonny Prince Charlie and not yet the licentious sot; another link with Canova, who was to make their memorial in the Basilica of St Peter in Rome. As another pointer to the sound basis for Corradini's popularity, Hodgkinson mentions that models of some of his later works were discovered in the Vatican in 1925 and at first attributed to Michelangelo. While still in Venice he made the celebrated three-quarter size Pietà in San Moisè, a fine work but one that still looks back to the previous century, for it expresses drama rather than tenderness, while the *settecento* marks the transition to the Romantic Age. The Pietà shows once more the importance attached to accuracy; here, as in few others, the Blessed Virgin has the features of a woman who has lived the hard life of a small town carpenter's wife, borne several children, is old enough to be the mother of a man of thirty-three and is mourning for her first-born. Earlier representations, including Michelangelo's in St Peter's, stress the idealized Pietà.

Hodgkinson has traced the provenance of two of Corradini's garden sculptures, now in the Victoria and Albert Museum. They were probably made for Frederick Augustus the Elder, or 'The Strong', Elector of Saxony and King of Poland, for royal wedding festivities in 1719. It was this patron's son who sent Algarotti to Italy on a shopping expedition twenty-four years later. In a picture of the fireworks on the Elbe in 1719 it is possible to make out Corradini's 'Time unveiling Truth', and eight years later five more of his statues appear in a print of the garden of the Holländisches Palais, later the Japanisches Palais.

Returning to one of the pair, 'Apollo flaying Marsyas', Hodgkinson draws attention to the realism of Apollo's fingers sunk into the flesh of Marsyas, visible in the photograph (plate 19). Corradini completed his masterpiece, the 'Verginità' in the Church of the Carmini in Venice, in 1721; Niero calls it 'the ideal portrait of an eighteenth-century lady, all dressed up in ribbons and finery' and Honour[4] refers to her as a proud beauty; my own feeling is that her attitude is improbable and possibly a legacy from the previous century.

In 1724 Corradini succumbed to the pictorial taste of the century and produced a series of gilded bas-reliefs for the luxurious upper deck housing of the last *Bucintoro*. Those that survive are a figure of St Mark, which is said to have adorned the door through which the wedding ring was thrown into the Adriatic, and two of the Muses, rather in the style of Goujon's nymphs in Paris. The next year he began the long task of restoring the Scala dei Giganti in the Doge's Palace, of which the statues are by Sansovino; it sounds as though Corradini may have resembled Sansovino in combining efficiency in sculpture with that in architecture.

Then came his wandering years. Vienna in 1730 and Court Sculptor (*Hofstatuarius*) to the Emperor Charles VI; Rome in 1740 and commissions for the Vatican; Corradini arrived in Naples before 1750 and produced *Pudicizia* (Modesty) on the monument to Cecilia Caetano di Laurenziana in the tomb chapel of the Princes of Sangro di San Severo; of all the veiled figures Corradini carved (at least a dozen) this is the most famous and one of the best. 'His work', wrote Hodgkinson, 'is wholly Venetian in character. The picturesque outlines, the play of light on limbs and draperies, the dancing postures and the modish details contribute to an effect of decorative elegance, which belongs to the world of Sebastiano Ricci and Tiepolo.' I wonder if he is not rather describing the spirit of the Rococo, to be seen at its best in France, even though Semenzato calls Corradini's work 'the over-dramatization of late Baroque'. Cecilia Caetano's monument was produced when the sculptor was over eighty, surely sufficient to stamp him as exceptional.

Corradini also carved furniture, much of it now in the Ca' Rezzonico. Ornate and impressive it may be, but the function of a chair is to be sat upon; ornately carved arm rests, over-embellished legs and a hard seat bring no balm to tired feet or a sore back.

The Bonazza family deserves a word. Giuseppe worked until 1730 and his sons continued after his death, Antonio being active about 1750. They are remembered chiefly for their work in the Church of SS Giovanni e Paolo (Zanipolo), for father helped in the stupendous Valier memorial on the right as you face the altar, and all of them contributed to the high relief marble panels in the Chapel of the Rosary, where they wage an eternal war for pre-eminence with those of Giammaria Morlaiter. A drawn game, I think; both are highly competent, but no more. But elsewhere old Bonazza did one group that is seen by the usual visitor almost every day; when Tirali planned the second Piazzetta, that which lies north of St Mark's Basilica and approaches the clock tower, he had Giovanni Bonazza carve the two lions which lie before the well, after whom the Piazzetta dei Leoncini is named. Again, in the Church of San Pantaleone the first chapel on the right has a group of St Anne, St Joachim and St Joseph, attributed to the Bonazzas. The realism of the first, the central figure, is the only noteworthy feature. And lastly, in the Civic Museum of Padua there is a Pietà by Giuseppe, looking rather defensive among the Canovas. The Blessed Virgin is elderly, as is right (eighteenth-century accuracy again), but very, very sentimental; 'in conformity with their age ... not our taste', says Semenzato.

Of the rest of the 'second-raters', it is difficult to make a short list. There is Giovanni Marchiori (1696–1778) who made the sybils near the entrance of the Church of the Scalzi, as well as the tympanum of the Church of San Rocco—to me his best work—and some of the statues inside. These last, a David and a St Cecilia are classed by Honour[5] as 'perhaps the most elegantly refined works of Venetian Rococo sculpture';

everything is realistic again, the head of Goliath is really that of a giant and we may be sure that if he had modelled a naked David he would not have committed Donatello's lapse of leaving him uncircumcised. As regards St Cecilia, so little is known about her that I cannot account for her supercilious expression. The statues on the façade of San Rocco are by Morlaiter, a sound workman. Marchiori's work is perhaps the more inspired and his sybils certainly display an exceptional elegance, even for the Age of Rococo.

What makes him the most interesting of all to me is the statue of St John Nepomuk that adorns the outside of one wall of the Church of San Geremia: it was this church which spent so much money provided by the poor priest Giovanni Zaniol (see page 87); the statue was carved by Marchiori and on its base is incised a sentence, by the sculptor himself, say the experts. It reads: '*Dixi secretum meum mihi*', Latin for 'I didn't squeal', an amusing sidelight on the mystery.

Antonio Gai (1686–1766) has great charm. I show one leaf of his bronze gate of the Loggietta at the base of St Mark's *campanile*, which gives an idea of the elaborate, yet elegant style of the artist. More of his work, reliefs in wood, can be seen in the Church of the Carmini (Santa Maria del Carmelo); it is not known for certain, however, how many are by Gai. All are dramatic and show great technical ability; the one which is almost certainly his shows the Madonna putting out a fire, or rather her scapulary performing the miracle, on 5 June 1599, when Giovanni Sereno's bakery at Salerno caught fire.

Giuseppe Mazza (1652–1740) is not difficult to happen upon, for the beautiful, blackened bronzes in the Chapel of St Dominic (where you *must* see the Piazzetta ceiling) in the Church of SS Giovanni e Paolo, are his; he also cast some bronze saints in the Redentore Church. But he must be passed over as a foreigner from Bologna and not a Venetian, not that this counted for anything; Casanova met many young non-Venetian Italians in Paris and refers to them as 'compatriots'. But my aim is primarily to show what Venice could do, either by giving birth to, or educating those who made her famous in her last century.

Giammaria Morlaiter (1699–1782) was a foreigner too, from north of the alps as his name implies, but he seems to have spent so long in Venice that his memory merits at least honorary citizenship. His output was greater than any of the others'; apart from the façade of San Rocco, already mentioned, you may see his reliefs along with those of Bonazza in the Chapel of the Rosary in SS Giovanni e Paolo and more reliefs, of New Testament scenes, in the Church of the Gesuati (who were a sect of the Dominicans); parts of the carved marble panels project so far that they are in the round. In real statuary he made many of the figures at the Church of San Marcuola, inside, of course, as the façade is unfinished. That of St

Anthony Abbott in the north-west corner is not only good sculpture but typical of its time. The saint holds a bell in his left hand and, by the eighteenth century, the bell had indeed become one of his attributes; but it dates back only to thirteenth-century France, when a special edict permitted the pigs of the Hospitallers of St Anthony to root round the gutters with impunity. In order to distinguish their pigs from the underprivileged, the good brothers tied a bell to each one; it was not long before St Anthony was pictured on a seal, walking in front of a belled pig, and a subsequent stage is shown in one relief in Palermo where the saint is accompanied by two angels, of whom one holds the pig and the other a bell.

We may now pass over several less distinguished sculptors and attend to the problem of Toretti. It is common for Italian names to be distorted —the grand tourists would say 'Canaletti'—so we should not be surprised to read of him as Toretto (remember also that the terminal -*i* can represent the father's or family name, e.g. Galileo Galilei). His recorded activity ranges from 1710, when he assisted in alterations to Udine Cathedral, to 1756, when a new pulpit 'with sculptures by Giuseppe Toretti' was installed in the Church of SS Apostoli; Bassi[6] writes of other statues of his finished in 1766, but without details. In between he worked on the façade of the Gesuiti Church, which fairly bristles with saints, and on its altarpiece of marble, representing God the Father and Christ seated on a globe; as the ensemble is of heavy marble it is not astonishing that the supporters below the globe look as if they are playing a rough game on a hot day. Realism? He made marble bas-reliefs for the Villa Manin at Passeriano and a statue of St Jerome for Santa Maria della Consolazione. But he should be best remembered for being Canova's first master.*

Andrea Brustolon (1662–1732) marks another aspect of the evolution of Venetian sculpture. I said that many sculptors came from Italian Switzerland: this one came from the Dolomites, where men spend their spare time, abundant in winter, with a knife and a piece of wood. I have seen, and bought, the products of their hobby in the country between Bolzano and Merano and local churches testify to the antiquity of their skill. Brustolon was born in the Zoldo Valley north of Belluno and used his Tyrolean skills for more elaborate work than Nativity cribs or horses. Much of his work is inspired and the pen-and-wash preliminary sketches are sometimes better than the final article. It would be interesting to trace the dates of his works, for the series suggests an eventual degeneration. A journey through the Zoldo Valley reveals a fine crucifix and two carved

* That is, according to many authorities. Honour[7] gives Giuseppe Bernardi as Canova's master and the dates for Bernardi's lifespan would allow Canova to be his pupil for about three years. In the Museo Civico at Asolo they exhibit works by 'Canova's master' Giuseppe Bernardi and when I wanted to know more about him one of the custodians told me 'Il Toretto'. Honour's dates for 'Toretto' make him die in 1743—fourteen years before Canova's birth—but see p. 100.

wooden altars at Mareson; at Pieve, a Madonna holding a rosary, of which I have shown the preliminary sketch (plate 21). Back in Belluno, in the Cathedral Baptistery, there is a fine John the Baptist, which retains its charm in spite of being gilded. Again in the Zoldo Valley the little village of Dont has a monument to its famous son, and a few miles further is what is considered his masterpiece—the ornate, painted, gilded altarpiece 'Of the Souls' near Selva di Cadore.

Brustolon is known chiefly for his furniture; as Honour[8] so acutely remarks, it is really sculpture which happens to have a practical function. Though overloaded with ornament and often inlaid, much of his work is worth seeing—the carved wooden statues in the right transept of the Church of Santa Maria dei Frari for example—but his furniture contrasts with the far more elegant work of contemporary English cabinet-makers. Nevertheless, it is interesting to see what the pick of a nation of wood-carvers could do. Corradini outlived him by twenty years, but while they were both productive, say from 1690 to 1730, their work in their respective media, marble and wood, may be compared.

We can also see another demonstration of the inter-relation of the arts, never more pronounced than in this century; the unity expresses itself in wood, marble or bronze reliefs that are made in pictorial fashion; in G. B. Tiepolo's liking for 'sculptured' forms in his larger works; in the role of sculptors in interior decoration, for example Corradini in the *Bucintoro* and Brustolon's decorative furniture; in the hand-painting of fans, snuff-boxes and bric-à-brac, and finally, perhaps most obviously, in the inter-dependence of architecture and sculpture that had reached its high point in the declining Baroque of the later seventeenth century.

Antonio Canova (1757–1822) brought Venetian sculpture to a climax and seems to have shone more brightly than any other. His natural gifts were obviously great, for such works as remain from before his move to Rome, when his mature style is supposed to have developed, are technically perfect. He has been called the greatest representative of the Neo-Classical school, but it is plain that his taste had already selected a style similar to the later Athenian before he came in contact with many examples of Classical sculpture.

He was born to a stonemason's family in Possagno and spent an unhappy childhood with his grandfather, owner of a marble quarry, after his mother's second marriage. Giovanni Falier, a Venetian patrician, recognized his gifts, rescued him from his grandfather's stern rule and sent him to study with Toretti in 1771, just before the latter's move to Venice; by 1773 his teacher was dead and Canova continued his studies with Toretti's nephew and pupil, Giovanni Ferrari, whose style was what the Germans call '*blühendes Barock*', or 'blooming Baroque'. Fussiness without function may have made young Canova long for the clean lines of the

Classical sculptors combined, as was only natural, with a foretaste of the Romantic Age; it was as though the Hellenistic masters had come to life again. Canova, in fact, became a Romantic whose sentiment took the outward form of Classical sculpture. Still under Falier's patronage he produced his 'Orpheus and Eurydice', begun when he was only sixteen. Contracts began to come in and the *procuratore* Pietro Pisani commissioned 'The Death of Procris'. At about this time he also produced 'Daedalus and Icarus', now at the Correr Museum, a marvellous study of an intelligent and affectionate father fitting out his son with wings. It is only in a cynical mood that we see Icarus as a child with a new suit and his father like a worried tailor at the first fitting. The comparison has a purpose, for it demonstrates how lifelike are Canova's figures, a complete departure from the stylized Baroque.

In 1780 he left for Rome, with a bursary from the Venetian government; the move, according to Semenzato, spoiled him, but the world did not agree. Now began the decades when Canova was given what Molmenti[9] calls 'exaggerated renown', and was proclaimed 'divine'. He had two exceptional and timely advantages: first, the painter Raphael Mengs, enjoying enormous prestige in the world of art, had successfully dictated a taste for the Classical before his death in 1779; and secondly Canova was encouraged by the influential British painter and collector Gavin Hamilton, who lived in Rome. It was he who suggested that Canova produce a 'Theseus and the Minotaur'; it made a tremendous impact and was hailed as beginning a new era in the plastic arts. He was next called on to design and execute a tomb for Pope Clement XIV, now in the Holy Apostles' Church in Rome, and later the tombs for Clement XIII and Pius VI, in St Peter's.

It was during this period of activity that he made the series of statues for which he is best known today, the rendering in marble of some of the most touching Greek myths, the 'Eros and Psyche' in the Louvre, the 'Venus and Adonis' at Possagno and 'The Three Graces' in the Hermitage at Leningrad. Much in the same spirit is his 'Penitent Magdalen' at the Villa Carlotta, Cadenabbia. Then international fame caught up with him and his genius was restricted to gratifying the great and near-great. Three statues of Napoleon were projected, but perhaps even Canova could not make him lovable, for the Emperor disliked them all; one is now in the Wellington Museum at Apsley House. A fourth, equestrian statue did not progress beyond the horse, but a famous bust of Napoleon by Canova survives in Florence's Pitti Palace.

The fall of Napoleon affected Canova and his works in many ways. He was asked by the Pope to go to Paris and attempt to procure the restoration of the art treasures looted from Rome, as he had done unsuccessfully during the Empire; his persistence in the face of obstruction by the major powers earned him a papal title. The other direct consequence was the disposal of his statues of members of the Bonaparte family: the celebrated semi-nude Pauline Borghese as Venus remains a Venus at the Villa Borghese, but her sister Elisa became 'Polyhymnia' and the Empress Maria Luisa 'Concordia'. The horse had no name to alter and therefore suffered only a change of rider: Charles IV of Naples.

An interesting extension of his last visit to Paris was a trip to London, to arrange the government's share in the expense of transporting the art treasures back to Rome. The Prince Regent was one of his many admirers and took the opportunity to order a tomb for the Cardinal of York, last of the Stuarts, in Rome. This now stands in the left aisle of St Peter's as the 'Stuart Memorial' and under it are buried the three exiles who visited Corradini's workshop so many years before. This is not the only indirect reminder that Canova was a Venetian. His lions on the papal tombs are reminiscent of those outside the Arsenal in Venice, brought there by Morosini a hundred years before.

Canova died in Venice and is buried in the mausoleum he designed for himself at his birthplace, Possagno. It may be objected that, when famous, he was no longer an exponent of Venetian art and that I have paid him too much attention; but Canova was born in the Veneto and his genius was apparent before he left for Rome. He was one more petal in the marvellous flower that unfolded in the last years of La Serenissima.

An appraisal of Canova's work, like all artistic judgments, is largely a matter of personal taste and, as I have said, should be so. During his lifetime he could do no wrong; today one reads that he eliminated all spontaneous and natural movement, so that his statues are cold and dull.[10] In my own opinion this was no more than a reaction from the exaggerated movement of the late Baroque; and, far from being cold, his imaginative works could be considered too sentimental, at least for our taste. But he was a herald of the Romantic Movement and therefore deserves to rank with Berlioz, Heine, Delacroix and Walter Scott; I reject the notion that 'classical' and 'romantic' art are always in opposition, for Canova studied nature through Classical models and combined formal beauty ('classical') with emotional intensity ('romantic'). Like other great artists he was many-sided. One thousand seven hundred of his pen and pencil sketches can be seen in the Civic Museum of Bassano and two of his water colours are in that of Asolo. Here too are some of his sculptures and copies of others, as well as his bust, by his cousin Domenico Manera; both this and the post-mortem sculpture, or possibly death mask, show the strong features, aquiline nose and high cheek bones that gave him his distinguished, ascetic look. A typically Venetian face, one may say, after seeing a number of portraits, busts and live Venetians.

*

From sculpture to furniture is a short step, which we have already taken once or twice; Venice, like most of Europe, followed France's lead in all that contributed to the art of living. There, interior decoration passed from splendour to refinement[11] and furnishings underwent the same change. The pompous style of Louis XIV was succeeded from 1715 by the lighter and more graceful *Louis Quinze* and it was not until the last quarter of the century that the trend to Classicism became obvious.

For most of the century, then, true Rococo reigned with its basically delicate and refined taste overlaid with more or less unnecessary, but always graceful, ornamental exuberance. At the same time the vivid colours of the textiles of the age of Louis XIV gave way to pastel shades, chiefly salmon, light blue, pale green and light yellow,[12] and 'the dainty luxury of gilt furniture, designed by Andrea Brustolon and upholstered in delicate silks, was matched by small, attractive works of art'.[13] Venice quickly followed France's lead in adopting *chinoiserie* and ornamental porcelain, introduced by Watteau and Boucher and the result of a lively interest in China, largely fostered by Jesuit missionaries, that had been increasing for a hundred years. Everything Chinese became popular and even criticisms of European governments were disguised as letters from mythical Chinese visitors. Venice had her turn in '*L'espion Chinois, ou l'envoyé secret de la Cour de Pékin . . .*' of 1769, nine years after Oliver Goldsmith's 'Chinese Letters'.

Decoration naturally included painting and the wealthy were able to employ genius—Tiepolo in the later years of the eighteenth century, Sebastiano Ricci or Pellegrini earlier. It is noteworthy that some of the greater artists worked both at home and abroad, once they were known for their ability as interior decorators. It was a Frenchman[14] who wrote that Venice held an important position in the department of interior decoration and that in furniture she competed with Versailles and Paris. Stucco, arabesque, medallions, and panelling enclosed a space in which graceful chests of drawers, chairs and wall candelabra enhanced their good taste, and variously coloured marbles, such as the *mandolato* of Verona, and smaller, tiled fireplaces lent further elegance to already attractive rooms. Mirrors and artistic picture frames all played their part; towards the end of the century, along with *chinoiserie*, we find furniture painted and lacquered.

The rich man's—and woman's—bed was a four-poster, with canopy and curtains, possibly a relic of more crowded times when dressing and undressing could be performed behind curtains for modesty's sake. Nothing is gained by a comparison of English with Venetian styles; we have the idea that ours were simpler and yet more elegant and that 'Chippendale' was a style. We may be right with regard to design, but Chippendale was a cabinet-maker and writer, prepared to make anything from the simplest to the most ornate, and his deserved reputation rests more on the quality of his workmanship than on his style.[15]

Trompe-l'œil was an offshoot of interior decoration when large spaces were to be treated, as we can see in the great ballroom of the Ca' Rezzonico, or in churches. So we meet anything from the crude attempt on the ceiling of Sant'Alvise to the perfection of the walls of the Gesuiti. This church has an interior of white marble with *intarsio* (inlay) of dark blue-green, making a pleasing pattern and, as Honour says,[16] suggesting a damask, an illusion heightened by the folds and tassels of a marble curtain of the same pattern over the pulpit.

Even commerce could not resist the general love of the exquisite. De Brosses tells us of a display of theriac on St Bartholomew's day,* with all the ingredients tastefully arranged, the vipers (an essential component) forming a scroll border.

The glass industry was one of Venice's proudest boasts, hence the refusal to allow their workmen to go abroad from Murano, even after rival countries had begun to use more up-to-date techniques. Glass candelabra, with ten or fifty branches for candles became more and more ornate: coloured glass was combined with white; flowers were blown, petal by petal, and stuck on at strategic points, and surfaces facetted to give the maximum glitter. In Venice such candelabra are too numerous to detail; elsewhere in Europe they can be identified in many public buildings by the observant sightseer, for instance in the Diputación, Barcelona. The end came in about 1775, when the old-established glass-blowing of Murano had been superseded everywhere else by the wheel and mould, and when the workmen of Murano persisted in rejecting every new idea that might have saved their livelihood.

In 1765 practically only mirrors were being exported, but the market was even then a small one, for the factory that La Lande visited employed only twelve men and these worked only two days a week. As well as mirrors, Venice had one secret that was always in demand, that of *lattino* glass; this is an opaque white, obtained by using a lead-arsenic compound, which formed the basis of the popular and expensive red painted glass. Plates carried a view of Venice, usually taken from a G. B. Brustolon engraving of a Canaletto original. There was one at Strawberry Hill, presumably acquired by Horace Walpole in 1741, perhaps the same as is now in the Jones Collection at the Victoria and Albert Museum.[17] As with most crafts glass-blowing ran in families; among the best known are the Miotti, who had worked at the sign of '*Al Gesù*' since the early seventeenth century and who probably made the Strawberry

* The pilgrim hospital on the Tiber Island in Rome is an annexe of St Bartholomew's Church and 'Bart's' in London may have been founded by a grateful survivor. Hence his feast day was the apothecaries'.

Hill collection; and the Briani, who made the great chandelier in the Brustolon Hall of the Ca' Rezzonico. Other specialities included glass bead manufacture and the *smalto* glass imitating porcelain which, at that time, was made at Capodimonte.

The industry did not die, but it degenerated until today it turns out monstrosities whose only unique feature is that they are produced by an out-of-date process. I have visited the display rooms of a flourishing firm with a rich buyer; there were giant fish, horribly tinted, impossible flowers in improbable colours, a multi-coloured cocktail cabinet (I am glad to say that it arrived in fragments when it was finally shipped abroad); the only glass object which I could not criticize was the bottle of Scotch whisky that was finally brought out to loosen tongues and purse-strings.

II

History Painting

The picture of Venice that I have sketched does not suggest the background against which serious art would emerge. And yet the eighteenth century was to see the most prolific flowering of the art of painting that Venice had ever known, comparable indeed to the great days of Tuscany two centuries before. How to account for it? Many are the suggestions proposed, but to each there are strong objections. Only Haskell, to whom I shall return, explains a part of the phenomenon to my satisfaction.

To my mind the two most important factors are: first, the fact that Venice, at the expense of influence and dignity, had steadfastly chosen peace without alliances for nearly a century. This formula for preserving the little she had left would not save her, but it may have postponed the end; furthermore it gave time for the 'rebirth' I have mentioned as a resumption of man's normal progress when liberated from the restraints of war and disease. A second factor may well have been the government's preoccupation with the trappings of wealth and power, now that the reality had vanished. To match the senseless ceremony of wedding the sea 'in token of perpetual subjection', we may observe that the only work commissioned for the Doge's Palace during the century (I omit a Doge's own plan for the Sala dello Scudo) was Tiepolo's 'Neptune offering to Venice the Riches of the Sea', originally in the Hall of the Four Doors. The glorification of Venice and her leading families was almost an obsession and though the state had little money to spare for painters, some private families still had plenty.

Haskell's explanation is based on the fact that many of the nobles were recently elevated; having bought the distinction they were looked down on by the older families and naturally sought every means of glorifying their own. I may add that we are dealing with a mercantile aristocracy, not with the kind usual in other countries, where ancestors had founded the family fortunes by brigandage. So it made little difference whether the present or previous generations had become ennobled; all had commerce in their blood and hence the desire to get value for their money when they commissioned a modern painter. The only value they could envisage was the promotion of their self-esteem and for this purpose paintings were commissioned with the object of glorifying their families, old or new. The Zenobio, for example, were not only new aristocrats but among the richest; in their palace* glorification had been largely entrusted to a French artist, but local talent was allowed to be represented by views and pictured myths in corridors and secondary rooms.

With wealth went a conservative taste in art and the painters of the previous century remained the favourites, even when such new masters as Pellegrini, Sebastiano Ricci and Amigoni were available. The consequence was that many Venetian artists found it easier to make a living abroad.

One of the few exceptions to the prevalent desire for self-glorification was Marco Foscarini; books were his passion and his pictures were said to have stressed the greatness of the learned. The only one for which he commissioned a well-known, though Roman, painter, was 'The Triumph of Venice', a reminder of La Serenissima's past glories. Of himself and his family there were no flattering allegories; perhaps he knew that they were unnecessary. But the newly promoted, and especially those of foreign or *terraferma* origin, knew what they wanted. The Labia, originally Catalan, had employed Lazzarini in the 1680s and earn our gratitude by later entrusting his pupil with an ambitious Classical programme. The pupil was G. B. Tiepolo. The Manins from Friuli—it was their 'country cottage' at Passeriana—were even responsible for a 'Manin style' through their willingness to spend constantly and extravagantly; this style is evident in the Gesuiti Church, paid for by the Manin family, and consisted of marble carved to imitate draperies.

A third and obvious factor was the increase in tourist trade, mentioned in connection with Consul Joseph Smith. It is clear that some of today's best known *settecento* painters lived from the souvenirs they painted, an industry which continued to flourish despite all competitors except one —the camera. View painting of the city, therefore, arose as a branch of landscape painting and, though its practitioners were despised by fellow artists and most Venetian patrons,† possibly brought more foreign money to Venice than any other branch of art, or even prostitution. Landscapes, too, were an attraction, even if they were not the forerunners of the picture postcard. The vogue for picturesque, wild scenery, waterfalls and sinister ruins, managed to survive well into the eighteenth century and, before it could die, was miraculously revived by the Romanticists, of whom one was to sing:

> Land of brown heath and shaggy wood,
> Land of the mountain and the flood . . .

---

* Now the Armenian College on the Fondamenta Foscarini.
† View painters were not even mentioned in Alessandro Longhi's *compendio* of 1762.

and Venice produced some passable landscape painters, as well as leaders in every other branch.

Patrons played a decisive part in the revival of art, and discriminating ones were of supreme importance. Such a one was Antonio Maria Zanetti the Elder. Rich and gifted, he not only studied art for its own sake, but showed talent as a draughtsman; more to the point, he was a collector and agent for art lovers from the rest of Europe. He revived a method for making *chiaroscuro* woodcuts in multiple colours. One can see a French colour engraving by a similar method, made by L. M. Bonnet (1769), in the Jones Collection of the Victoria and Albert Museum. Antonio Maria Zanetti the Younger was a cousin and is remembered chiefly as an art critic.

To guide the reader among a spate of unfamiliar names is no easy task and it is better that he should have a few stepping stones. I therefore mention four of the best known—their names may already be familiar—and hope that most of the others can be thought of in relation to them. Thus, for instance, Giambattista Tiepolo, the greatest history painter of them all, had a son Gian Domenico whom we shall discuss; Pietro Longhi, regarded as *the* painter *par excellence* of genre, intimate scenes of daily life, had a son Alessandro who painted portraits; Canaletto, the most famous of the view painters, leads us to a nephew, Bernardo Bellotto and a successor, Francesco Guardi; Rosalba Carriera, whose portraits reached every part of Europe and whose style was zealously copied, serves to orientate a lesser artist, the history painter Pellegrini, who was her brother-in-law.

With these four outstanding artists as the cardinal points, the reader may confidently wander in the maze of lesser lights, certain of coming back to a point of departure. Let us tabulate them:

History	G. B. Tiepolo—his son Gian Domenico
Genre	Pietro Longhi—his son Alessandro
View	Canaletto—his nephew Bernardo Bellotto
Portrait	Rosalba Carriera—her brother-in-law Pellegrini

A favourite remark on the subject of painting is: 'In the eighteenth century Venice is the only city of Italy with an original school of painting.'[1] No doubt a correct summary, if it is remembered that Venice had no school, in the sense of an educational establishment, until a guild* was formed in 1679 and the Academy in 1750. But even this was not satisfactory, for on at least one occasion a visitor, seeking an interview with the president, was told that he had not been seen at the Academy for two years. And there was a perpetual squabble between the *Collegi* of painters and sculptors on the one hand, and the Academy on the other. To antici-

* The *Collegio dei Pittori.*

pate, Valcanova tells us that the Academy was reorganized by a decree of 1807, issued by Eugène de Beauharnais.* The new post of 'Keeper' was given to one Pietro Edwards who had been a pupil, member and president of the old Academy. (Was he, I wonder, a descendant of the other Pietro Edwards, official picture-framer and freelance painter in 1728?)

Venice's painters showed such differences among themselves in style, subject matter and medium that it would be a mistake to lump them together in a 'school'. It is, however, true that many of them were original in their own sphere, that the government encouraged their efforts, though not with open purse-strings, and that the public showed a praiseworthy discrimination. On 2 June 1743, the whole parish celebrated the unveiling of Tiepolo's ceiling in the *Scuola*† of the Carmini and the same enthusiasm marked the same function in the Church of the Pietà on 2 August 1755.

Artists had their vicissitudes and, if we hear of the wealth accumulated by the lucky few, we may also judge of the struggle that marked the career of the rest; thus a Guardi, either Francesco or his elder brother Gian Antonio, took boarder-pupils, one of whom was Casanova's bro-ther.[2] The guilds were becoming poorer too, along with the rest of Venice, and could no longer afford to buy masterpieces, with the result that some artists began painting exclusively for the tourist souvenir trade, and others accepted engagements abroad. Thus specialization was born: Canaletto must limit himself to views of Venice, Longhi to genre paint-ings, and Tiepolo, summoned to Würzburg and Madrid, must paint his frescoes in the grand manner consonant with the dignity of his paymaster.

But so prolific and so numerous were her artists that 'there are probably more paintings in Venice than in all the rest of Italy, and certainly more than in France'.[3] Another reason given for this outburst of painting is the excellence of Venetian models; certainly the history and portrait painters left us some fine faces, magnificent bodies and interesting characters.

I wonder how many artists worked, made a living and even a reputa-tion and are today forgotten? The question occurred to me when I caught sight of a plaque at No. 6 Via Roma, Verona: 'GIAMBETTINO CIGNA-ROLI (1706–70) was visited in this house by the Emperor Joseph II (1769) who greeted him as the greatest painter of the time.' Today this eight-eenth-century Ozymandias is remembered, if at all, as the founder of the Academy of Verona; although some of his oil paintings can be seen on the ceilings of the Palazzo Labia in Venice. So with many of those whom Monnier calls the '*petits maîtres*'; only the specialist can tell you of F. Fontebasso, M. Morlaiter the painter, D. Maggiotto, G. Pozzoli, A. Joli,

* Napoleon's stepson and viceroy of the 'Regno Italico' that included Venice after the defeat of Austria at Austerlitz in 1805.
† Various guilds had art collections in their chapels as a means of displaying their wealth and taste.

P. Gaspari, G. Moretti, F. Battaglioli, A. Visentini, V. Damiani, who did Gothick revival decoration in Lincoln Cathedral in 1728,[4] and a hundred others whose works hang in the worst-lit corner of some humble civic museum or whose names are mentioned casually in a diary of those days. And what of the forgotten provincials? Brescia, for instance, was famous for its painters of *trompe-l'œil* perspective frescoes in the eighteenth century, but no guide I know mentions them today.

I have classified painters of the Venetian *settecento* in the manner of Levey (1959). What of their ancestry? Taking 'History'* first, we find a direct line from the Renaissance painters Veronese and Correggio to Luca Giordano, a Neapolitan who absorbed the spirit of the Venetian Renaissance and handed back the product of this and his own high Baroque manner.†[6] Again, Tiepolo, who is regarded as the greatest of them all, may well have derived some of his ideas from his teacher Gregorio Lazzarini (1655–1730), who in his turn learned from Giulio Carpioni, a pupil of Alessandro Varotari ('*Il Padovanino*') whose father Dario was a pupil of Paolo Veronese. And the glorious sky scenes, in which Tiepolo makes lighter-than-air *putti* frisk and tumble in the aether, come in a direct line from Correggio, whose heavenly figures were described by a canon of Parma Cathedral as a 'hash of frogs' legs'.

Then we have another, indirect line through Piazzetta, whom Charles Blanc[8] called 'a Venetian Caravaggio'. Not without reason either, for Piazzetta's teacher Crespi of Bologna developed a style which, though it resembled that of the Dutch School, was in fact derived from Caravaggio. And Caravaggio served his time with Simone Peterzano of Bergamo, who claimed to have been a pupil of Titian; the last, of course, was the main influence in shaping Paolo Veronese. Antonio Balestra (1666–1740) was another who had some influence, for not only does all eighteenth-century painting in Verona go back to him, but he was for a time Pietro Longhi's teacher.

When we consider the landscape artists and view painters, the line goes back direct to the Netherlands, and from Dutch Baroque came such early influences in Venice as Richter of Sweden and Heintz from Germany. When the latter's production could no longer keep up with the demand, Carlevaris and Canaletto came into their own. Another foreigner, Gaspar van Wittel (Vanvitelli) was more obviously Dutch than Carlevaris, who was born at Udine, even though his name is sometimes spelled 'Carlevarijs' in Dutch fashion. At Udine we can see two of Carlevaris' views: the first is a bird's-eye view of the town, painted from an imaginary hill,

* The word, as used here, means 'the noblest form of art and consists of generalized representations of the passions and intellect as symbolized in classical history or mythology or in subjects taken from Christian iconography.'[5]

† 'We must remember that it was Correggio and the Venetians who took the world of mystery and revelation and made it palpable, majestic, of flesh and blood.'[7]

with fictitious figures in the foreground, and the second a view of Venice's Piazzetta, with such disregard of perspective that San Giorgio seems both too near and too large.

Sebastiano Ricci is the first important figure among the history painters; he was not only one of the first Venetian artists to visit England, but had an influence on contemporaries and successors far greater than his merits would suggest. You may remember him, if you wish, as the plagiarist or, to be kinder, as an unconscious mimic. Gioseffi qualifies his work as exaggerated *chiaroscuro* and Mannerism, as though that was an unpleasant disease, but plays safe by adding 'a true originator of a new style'. Levey[9] stresses his plagiarism, especially where Veronese is concerned; he reminds us of the time Ricci deceived Charles de la Fosse with a pastiche made up of Veronese, passing it off as his own, and was told: 'Paint nothing but Paul Veronese's and no more Ricci's'; Chastel classes him with Magnasco, painter of melodramatic scenes and strangely enough Magnasco is the very man whom Sebastiano's nephew, Marco Ricci, is alleged to imitate. My subjective impressions vary, as will yours. There are paintings which arrest one by their luminosity, such as the ceiling in San Marziale; there is excessive emotion in others, for instance in 'Esther before Ahasuerus',[10] though the composition is satisfying and the brushwork competent in so small a canvas. In the Gesuati in Venice 'Pius V with St Thomas Aquinas and St Peter Martyr (or St Vincent Ferrer?)' makes the most of *chiaroscuro* relief and the Palladian background is, as you might expect, typically Veronese.

I am inclined to be charitable to one who was great in his day, even if eventually overshadowed by one greater. I think of Brinton's words, 'Sebastiano's translations of Veronese into eighteenth-century style were an important influence on the young Tiepolo.' At St Peter's in Belluno and in the adjacent convent are some of Sebastiano's most natural works, in fresco, with good drawing and fresh colour. But in the Venice Accademia we touch the depths, for there is a painting without a spark of life ('The Dream of Aesculapius'); I once heard a stranger remark of this, that though Sebastiano Ricci could sometimes equal Veronese at his worst, this was not such an occasion. And yet it was Sebastiano Ricci whom Mariette called '*un fort beau génie*'; perhaps our own tastes are just as impermanent. For there was no doubt about the reputation he enjoyed in his own day. Though he did little work for the patricians of Venice he was frequently employed by the Church and by Consul Joseph Smith, who began his own collection with a judicious selection from Sebastiano's works.

Sebastiano Ricci spent much time away from Venice, at the Court of Turin and in England. Here he was regarded as an innovator, which implies that either the eighteenth-century Englishman knew nothing of Veronese or that modern commentators should modify their views. He was employed by Lord Portland, for whom he painted a series of religious pictures in which, twenty years later, Vertue saw '. . . noble free invention; great force of lights and shade with variety and freedom in the composition of the parts'.[11] Far more important was his work for Lord Burlington whose Burlington House had its walls covered with Sebastiano Ricci frescoes long before the Royal Academy hung its own selections; many of the former were removed to decorate Chiswick, the Burlington–Kent version of Palladio's Villa Capra (La Rotonda) at Vicenza. Among these is the evidence that 'Sebastiano Ricci was the true innovator of a new style' and that the 'new painting peopled the sky with flying allegorical genii in scattered order'.[12]

As well as all this he found time to collaborate with his nephew Marco and paint figures into the younger man's landscapes. He had firm friends in Venice, among them the peerless Goldoni, who dedicated to him *Il Filosofo Inglese*, and had a following of pupils, from among whom Fontebasso not only did the ceiling paintings for the Gesuiti, the Stations of the Cross in Santa Maria Zobenigo (now gutted by restorers) and other works in Venice, but the decoration of St Petersburg's Winter Palace. To make up your own mind about Sebastiano Ricci, first steep yourself in Veronese's works and then follow Ricci's in Belluno, Venice, the Galleria Sabauda in Turin, the Pitti Palace in Florence, London's Chelsea Hospital and wherever else you can; then pass judgment.

Among Ricci's many pupils, Giovanni Antonio Pellegrini (1675–1741)* stands out, if only for the fact that he was the very first Venetian painter to visit England; Honour,[13] in fact, calls him the best of the errant Venetians of the *settecento*. The occasion of his visit makes a strange story; five years before, Rosalba Carriera, destined to become the most famous of all Venetian portrait painters (though she worked chiefly in pastel), had been noticed and encouraged by an official of the English Embassy. In 1707 Lord Manchester, the ambassador, returned to Venice, an occasion commemorated by Luca Carlevaris in an oft-reproduced documentary painting. A year later he quarrelled with the Venetian government and returned to England, taking with him Rosalba's brother-in-law Pellegrini and Marco Ricci, nephew of Sebastiano; both artists were in their early thirties. Pellegrini might be remembered for his English paintings alone, for one of them, 'The Musicians' at Kimbolton Castle, the seat of the Earl of Manchester, demonstrates what Levey[14] means when he writes of him as a 'graceful and lyrical' painter, and ' . . . probably the first of the Venetian history painters to paint decorative scenes as such—pure fantasies without any story or subject.' Apart from this solitary example he has little excuse for intruding in these pages. However, I can recall one Pellegrini painting in Venice, rather ambitiously entitled '*La Pittura*';

* *Pellegrino*, fittingly enough, is Italian for a wanderer.

to me it seems flat and undistinguished. Canaletto's skill deserted him in England; perhaps the spell worked the other way with Pellegrini.

His connection with France had some interest too. Among the manifestations of the looser rein of Louis XV was the new financial credit scheme invented by John Law; its climax was the Mississippi Scheme which suffered the same fate as the South Sea Bubble and, like it, was symptomatic of the times. Before the crash the Banque Royale commissioned a Mississippi Gallery and the symbolic decoration was entrusted to Pellegrini. We learn that it was a panegyric of royalty and commerce combined. The King, the gods of Olympus and financiers were all portrayed to their advantage, and symbolism was even stretched to show the Seine embracing the Mississippi. Unfortunately the old Banque was burnt down.

It is strange that another Venetian, Jacopo Amigoni (1675?–1752) attained success shortly after through the patronage of a Mr Styles, who had made a fortune out of the South Sea Bubble.[15] Amigoni had also found prospects in Venice poor for any save the celebrities, while a future abroad was bright even for the worst. Not that he could be thus described; on the contrary, Amigoni's drawing and brushwork were excellent, when he chose to take his time; it is only in the absence of feeling that his history painting is often second-rate. Though hailed as a representative of the Rococo, his style showed none of the grace and gaiety that characterized, for instance, Boucher in France. His work in Bavaria, where he spent his first ten years abroad, was pastoral and mildly erotic, appealing more to sentiment than to wit.

In England Amigoni's success as a history painter was not striking and he was forced to practise a form of painting for which he had special aptitude—portraits. Here his success could not be doubted and when he left for Venice in 1739 he took with him a fair amount of earned income. But by this time the Rococo masters had become so well known that his work showed up as dull by contrast; anyone who comes upon his 'Venus and Adonis' in the Accademia Gallery without warning will agree. Some of my reaction may be caused by the Flemish influence he shows, something best left to the Flemings, who know how to use it. Gioseffi[16] mentions how he '. . . restrained the impetuous and capricious exuberance in composition inherited from the Baroque'. Whether or not Gioseffi is right, most are agreed that Amigoni was not a true exponent of the Rococo and anyone who has seen his composite portrait (in the National Gallery of Victoria, Melbourne) will admit that this was his true vocation.

In 1747 he was invited to Madrid to become court painter to Ferdinand VI, a task which was principally portraiture, and difficult portraiture at that, of a family notorious for its ugliness. Amigoni, like Luca Giordano who had popularized Italian art in Spain, was a Neapolitan by birth and was followed to Madrid by yet another southerner, Corrado Giaquinto, who is said to have had more influence on Goya than any other painter,[17] and finally by the Tiepolo family. So it is possible that Madrid owes its Tiepolo frescoes indirectly to Amigoni.

I have put Sebastiano Ricci and Jacopo Amigoni together for more reasons than chronology. Essentially history painters, they were almost unemployed in the decoration of Venetian palaces and were better known outside their own country. From Amigoni's experience we learn another fact: that the English who had done the Grand Tour did not like history painting in the grand manner.

Gian Antonio Fumiani (1643–1710) deserves mention as one who began the trend away from the *tenebristi.* Some of his paintings show the restlessness of the century he was leaving behind, but in many respects he is to be admired. The huge ceiling painting of San Pantaleone, Venice—the greatest canvas in the world, if size is the criterion—is a remarkable demonstration of vertical perspective, as is the ceiling over the high altar. We have the illusion of looking up steps at a series of episodes, a device that was to come into greater favour. A good example is the ceiling of St Ignatius in Rome, where we have the same vertical perspective, the problem of limb foreshortening that intrigued Correggio and the resulting 'hash of frogs' legs'. Another example is the face seen from a viewpoint below the angle of the jaw. All history painters had to learn to deal with this view and it enabled G. B. Tiepolo to obtain some of his most dramatic effects. Ceiling art, in fact, played its part by shifting the viewpoint to below the subject and therefore demanded a new range of virtuosity, which was given the Italian name *sotto in sù*. It was left to Tiepolo to make the most of it.

If I limit myself to a handful of painters it is not for lack of material; in fact their number was so great and their performance of such high standard that they can be criticized only by comparison with a genius such as Tiepolo. Even the least known (at least to the amateur), Pozzoli, Maggiotto, Novelli, have at times reached heights which could ensure them immortality, if it were not for the unevenness of their work. We must therefore pass over scores in order to discuss a few, distinguished by originality or by a persistently high standard; but any day we may hear of the discovery of Nicola Grassi, Antonio Zanchi or Giovanni Migliara and confess that we overlooked them because the crowd was too big, and that the deficiency lay, not in their work but in our judgment.

---

* Latin *tenebrae*, darkness; hence those who relied on *chiaroscuro*, the contrast of light and shade, for their effects. One of the features of the eighteenth century was the revived use of colour to enhance the three-dimensional effect of paintings, as practised by the great Venetians of the Renaissance.

In their own day there was what Levey[18] has called the 'grand trinity' of Pittoni, Piazzetta and Giambattista Tiepolo. The last is by general consent so far above the rest as to warrant a chapter to himself; the others can be considered here. Giovanni Battista Pittoni (1687–1767) was a few years older than his great rival, Tiepolo. At the time, however, the Venetians saw little to prefer in any one member of the trinity; if I have to sum up the outstanding characteristic of each artist, I should credit Pittoni with colour, Piazzetta with the manipulation of tone values and Tiepolo (apart from transcendent genius) with light.

Before condemning Pittoni's work out of hand we must take account of the customer's requirements. Drama was wanted in history painting, or even melodrama based on the old classical themes of heroism and self-sacrifice, preferably applicable to the purchaser or his family. The Germans were as prone as many Venetians to these quaint survivals of the Baroque and as Pittoni generally painted mostly easel pictures where Tiepolo preferred fresco, he was much in demand in that country, for it was cheaper to import a canvas than a fresco painter and Pittoni had the knack of turning Bible stories into melodrama.

When Algarotti returned to Venice to commission pictures for Augustus III of Saxony, he went with an intelligent aim, that of fitting the painter to the subject. Though many decry him, there is little doubt that Algarotti had an artist's insight and that his reasoned approach had much to recommend it. According to him, Pittoni was 'distinguished for painting the vestments of priests ... and gladly decorates his compositions with architecture.'[19] A fairly representative work hangs in the National Gallery[20] and brings out the *sotto in sù* views of the face that were by then commonplace. The excessively rosy complexions may be due to age thinning the upper layers of paint and allowing the red priming, a favourite of Venetian painters, to become more accentuated than ordinary flesh tint requires.

Three of his paintings hang in the Venice Accademia: an Annunciation, in which the Archangel Gabriel is a female—which would never have done for the precise Algarotti; a Maddalena which today we consider over-emotional; and the well-known 'Sack of the Temple of Jerusalem', a fair enough presentation of an important event, but containing too much movement for most tastes. To make it worse, the composition shows at least four simultaneous actions, so that the eye becomes as restless as the painted figures. More typical works of Pittoni hang in the Civic Museum in Padua, where a 'Baptism of St Daniel' is crisper and shows the bright colours for which Pittoni was known. Gioseffi[21] considers his 'Diana and Actaeon' in the Civic Museum, Vicenza to be his best known work—an Arcadian, idyllic composition with beautiful flesh tints and richly coloured draperies whose folds recall Tintoretto; a tiny Actaeon, being devoured by hounds in the background, hardly disturbs the afternoon's tranquillity.

Giambattista Piazzetta (1683–1754) is admittedly the greatest of the second class and, if Tiepolo had not existed, would possibly take his place today in popular esteem. A slow and careful worker, he never achieved the sure touch and light-filled scenes of the Rococo and, in fact, plodded along the old lines while retaining a magic of his own. This consisted, as I have said, of tone; by this I mean that he usually confined himself to sombre colours, red, brown and chocolate.[22] A master of *chiaroscuro*, he naturally needed a sombre ground for his contrasted highlights; this led to the usual drawback of selecting gloomy skies and murky clouds, quite the wrong environment for a gay Rococo ceiling that is supposed to give you the essence of pellucid skies with saints, angels and *putti* engaging in their endless acrobatics. And yet his choice of colour made his task far more difficult, for he had to produce his effects without chromatic aid; he deliberately abandoned the part played by colour in composition, established by Titian, Tintoretto and Veronese, who could counter feeble lighting with a brilliant splash of colour.

Piazzetta is included among the history painters though, in fact, much of his work should be classed as genre, and some as portraiture. He was beginning to get results with these and with pastoral paintings, when Algarotti, in about 1742, commissioned 'Caesar and the Corsairs of Cilicia'; shortly after, Piazzetta, intoxicated with the drama of the Classics, painted 'Mucius Scaevola at the Altar', now in the Palazzo Barbaro Curtis, and 'The Death of Darius' in the Ca' Rezzonico. Here, as nowhere else, you can judge the dramatic effect he obtained with his restricted palette; you can also see how outdated was his monumental style. Once more Algarotti showed his acumen: 'Piazzetta' he said, 'is a great draughtsman and a good colourist but has little elegance of form or expression.'[23] The 'Caesar' is lost for ever but the two survivors, now representing Piazzetta's only Classical paintings, give an idea of his versatility.

Being a slow worker, 'neurotically slow' according to Levey,[24] Piazzetta was unsuited for fresco work, where everything the artist has to say must be recorded while the plaster is still wet. His only work of this kind is the celebrated ceiling in the Chapel of St Dominic, the last chapel on the right in the Church of SS Giovanni e Paolo. It is an impressive work, but a trifle heavy; La Lande, himself a child of the Rococo, wrote that it was 'badly composed, the light blazes all over and its colouring is wrong'. He takes a great deal on himself; others maintain that the light, compared with Tiepolo's many masterpieces in this field, is dull and La Lande should have known that Piazzetta had his own ideas about colour. I agree with him, however, that the perspective in the concave ceiling was very difficult, but foreshortening and vertical perspective were by now an everyday exercise for the *settecentisti*. The same heaviness, inseparable from Piaz-zetta's style, mars one of his best works, the 'SS Vincent, Hyacinth and Lorenzo Bertrando' in the Gesuati Church. In a wall painting it is support-able, but in a ceiling fresco such as that in the Chapel of St Dominic one has the feeling that the figures are kept aloft only by an effort of levitation. And for all that, Piazzetta's work is as much in advance of his contempor-aries as Tiepolo's is ahead of him.

Piazzetta's gift is for genre and even one of his 'history' paintings, 'Rebecca at the Well' is a wonderful exercise in genre and could equally be entitled 'The Pander and the dumb Blonde'. Where he was so superior to other Venetian genre painters was in his aptitude for portraits; each subject lives in his own right; see, for instance, two of the three figures in the enigmatic 'Idyll on the Seashore' at Cologne or 'The Boy with a Whistle' at the Ca' Rezzonico. His sitters are ordinary people, even when they are dressed up as kings or bishops, though his peasants never have the realism of Giacomo Ceruti's (*fl.* 1724-38) underdogs as seen, for instance, in the Pinacoteca Tosio-Martinengo of his own town of Brescia.

Unlike Ceruti, Piazzetta did not stress their squalid lives and, unlike Murillo, he never idealized poverty and made you feel that those sores didn't really smell and that the ringworm wasn't really infectious. That he showed the sitter's character as well as his features is evident in the portrait of his patron Marshal Schulenburg, in the Castello Sforzesco, Milan, and in his own self-portrait in the Carrara Academy, Bergamo, showing an impatient, self-indulgent man of middle age; perhaps his notorious slowness was a deliberate attempt to curb an impulsive nature. In the same room is one of Ceruti's less revolting sitters, the 'Portrait of a Girl' with a fan—a remarkable piece of work.

We cannot leave Piazzetta without a mention of his book illustrations. One of his patrons was the publisher Giambattista Albrizzi and for him Piazzetta produced an inexhaustible supply of drawings, views, genre scenes, *putti*, *chinoiserie* and other irrelevant vignettes, all so different from his heavy painting style as to suggest that he could not be their author. 'His drawings', says Pallucchini,[25] 'show a profound feeling for the character and mood of his subjects' and Algarotti chose him to engrave the frontispiece for his *Neutonianismo per le dame*.[26] He is less successful when required to represent dramatic scenes, which show the same absence of grace and lightness as distinguish his history pieces from those of his Rococo contemporaries. In 1745 Albrizzi produced a sumptuous edition of Torquato Tasso's *Gerusalemme Liberata*—whose classic stanzas the gondoliers would sing—dedicated to the Empress Maria Teresa of Austria; the edition had the support of connoisseurs from all over Europe. Piaz-zetta was the artist; dramatic scenes were few and of his seventy drawings the pastoral scenes were regarded highly, especially in France; rightly so too, for Piazzetta achieved a suggestion of Boucher and indeed had by this time taken on what could pass for French sophistication, 'as he showed in 1747 when designing a frontispiece for the most unpromising of books, Platnerus' *Institutiones Chirurgicae*. Meanwhile in Venice the Guardi brothers plagiarized his illustrations for the *Gerusalemme Liberata* in a series of large decorative canvases depicting scenes from the poem.'[27]

12

The Portrait and Landscape Painters

The seventeenth century had been remarkable for portraits and the craving for immortality that it represents persisted into the eighteenth. Discussion of the subject must necessarily distinguish the specialist portrait painter from the general artist who does the occasional portrait. Definitions, too, are unavoidable and it is as well to be precise as to what constitutes a portrait; thus, for example, a history painting in which a model has been perfectly reproduced must not be confused with a portrait, for the object of the latter is to present, not only the sitter, but the artist's impression of the sitter's character. In the former, on the other hand, the features may be those of the model, but the character should be that of Cleopatra, Mucius Scaevola or whoever else is represented. Let us begin with a few examples of painters who did not specialize in portraits.

Amigoni was mentioned as the history painter who rounded a nasty corner in England by painting portraits in the new style and with great efficiency. Antonio Balestra did a competent self-portrait which hangs in the Castello Gallery of Verona. The peerless G. B. Tiepolo did an excellent portrait of the Prince-Bishop of Würzburg in the staircase fresco of the palace there, and another in oils, now in the Querini-Stampalia Collection, of the *procuratore* Giovanni Querini; furthermore, either he or his son Domenico incorporated both their portraits in a fresco in Madrid. Piazzetta's portrait work has been mentioned and it will suffice here to note that both Pietro Longhi (the genre painter) and Francesco Guardi (the view painter) produced competent portraits.[1] Though not a Venetian, Raphael Mengs may be mentioned, as his excellent portrait of a gentleman hangs in the Venice Accademia. And even Canova, the prince of sculptors, did a portrait in oils of a rich German collector, Gottlieb Swaier, which hangs in the Correr Museum. So it seems that a competent, if not masterly, portrait was within the powers of any professional painter, whatever his speciality.

Of the specialists, I begin with one whom Honour[2] calls 'the best seventeenth-century Venetian portrait painter', Sebastiano Bombelli (1635–1716), who is represented three times in the Pinacoteca Querini-Stampalia. His portraits are full-length, a fashion which had become general though, as Levey[3] points out, it was originally reserved by Titian for only the grandest subjects. Bombelli's portraits stress the gorgeous colours of the patricians' robes (those preserved in the Correr Museum are somewhat faded) and take us back through his teacher Guercino to Veronese and Titian. I agree with Levey that the rank counts for more in these portraits than the sitter, if you can call him that when he is standing or kneeling.

The next in seniority is Vittore Ghislandi, or Fra Galgario (1655-1743); I am glad to write that my own admiration for this artist was shared by the great patron Cardinal Pietro Ottoboni, a Venetian who had an uncanny eye for talent, even if his influence occasionally spoiled it later. Luckily Fra Galgario refused the Cardinal's invitation to Rome and I can see no sign of deterioration in his work at any stage. The group of his portraits in the Carrara Academy of Bergamo is outstanding, if only because it contains one of Tiepolo, when he was about thirty-six years old. The face is blunt-featured and has a slightly quizzical expression, as though he could never quite suppress the humour that was bubbling behind it. In features alone there is a hint of Goya, though of course the styles, and indeed the whole outlook of the two masters were different.

It is only fair that the Ghislandi family of artists should have a hall named for them in the Museo Poldi-Pezzoli in Milan, the Sala dei Ghislandi, in which there are several portraits by Fra Galgario, including the well-known 'Man in the three-cornered Hat'; in this room you may quietly compare him with the effects obtained by Guardi and Canaletto in their own branch of painting. If any proof were needed that Venice and the *terraferma* teemed with talent in the eighteenth century, the fact that Fra Galgario is left out of so many accounts of the artistic revival should be adequate.

Pietro Longhi's son Alessandro (1733-1813) was a specialist in portraits, and a good one. Perhaps his father's influence had something to do with it, for Pietro's genre paintings had to be realistic and often produced satire, while his son's portraits are noted for their detachment. How far the son's skill exceeded the father's in this branch of painting can be seen in the Pinacoteca Querini-Stampalia, where Pietro Longhi has a portrait of Andrea Querini (Room XVIII) and Alessandro one of the *procuratore* Daniele Dolfin IV (Room I).

One of Alessandro's most penetrating studies is a full-length portrait of Antonio Renier in the Padua Civic Museum, contrasted by Levey[4] with Gainsborough's 'Lord Howe'. One can understand, looking at the smirking face of the *bon viveur*, how Levey could label him a symbol of Venice's decline, especially as he takes him to be a naval officer, though he describes him as a 'naval official'. In fact Levey mistakes the sitter for one Jacopo Gradenigo and the comparison loses force when we dis-

cover that Gradenigo was an administrative officer, not a sea-dog at all
—a lagoon-puppy at the most.

One of Alessandro's most sensitive portraits, though done with the
dispassionate eye of a scientist, is that of his patron Carlo Lodoli, in the
Venice Accademia. An engraving aroused considerable interest and
opposition, partly because of the inscription comparing Lodoli with
Socrates; they at least had one thing in common: busts of Socrates and the
portrait of Lodoli show exceptionally ugly subjects. It may be of interest
to mention that Lodoli, a Minorite brother, was among those who used to
meet at Joseph Smith's house, suggesting that the latter cannot have been
quite the shunned eccentric that is alleged.

Alessandro crowned his achievements with the portraits of Carlo
Goldoni that hang in the Correr Museum. For once he loses his objectivity;
Goldoni was an intimate friend of his father, Pietro Longhi, whom he had
even mentioned in a sonnet as the worshipper of a sister Muse. Some
believe that Alessandro was far more likely to have been the real friend,
maintaining that the playwright's true counterpart was the painter of
candid portraits rather than of genre. Whichever it was, it points out that
three prominent Venetians, Goldoni and the two Longhis, followed the
tendency of the eighteenth century in their emphasis on realism or, if you
prefer, accurate detail. Alessandro revealed something of the man behind
the brush in publishing a compendium of biographies of contemporary
painters, illustrated with engravings of their portraits. It tells us why his
work is still so attractive, for to the imaginative viewer every portrait he
painted is a biography.

So far none of the painters discussed has been a typical product of the
Rococo. Elegance, grace, frivolity, all are missing; it was left for a woman
to realize that portrait painting could embody all three, and she did so at
the outset of the century. Rosalba Carriera (1675–1757) was the most
famous, over the largest area, of all Venetian artists of her time. No one
would contend that she was a greater artist than G. B. Tiepolo, or a more
discerning portrait painter than Nazario Nazari, who in this account has
to make way for more interesting personalities. Nor can one claim that her
pastel medium was original or even fully exploited in her hands. Her over-
whelming success was due to the happy touch of frivolity, the coyness that
is for ever promising something more; some of her subjects were Venice's
noblest, gayest and most voluptuous beauties, others the rich visitors who
felt that they had missed an important part of the Grand Tour if they came
back without a Canaletto and a Rosalba. Most of the pretty ladies were
bought up by the Germans and Scandinavians* and we run across her

---

* Frederick IV of Denmark and Norway commissioned miniature portraits of the twelve
most beautiful and famous Venetian women. All were patricians and the names of eight are
recorded.[5]

pastels in the most unexpected places. She ushered in the spirit of the Rococo, and that at the turn of the century. Tiepolo and Canaletto were toddlers, Pietro Longhi, Francesco Guardi and the landscape painters Zais and Zuccarelli were still unborn; it was a quiet, sober spinster, a model of bourgeois propriety, who introduced the fashionable world to the graceful felicity which came from France and found its home in Venice.

Rosalba began as a designer of patterns for the rapidly dying craft of lace-making; dying because Venetians who had been taken to France by Colbert were able to inspire the development of a great industry. The next step was the embargo on the importation of Venetian lace into France, and the last was the sale in Venice itself of lace made in France, the Low Countries and England. Such cut-throat competition had the welcome result of diverting Rosalba from her profession to that of painting the lids of snuff-boxes, whence she graduated to ivory plaques. So attractive were her miniatures that the English ambassador's first secretary, Christian Cole, persuaded her to take up pastel portrait work in 1703.* Some say she took lessons from a Frenchman, Jean Stève; others name Felice Ramelli. We know that the ambassador himself was instrumental in taking Rosalba's brother-in-law Pellegrini to England five years later. Her success among Venetians was immediate and even greater among visitors, for her fame spread with uncanny speed; much of this may have been due to Joseph Smith, for she was among the first artists he employed. In 1715 Venice welcomed the rich French banker Pierre Crozat, who had discovered Watteau and was now overwhelmed with admiration for Rosalba. They kept up a correspondence and among other matters discussed sending some of her pastels to Paris, in exchange for one of which Crozat promised her a Watteau or, if she preferred, the money.

Crozat also urged her to come to Paris, and this she did in 1721, accompanied by her unmarried sister and assistant Giovanna, or 'Nenetta'. Her welcome was a triumph and her stay as Crozat's guest a round of work and entertainment. Among others, she did a portrait of John Law the financier, still the wizard who helped people make a fortune overnight. Was this, perhaps, the portrait that Horace Walpole bought years later in Venice, when he saw Law's widow? It is just the sort of thing Law could have taken with him when he fled and would have been a negotiable asset. French artists were impressed with Rosalba's results; she was, in fact, the only Venetian artist among the 'moderns' to interest the French, and not for her looks either, for these were of the plainest.

Then back to Venice, where she had no respite either, for she was hard put to it to keep up with the demand. Her prices were not excessive—perhaps she could have gained time by raising them. But she did not have Canaletto's financial estimate of his own capabilities. She charged 50

* It is difficult to reconcile this with a report that she was already famous in 1700.

zecchini* for a miniature and from 20 to 30 for a pastel portrait, depending on whether hands and flowers were to be included. Her other rewards were commensurate: the Academy of St Luke in Venice elected her a member in 1705, and that of France in 1721. When she went to Vienna in 1730 she was also given a splendid welcome, but it is said that her success there hardly matched that in Paris; nevertheless she found plenty of work and though she refused invitations to many of the German courts there was no lack of German buyers.

Her beloved Nenetta died in 1738 and in 1746 Rosalba became blind. An operation restored her sight for a few months,† but then permanent blindness followed. I need not stress what this meant to one who saw life so vivid and so pleasant. Her last months were rendered less tragic for her and more for her friends by a terminal madness, and she died on 15 April 1757.

Monnier describes her home life; the Carriera house was in the street where Goldoni was born. He tells us of her mother, the sprightly but shrewd embroidress, of her sister Angela who married Pellegrini, calling him her *burattino*, her poppet, and her dear Nenetta. It was a happy, bourgeois household, a worker's home. Good books, old friends, a spinet, a violin and the magic box of crayons. There, on the wall, was the Watteau picture; we might have guessed that Rosalba would prefer it to the money.

The sisters prepared the backgrounds, Rosalba drew or painted, and under her hand appeared the faces of the gay women of the aristocracy; pale, powdered faces, it has been said, lacking any sign of interest,‡ and over all a veil of tedium, herald of the inevitable end.[6] Valieri's comment does them all less than justice; her sitters show their personalities, but only to the sympathetic. It was abhorrent to Rosalba's nature to declare her own sentiments or to expose too blatantly those of her sitters; her art was delicate, sensitive and refined. Such was the respect accorded her that it used to be said jokingly, that to find Rosalba a suitable husband it would be necessary to bring Guido Reni back to life.§ Her male sitters are somewhat lifeless compared with the female, but their decorations glittered.

* From the Arabic *zecca*, a die stamp and hence the mint. As an indication of the value of the zecchino, Haskell mentions that the richest family in Venice had an annual income of 32,000 and that 15 *per annum* provided bare subsistence.

† The operation of couching cataracts goes back to the first century A.D. The operation came to Europe with the Arabs of Spain. It was practised in England as late as 1780 and in Germany up to 1820. Biographies of the time are full of these sad accounts; the immediate result of pushing the opaque lens flat in the back of the eye are brilliant, but permanent inflammation and blindness are almost invariable after a short time. Hence the cataract couchers of the East are usually itinerant practitioners.

‡ This is hardly fair: Rosalba was the first Venetian to introduce coquetry into portraits and represent what then passed for sex appeal without a gross display of flesh.

§ Reni was the most famous painter of his day; Ruskin's criticism relegated him to temporary oblivion.

Princes, electors and dukes passed through her studio and the Duke of Mecklenburg used to play the viola while Rosalba accompanied him on the spinet. She was eager for life and saw as much of it as she could, walking, chatting, playing cards, passing among the crowds but not of them, apparently unconscious of her own ugliness. She even made a self-portrait that cannot have flattered her. A simple life, productive and joyous, wearing her fame lightly and happy to spend her evenings at home, with Pellegrini making sketches of poor, sleepy Nenetta, who had been up since sunrise, busy with her household tasks and charities. If the picture is not that of eighteenth-century Venice as told by foreigners, it is probably more accurate.

Her work was portraiture, but occasionally we find something else, the miniatures and snuff-boxes of her youth, a painted fan. It would be virtually impossible to enumerate her sitters; the English were always on the doorstep. We find a Thomas Coke of Norfolk, possibly the father or grandfather of the first Earl of Leicester, among her many portraits. If you were an aristocrat you did the Grand Tour. If you did the Grand Tour you went to Venice; and that of course meant having your portrait done by Rosalba. For her the invention of the century would have been one seen by La Lande in 1765 and called 'recent', a method of fixation discovered by Loriot; she probably used oil painters' varnish.

Her importance in the field of art goes far beyond her own works; when she was in Paris her results with pastel stimulated others. The most important was Maurice Quentin de Latour (1704–88), who gave up oils completely in order to develop Rosalba's method. Considered the best portrait artist in France, he carried over to crayon a trick of accentuating curves and shadows with brush strokes, and imitated the oils most successfully. This is just one of the devices that made his work superior to Rosalba's, and Jean-Etienne Liotard in his turn gives his pastels even more life and reality. Liotard's famous 'Chocolate Girl' (Mademoiselle Baldauf) was bought by Algarotti for the Elector of Saxony, presumably in 1745, when Liotard did Algarotti's portrait in Venice.

So the circle is complete and even though her French and Swiss followers obtained results beyond her reach, Rosalba was the pioneer and deserved all the praise she received. Though she had no school in the accepted sense, her sisters helped her and she had at least one pupil, Felicità Sartoni. This lady married a councillor of Augustus III* and worked in Rosalba's style in Saxony. Augustus himself had visited Venice while still Crown Prince; Rosalba did his portrait at that time and such was his admiration for her work that he had his agents subsequently buy over 150 of her pastel portraits.

* More properly Frederick Augustus III of Saxony (Elector) and Augustus II of Poland. It was for him that Algarotti bought so many pictures, including 'The Chocolate Girl'.

We get an insight into the taste of the time when we hear that Rosalba was scornful of Zuccarelli because he was a mere landscape painter. You would scarcely believe that this branch of art, though it began with van Eyck and other Flemish masters, played an important part in Renaissance painting in Venice. Tracing its development through Mantegna and the Bellinis is an interesting exercise; by the early sixteenth century landscape had in some cases become the main subject and the figures, as for instance in Giorgione's 'Tempest', seem merely incidental, if enigmatic. But landscape without figures was not to be considered worthy of a real painter until the Dutch Baroque School showed how satisfying it could be. Even so, and over a century later, it was still despised in Venice, though Domenico Tiepolo was including it, to their advantage, in many of his genre paintings. Landscape was more suited to the British temperament than the Italian and it was possibly for this reason that those Venetians who were successful landscape painters had been in England. In addition, Joseph Smith, with an eye to the English market, was a keen and discerning purchaser; it is worth noting that the collection he sold to King George III contained no landscapes by Zais, who had never been to England, though Zais was a close friend of Smith.

Marco Ricci (1679–1729) was the nephew of Sebastiano and, like him, came from Belluno. Perhaps it was the noble scenery of the Dolomites that urged him on to landscape work even if, like most painters, he could turn his hand to almost any branch. He and the other landscape painters I shall discuss inherited from the previous century what was tantamount to an early Romanticism—dark woods, thunderous skies, crags and waterfalls tend to occupy the scene and a few figures in the foreground reflect what light there is, while ruins of a castle or church add the impulse to moralize. The savage, threatening background was the legacy of Salvator Rosa; the quiet figures in the foreground recall Claude Lorrain.

What is known about Marco's personality does not endear him to us. He is said to have accepted the Earl of Manchester's invitation to England to escape the consequences of killing a gondolier who had criticized his work; he returned after falling out with his travelling companion Pellegrini. But he did not quarrel with his uncle, who patiently painted in the figures of Marco's landscapes. Later in life he changed from oil to gouache, perhaps coincidentally with the short-lived craze for water colours that came to France.

There are oils of his in the Accademia and the Pinacoteca Querini-Stampalia, but they do not impress me. For one thing they are not always hung to get as much light as they need; possibly they could do with cleaning too. Where, in fact, is the sparkle of the Rococo? There is also a feeling that you have seen the identical picture before, not, as was the case with his uncle, because you did see some of it in a Veronese, but because one waterfall looks very much like another. To me there seems little reality and the explanation is possibly a simple one: Marco Ricci, like many another Venetian painter of the *settecento*, was a scene painter for the theatre. When the Earl of Manchester returned to England in 1708 with Marco Ricci and Pellegrini, the Haymarket Theatre was getting ready to produce Scarlatti's *Pyrrhus and Demetrius* and the scenery was to be by 'two Italian painters lately arriv'd from Venice'.[7] His paintings, then, may be just so many set pieces.

An interesting comparison may be made between Marco Ricci's 'Storm at Sea'[8] and C. J. Vernet's seascape, commissioned by Stanislaus Poniatowski, King of Poland; it is said to have been painted in 1773 and eventually acquired by Clive of India.[9] The compositions are almost identical, a stormy sea, a three-master almost on her beam-ends, a bluff on the left crowned with a tower or lighthouse. I have seen Vernet's seascapes described as 'theatrical'; surely this applies to Marco Ricci too, and we should remember that Watteau began his artistic career as a scene painter. The similarity in Ricci's and Vernet's paintings does not imply plagiarism; it simply demonstrates the taste of the day. Perhaps we shall be more kindly disposed towards Marco Ricci when we remember that he, like others of the day, did a series of operatic caricatures so amusing that Smith bought them for his collection. We have to lament his death by suicide at the age of fifty.

Francesco Zuccarelli (1702–88), though born in Florence, spent his working life in Venice, except for fifteen years in England. I cannot pretend enthusiasm for any of the eighteenth-century Venetian landscape painters, Zuccarelli least of all. But this is a personal reaction and not shared by the experts. To me he is monotonous and repetitive and above all presents nothing which can be classified as Venetian Rococo, unless we accept the *capricci* that he produced in collaboration with the engraver Antonio Visentini. The best known and most topical is their 'Burlington House in an imaginary Setting';[10] here we have Boyle and Kent's version of Palladio, a section of banal landscape and a few posed figures in the foreground. The landscape adds nothing to the architecture and the mansion does nothing for the landscape except mercifully to screen three-quarters of it.

Another activity was the setting of classical and mythological scenes in the country, such as the 'Rape of Europa' in the Venice Accademia, a hackneyed subject treated in the old-fashioned way. It is strange to read that in Algarotti's scheme for getting the most suitable man for each subject Zuccarelli was chosen for out-of-doors subjects such as 'The Hunt of Meleager and Atalanta'—straightforward history painting. He even tried his hand at genre and in the Accademia is his 'Bull-baiting' with the usual landscape setting. I have the impression, in fact, that for anything but the English market Zuccarelli had to liven up his landscapes with genre, mythology or religion, the first two preferably with breasts. With it all he seems to have been popular, much more than the town painters who have ousted him today; perhaps it was his personal charm, or the fact that he was willing to lend his landscapes to any theme. Critics and patrons competed in singing his praises; in fact the Elder Zanetti said that he could not do so enough, while G. B. Biffi called him '*Il mio Zuccarelli*' and added, 'Thanks to you we do not have to envy the ancients.'[11] Having seen his 'Bacchanal' and 'Rape of Europa' I agree with the last remark.

Giuseppe Zais (1709–84) is regarded as a more satisfactory interpreter of landscapes; Smith, it is said, patronized him only because Zuccarelli was in England and, I may add, because they were friends. Certainly Zais infuses more life, either through genre or biblical subjects, and there are even *capricci* with ruins; but there was obviously no room for many landscape painters, except in England, which Zais never visited. He lived on in want and is bracketed with Guardi as one of the most neglected masters of the day. It is just possible that Zais arrived too late and Guardi too early to catch the fancy of the public.

The last of the landscape artists* is Antonio Diziani (1737–97?), whose 'Four Seasons' can be seen in the Padua Civic Museum. From these and other of his paintings that I have seen, I would say that his work is as dreary as that of the other landscape artists. My impression is that there was little typically Venetian and nothing Rococo in their work. There was simply no room for them in the century that saw Watteau and Fragonard.

---

* I omit view painters, like Marieschi, who did occasional country scenes, the landscape backgrounds of some of Domenico Tiepolo's frescoes and, of course, Guardi's lagoon scenes.

13

The View Painters

Though they were looked down on by the Venetians, the painters of views in eighteenth-century Venice were possibly of more value to the State than any of the other specialists. The Grand Tourist needed souvenirs, a portrait by Rosalba and a selection of views of the city painted or engraved with accuracy and sympathy, the forerunners of the picture postcard. The atmosphere of exuberance and licence, the strange appearance of masquers and the entertainments offered, all gave the visitor material for his memories and, says Levey,[1] 'There might even exist a sort of therapeutic value in delineations of Venice, and when the valetudinarian Mr Woodhouse in *Emma* needs to be entertained, Jane Austen has Mr Knightley produce engravings of "some views of St Mark's place, Venice. ..."'

The paintings, engravings made from them, and even tableware which embodied copies of such engravings were in great demand everywhere but in Venice itself, where view painters were rated even lower than landscape painters and where Canaletto, at a time when he had achieved international fame, had great difficulty in being elected a member of the Academy. Alessandro Longhi does not even mention view painters in his *Compendio*. Not that city views were a strange innovation, unknown elsewhere, though it is difficult to be precise about the origin of this branch of painting. There is Vermeer's 'View of Delft' which had important consequences; unfortunately one of them led artists to the open country to paint landscapes, and the other to pay exclusive attention to the foreground figures and so to genre scenes.

It is unlikely that Northern Italy was the home of the true townscape, but once it arrived what more appropriate subject than Venice could be chosen? Even in Venice, though, it was not the Italians who introduced townscapes but northerners, including Heintz from Germany and Richter of Sweden. With the exception of El Greco's painting of a storm over Toledo, Velázquez ('View of Zaragoza'), Hollar, to whom we shall return, and no doubt a few others, city views seem till then to have been Flemish or Dutch. From the Low Countries the idea may have spread, not only to Spain, but to England, for townscapes of the early eighteenth century are by no means rare; that of Broad Quay in Bristol[2] by Peter Monamy is in every way comparable to the Venetian paintings we shall discuss, with its emphasis on perspective, its meticulous detail and its groups of figures—even Canaletto's almost invariable dog in the foreground. And even this may have had an English ancestry, for Wenceslaus Hollar the Bohemian was active in England in the middle of the seventeenth century and on his return from the Low Countries engraved his views of London after the Great Fire; Thomas Johnson was his follower and his 'documentaries', comprising view and genre together, may be seen in engravings in the Prints Department of the British Museum.

The same tendency, to use the townscape as a medium for presenting events of greater or less importance, is seen in Joseph Heintz's seventeenth-century 'Procession of the Patriarch' in the Correr Museum. Gaspar van Wittel (Vanvitelli) has a view of Venice in the last years of the seventeenth century, now in Madrid's Prado Museum, where one may also see a much earlier view painting, that of Zaragoza by Velázquez. The first whom we can consider a Venetian painter of *vedute* was Luca Carlevaris (1663–1730), born at Udine in the *terraferma*. He seems to have been well recognized as a reporter-painter, for he was commissioned to record the 1707 return of the English ambassador, the Earl of Manchester and those of three other ambassadors from various countries, as well as the regatta in honour of Frederick IV of Denmark.

This seems to have been the chief employment of the *vedutisti* at home; their main income derived from the sale of small souvenir pictures to tourists, but patrons from other countries in Italy, and especially publishers with an eye to the foreign market also did their share. Thus Carlevaris illustrated *Le Fabbriche e Vedute di Venezia* (Buildings and Views of Venice) in 1703 with engravings designed for travellers. It is not therefore surprising that so few of his paintings are to be found in Venice and the Veneto; in fact the only two I have seen there were at Udine. The first is a bird's-eye view of the town, from an imaginary hill with rustics in the foreground; the other is of the kind that sets a fashion, a view of the Piazzetta of Venice, with a part of San Marco and the Doge's Palace on the left and the Island of San Giorgio with its Palladian church in the foreground. It is all purposely distorted; San Giorgio is too near; the foreground figures are exotic and probably represent Albanians. All in all, this appears to be an early attempt at taking liberties with a scene in order to heighten the effect. Carlevaris' successors were to go to greater lengths and mix up portions of views taken from different parts, or even invent parts, and present these flights of imagination and draughtsmanship as *capricci*, or fantasies. In Guardi's pictures they open up a new field of art and many prefer them to the meticulous record of a well-known scene.

When Algarotti commissioned them he even specified the buildings which should be juxtaposed.

Carlevaris liked to regard himself as a man of learning, not as one of the despised class of landscape or view painters; hence perhaps his delight in scenes of Venice's grandeur, the gorgeous processions, the winged lion of St Mark above the milling crowd, the gilt barges, the decorated *bissone*. Perhaps the most telling criticism of him and his predecessors is the gaudiness of the scene; it was for Canaletto to show the way to paintings that satisfy the eye as well as the archivist. In the British Museum there is an etching by Carlevaris of the Rio dei Mendicanti; the highest praise it could earn was that Guardi took it as the scene of what many consider his most attractive painting. It is always interesting to see preliminary sketches and in those of Carlevaris,[3] both drawings and oils, there is evidence of great attention to costumes, so much so that several figures consist solely of clothes, with absent hands and features only lightly suggested. Here we can also see drawings of gondolas with *felze*, the detachable, black cabin tops which give such an air of intimacy.

Giovanni Antonio Canal, known as Canaletto (1697–1768) was the son of a scene painter. Where this was prejudicial to Marco Ricci in making his landscapes too theatrical it was turned to good use by Canaletto, who realized early in life what an important part is played by attention to perspective. He is said to have owned a camera obscura—there is one marked 'A. Canal' in the Correr Museum—and it seems that he used it for the preliminary lay-out and then painted in the rest at leisure or had his assistants share in such work. His strength lay in the marvellous sense of depth that accurate perspective gives, and the introduction of contrasting light and shade; it is in Canaletto's paintings that we first realize what magic lies in the clear light of Venice, but it was left to Guardi to present the more usual pearly light of spring and autumn and the misty distances of the lagoon. Canaletto does not allow distance to interfere with detail; what the eye can see, he can reproduce[*] and his strength lay in seeing what others passed by.

One of his earliest and best paintings is the Campo San Vidal, known as 'The Stonemason's Yard'.[4] It shows building operations that must have been in progress, for there is no evidence of a permanent yard, though the well-head and the houses on the right survive. Levey[5] inclines to a date between 1726 and 1730, which would put it between Canaletto's early and later styles. It marks the heights to which this great artist could attain before his work became mechanical in order to satisfy the increasing demands of the tourist trade. It also demonstrates what an artist can see

---

[*] Even a small amount of water vapour in the air may render distant objects less distinct. Canaletto always paints as though atmospheric humidity was nil, which must be almost unknown in Venice.

where others pass by without a second glance. Venice is the last place to look for his best pictures; some are in England, others, according to Gioseffi, in Rome and Milan.

With the help of Joseph Smith, who has been suspected of monopolizing Canaletto's works and exploiting them, he found more work than was convenient and the standard deteriorated. When the demand in Venice fell off he went to England and to disappointment. Though he did some fine paintings, the old sureness had gone; the light did not, perhaps, suit his style, for there had been complaints about the coal smoke in London since the days of Elizabeth I. There was grumbling and even some talk of a substitute having been sent in place of the great 'Canaletti'. Among the works dating from this period of ten years' desultory painting in England, is the view of Eton College.[6] Its chief interest is that the details are highly inaccurate—so unlike the old Canaletto!—and additions do not seem to have been made to help the composition. It is, in fact, a *capriccio* without an organized theme. The college buildings derive no advantage from the imaginary ones along the horizon; it has been suggested that Canaletto made his drawing and the final painting from an inaccurate engraving. Certainly he would never have been guilty of altering a view in this way as a mere whim. Perhaps the rural setting of Eton made him unsure, for he was essentially a city man. This alone would be enough to make him unpopular with the English aristocracy of that time; furthermore, he knew the value of his work, not in any abstract artistic sense, but judged by the demand. Hence the frequent complaints of his grasping nature.

Canaletto was an artist who combined accuracy with emotional appeal. His views of Venice tell us exactly how the parts he painted appeared at the time, and yet there is something about the light, the colour and those so necessary figures that no camera study could evoke. He was deservedly the most popular painter in Italy. When Mrs Piozzi was there, nearly twenty years after his death, she wrote disparagingly of the state of painting in Venice and remarked that Angelica Kauffmann, the Neo-Classicist, chose to live in Rome. Mrs Piozzi did not know that Angelica was proud to own two very fine views by the Venetian Canaletto.

During his lifetime his speciality was, as I remarked, very much looked down on and it was not until two years before his death that he was elected to the Venetian Academy. His *morceau de réception* still hangs in the Accademia and consists of a *capriccio*, or what he called a *veduta ideale*, which is entirely imaginary, instead of incorporating portions of various views. The colour adds little to the pleasing effect of the fancy and reminds us that Canaletto was as competent with pen, pencil and burin as he was with the brush. He did not, however, make much use of this gift, but in 1735 and again in 1742, just before his visit to England, he collaborated with the engraver Visentini, with whom he published a total of thirty-eight plates.* There has been ample discussion about the series[7] which was dedicated to 'J. Smith *cons*' and signed 'A. Canal'. Those that Canaletto himself made were dedicated '*Al Illmo Signor Giuseppe Smith Console di S. M. Britanica*'. Canaletto's drawings, though intended only as preliminary sketches, are among his masterpieces and the whole series (or its reproductions) is under lock and key at the Carrara Academy in Bergamo.

Of Canaletto's views in the National Gallery I am particularly interested in the '*Scuola di San Rocco*',[8] showing the annual procession of the Doge to the headquarters of the confraternity of St Roch; thus was commemorated, on the Saint's feast day (16 August), his intercession when the plague was ravaging Venice in 1576. The faces in the crowd have two peculiarities: first they are so sketchily portrayed as to be quite at variance with Canaletto's usual practice; this must be why at one time Tiepolo was seriously suggested as a collaborating figure painter. The second point is that certain faces seem to be repeated, with variations in the colour of headgear and clothing, suggesting an economy in the preliminary *modelli*. A little roof garden on stilts is also seen and, judging by other views, appears to have been a common addition to houses at the time.

Another peculiarity of Canaletto, at least in his maturer work, is the use of white dots on objects or people, even when they are in the shade; they can be seen sparingly in the 'Regatta' at the National Gallery[9] and profusely in two views of St Mark's Square,[10] which are later. They are certainly effective in livening up the whole picture, especially where a large area is in the shade, with consequent toning down of colour.

It is an education to look at Canaletto's and Francesco Guardi's view paintings almost side by side. It can be done at the National Gallery and in the Carrara Academy in Bergamo, and almost invariably Canaletto comes off second best. In some ways he is as old-fashioned as Carlevaris, perhaps because he too was commissioned to paint scenes from the *Sensa* as well as regattas and processions; his foreground figures often appear static in comparison with Guardi's; and he nearly always misses the evocative quality of Guardi's freer hand and the soft light that suffuses the lagoon. On the other hand he shows the virtues of method, untiring application and what Phillips calls 'almost monotonous tranquillity'.† And that is why he remains today the king of Venetian view painters, that rare phenomenon of an artist who achieved an international reputation in his

---

* The first fourteen comprise views of the Grand Canal, and there are engraved portraits of Canaletto and Visentini. The former is engraved by Visentini after a painting by G. B. Piazzetta and shows a good-looking man in a periwig, of any age from eighteen to fifty. He was actually thirty-eight.

† The largest collection of Canaletto's paintings are, as might be expected, in England, whence came his usual customers. The Royal Collection at Windsor contains the whole series that Joseph Smith sold to King George III and that at Woburn Abbey is based on the views commissioned in 1740 by the Duke of Bedford.

own day and has kept it for two centuries. For pure utility an accurate reporter, such as Canaletto, has proved to be indispensable; an example is his representation of the Prà della Valle (at Windsor). Without it, we should be less impressed with Andrea Memmo's efforts.

Canaletto's sister Fiorenza was the mother of Bernardo Bellotto (1720–80); he was trained by his uncle and produced works which, at their best, were often mistaken for those of his uncle at his worst. In fact he signed himself 'Bernardo de Canaletto' and is still known as Canaletto in Poland, where he spent his last years. So while Canaletto was mistaken for an impostor in London, Bellotto in Eastern Europe was adding to confusion by being taken for his uncle. Even now there are paintings which it is difficult to attribute to one or other; when they are Bellotto's, they date back to the period before he abandoned the formal character he had learned in his uncle's studio.

He seems to have been a restless man: for a time he wandered through the Veneto, painting in Padua and elsewhere; then, in 1747, when his uncle left for London, Bernardo went to Dresden, where he worked for Frederick Augustus III. When he finally settled in Poland in 1768 Stanislaus Poniatowski, the last king, was already on the throne; for him he painted those views of Warsaw which combined his uncle's accuracy with glimpses of genre and a style which seemed to deny the mathematical. Nevertheless these same views proved essential to the architects commissioned to rebuild ruined Warsaw after the destruction of 1939–45.

Most of Bellotto's work remains in Eastern Europe. Of the few found elsewhere the Jones Collection[11] has a *capriccio*, a view with two bridges dating from his Venetian days, and the Accademia in Venice one of the Scuola di San Marco. Like his uncle, he drew in perfect perspective and used white paint in tiny streaks to stress highlights, a mannerism adopted by many others. Two more *capricci* are in the Civic Museum of Asolo and another in the Carrara Academy of Bergamo. This is noteworthy in that the foreground of the Roman forum, including the Arch of Titus, are an accurate reproduction, while the only fanciful part is that seen through the arch.

To the casual visitor Bellotto's paintings may give as much pleasure as his uncle's; it seems, in fact, as if a modern expert is needed to distinguish some of them. Thus Clive of India bought a 'Canaletto' view of Verona harbour in about 1773 for 140 guineas, that turned out to be by Bellotto. In 1972 an acknowledged Bellotto view of Verona, possibly the same one, was sold at a London auction for £300,000. Which suggests that quality is not the only consideration in pricing a work of art.

There were other view painters at the time, for the market was bullish. Some, like Francesco Tironi did little but copy Canaletto's views, and their works still turn up at sales outside Italy; others gave up landscape painting to take up urban views; Michele Marieschi, for instance, anticipated Guardi in the freedom of his brushwork and would undoubtedly have completed a famous trio, along with Canaletto and Guardi, if he had not died young. Four of his views—probably *capricci*—hang in the Venice Accademia and impress chiefly by their dark tones. But careful study shows that they are all drawn with precision; perhaps the dark tints are a carry-over from the gloomy landscapes that Zuccarelli, Zais and Diziani (who was possibly Marieschi's teacher) favoured, in common with the previous century's *tenebristi*. His most entertaining, if least original views are the celebration pictures, subjects which so many artists painted. He seems to have been equally at home with the burin and the needle, and his engravings, like those of nearly all his contemporaries, are always attractive. In 1741 he produced a book of illustrations designed for the tourist market and of such high quality that Fragonard, years later, held them in great esteem.

One who relied on engraving to the exclusion of painting was Giambattista Piranesi (1720–78), architect and artist. Little is known about his training, but it has always struck me as suggestive that Canaletto was in Rome in the year that Piranesi was born and brought back sketches of ruins that he worked up much later. Piranesi followed him twenty years later and stayed on. His romantic, but accurate views of Classical Roman ruins are famous and widely distributed, as befits the work of a craftsman who could draw four thousand impressions from a single copper plate. He used to describe himself as a 'son of Rome', but his signature always bore the designation 'Venetian architect'. His views of the ruined forum, aqueducts and even *capricci* in the form of imaginary prisons played a great part in the Classical revival that superseded the Baroque and Rococo and may even have stimulated Gibbon to produce one of the world's classics. Professor Murray does not play down Piranesi's Venetian origin and in fact draws attention to the relationship between his etchings and the *vedute* of Venice. As one who, unlike Professor Murray, has nothing to lose by an ill-formed guess, I like to think that Canaletto played a part in Piranesi's education and that his sketches of Rome set the great engraver on the path that led to fame.

Successors who painted views in Venice were few. Giuseppe Bernardino Bison (1762–1844) imitated Canaletto's style and Giovanni Migliara (1785–1837) tried to repeat some of Guardi's effects; but it was Richard Parkes Bonington (1802–28) who was the only worthy successor of the masters. In his short life, and working usually with water colours, he alone, more than Turner, Whistler, Manet, Renoir or Monet, recaptured the feeling of Venice and the Venetians, as presented by Canaletto and Guardi.

Canaletto's influence is invoked again in the mystery that surrounds the

21   Andrea Brustolon: sketch for Madonna of the Rosary, which can be seen at
Pieve in the Italian Tyrol

22   Antonio Canova: Daedalus and Icarus. The great inventor is fitting his son with wings which, alas, will not stand up to the sun's heat. When the wax melted Icarus fell to his death

23 Alessandro Longhi's portrait of Carlo Goldoni. Both painter and playwright were highly talented and meticulous workers. One may feel that the portrait expresses their sympathy

24 Antonio Canale (Canaletto): an engraving by Antonio Visentini from G. B. Piazzetta's lost painting. The artist was about thirty-eight at the time it was made

25   F. Guardi: Sketch for *La Sala del Ridotto* which now hangs in the Ca' Rezzonico
There are numerous other sketches for this work in the Venice Correr Museum.

26   Design for a *bissona*, one of the types of skiff used by Venetian patricians on state
occasions. Note the concession to the vogue of *chinoiserie*. F. Guardi

27   *Il Concerto* by P. Longhi, 1741. While the musicians fiddle away earnestly, two clerics are oblivious, completely immersed in their card game

28 Fresco on the ballroom ceiling of the Ca' Rezzonico, by G. B. Tiepolo. It is entitled 'The Nuptial Allegory' and the bride is riding in Apollo's chariot. Tiepolo had previously used the lower view of the four white horses with great success in the Kaisersaal at Würzburg

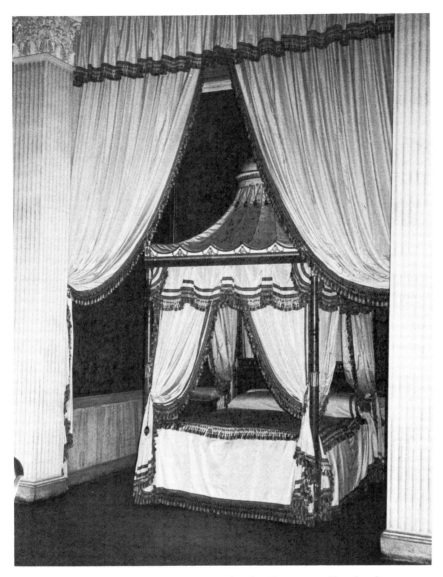

29 The Viceroy's bed at the Villa Pisani, Strà. The Viceroy was Napoleon's stepson
Eugène de Beauharnais

30   G. B. Tiepolo: Angelica staunching the wounds of Medor. A drawing for the frescoes of the Villa Valmarana

training of Francesco Guardi (1712–93). He began as a figure painter in
the studio of his elder brother Gian Antonio and considerable doubt exists
as to how much Francesco did, and how much Gian Antonio. Informed
opinion[12] states that Francesco's figure painting reflects the influence of
Sebastiano Ricci in his lively, light touch and of Magnasco* in his vigorous
brush and bold painting. We must, however, realize that the Guardi
'dynasty', as Gioseffi[13] calls them, were quite openly plagiarists and had no
qualms about appropriating ideas or views of others; the '*Rio dei Mendicanti*', my own favourite among all Francesco's townscapes, is a reproduction in colour of a Carlevaris engraving and it has been suggested that
his pale, bright colour may owe something to his brother-in-law, G. B.
Tiepolo. Again, after Piazzetta's book illustrations for the *Gerusalemme
Liberata* had been acclaimed for the masterpieces they are, the Guardi
brothers produced a series of large canvases which altered only the size
and the medium of Piazzetta's work. As regards the old belief that Francesco Guardi was a 'good pupil' of Canaletto, we have only one isolated
remark of 1764 on which to base it. Until 1760, when Gian Antonio died,
we have no record of Francesco being interested in anything but figure
painting. Few examples of these can be found today, but four, incorporating the *sotto in sù* viewpoint, are in the Palazzo Labia in Venice. It was after
his brother's death that Francesco Guardi seems to have specialized in
vedute.

Modern opinion holds Guardi† in the greatest esteem, perhaps because
he never achieved the almost photographic reproductions of Canaletto.
This failing, if it can be so called, was responsible for much criticism in
Guardi's lifetime; the Englishman John Strange, for instance, thought
him 'too spirited' and begged his representative to tell Guardi that his
drawing must be 'not just clear, well finished and *a pair*, but also coloured
exactly'. We can now understand why Guardi was considered to miss the
'truth' of the views that he painted.[14]

So much has been written about Guardi that it is unwise to be dogmatic.
Some see in him the forerunner of the Impressionists, others deny it;
surely it is of interest to no one but an art critic. In his views he sacrificed
Canaletto's tranquillity to the faithful portrayal of the bustling Queen of
the Adriatic, 'its restless waters, its weightless skies'.[15] He invented ways of
producing effects more powerful than those previously obtained by frank
reproduction; to base on this the claim that he anticipated the Impressionists is as logical as calling Beethoven the father of jazz because he sometimes used syncopation with considerable success. Guardi had something
original to say; let us see how he set about it.

First, his drawing. Like all the *settecentisti* this was usually meticulous and,

* Another of the Salvator Rosa persuasion, often indistinguishable from Marco Ricci.
† From now on the surname refers to Francesco, unless otherwise stated.

even if the final painting gives the feeling of freshness and freedom that suggests a dashing style and rapid brush work, the preliminary drawing shows how much time and care went into its preparation. Thus, when La Serenissima commissioned four paintings from Francesco Guardi to commemorate Pope Pius VI's visit of 1782, his preliminary study of the interior of SS Giovanni e Paolo shows the most careful draughtsmanship and faultless perspective, with less suggestion of impressionism than many of G. B. Tiepolo's pen and wash sketches.[16] But the finished painting: what a wealth of light and movement! You would think that the figures were the only part that Guardi bothered about and the perspective, which had cost so much labour in the drawing stage, is simply a setting which would be noticed only if it were incorrect. Then there are his 'squiggles', as Levey so aptly calls Guardi's foreground figures. From the comparatively complete pen-and-wash visitors at the Sala del Ridotto, to the apparently juvenile, wriggly pen strokes of his drawing for 'The Bull-Baiting',[17] Guardi reveals himself as a master of the difficult art of capturing atmosphere with only the essential lines; but every line tells. Then there are the careful designs for *bissone*, the patricians' skiffs that accompanied the *Bucintoro* on state occasions; in one the gondoliers in Chinese costume reveal the topical appeal of *chinoiserie*.

The colouring of Guardi's paintings is even more likely to support those who consider him a forerunner of the Impressionists. Apart from scenes of outdoor, official occasions such as the Doge's annual wedding ceremony, in which he copies Canaletto closely—suspiciously closely in fact—colour is laid on with all the power of moderation. Nothing is brilliant except the light of Venice and even that is not the cold, clear, hard light of Canaletto. His townscapes are usually so posed that they might justifiably be called 'The Crowd in the Piazza di San Marco' or 'Gondolas and Fishing Boats in front of Santa Maria della Salute'. For all is light and movement and the lightest colours are kept for those who are doing most of the moving. There is light and shade, of course, but nothing as theatrical as Canaletto's; we can, in fact, picture Guardi drifting through canals or across the lagoon in his mobile studio and taking the light as it comes, now pearly, now hazy, rarely bright and clear, always mobile and elusive.

The figures themselves, so effective in the preliminary sketches, are doubly so with the help of colour and brush strokes. The first paintings known, believed to be by the two brothers Guardi, are in the organ loft of the Church of Angelo Raffaele, Venice, and illustrate the story of Tobias. Being where they are, they are intended for viewers at a distance, and their technique reveals the artists' skill. I am strongly reminded of Manet's 'Road Menders in the Rue de Berne'[18] when I see the Tobias series; but this does not make the Guardis pre-Impressionists either; at the most they could be called pre-Manet, and then only one aspect of Manet's style.

Most commentators refer to the flickering, restless light of Guardi's view paintings and it is difficult to better the description. Levey[19] writes that Guardi seemed to agree with Constable's remark that the best lesson he ever had was: 'Remember light and shade never stand still.' Is this perhaps why one of his architectural *capricci*[20] has shadows in the shaded foreground and bright background going in opposite directions? There seems to be no surface which could reflect light sufficiently to throw a secondary shadow. Did he paint half the picture in the morning and finish it after luncheon? Or did he combine two separate views in his *capriccio*, one facing north and the other south? No matter; Guardi's fantasies are so constructed that they appeal to the intellect as well as to the eye and, with a lesser painter, one would not even notice an apparent oversight. The very next painting in the same gallery[21] also seems to be a *capriccio* and is popularly entitled 'The Treasure Seekers' though there seems to be no documentary evidence for this belief. Note how few brush strokes were needed to show eagerness, fatigue, greed and loneliness; they are all there and it makes Levey hard to believe when he writes[22] that 'Guardi's handling is really an inspired accident rather than a scientific method of vision'. Once you have seen those two figures at work in front of the ruined arch you cannot care if the title is or is not inspired by truth; contrary to all reason, you *know* they are digging for treasure.

We should not leave the Guardi brothers without a mention of their genre paintings in the Ca' Rezzonico. Two famous pictures hang there, the '*Ridotto*', which has the whole room named after it, and the '*Parlatorio*' which hangs in the same room (see plates 1 and 2). These are pure genre; everything is subordinated to portraying the activities of the subjects. In the '*Ridotto*' one may study the various types of mask, the men with the white, grotesque *larve*, the women with masks of black satin, the half-mask or the oval *moretta*. Two women are without the *bauta* and might be servants, though it is possible that they are deliberatly flaunting their looks in the hope of making enough money to gamble. Here too, among the men with their black, three-cornered hats, their black *baute* and crimson cloaks, there is one using a muff, others in a bar in the background; the only ones unmasked are the two barmen and the patricians, identified by their full-bottomed wigs, who are dealing cards which will shortly join a dozen others on the floor. Fiocco[23] reproduces and discusses a second version of the '*Ridotto*',* presumably in a private collection, with only one patrician dealer; he also points out resemblances between female figures, one in each painting in the Ca' Rezzonico, but adds that Francesco Guardi had more imitators than any other artist, ancient or modern. And

* Possibly the one sold at Sotheby's in 1972.

what if other experts are right, and these two pictures are not by Francesco at all, but by his brother Gian Antonio?

The '*Parlatorio*', or Nuns' Parlour, shows a scene described by Casanova and by many tourists. Behind a grille in their parlour sit the nuns, in fashionable dresses and jewellery, but with short hair that detracts in no way from their looks; talking to them through the grille are their visitors, who include the two fashionably dressed boys, sword, lace and scarlet heels proclaiming their aristocracy, watching a Punch-and-Judy show. The authorship of these two paintings was for a long time disputed. At first it seemed obvious that Pietro Longhi, archetype of the genre painters, must have been responsible. Then second thoughts crept in; why was the style so much less artificial than that of the known Longhi's? Surely Francesco Guardi was a more likely author. But the date, and much intrinsic evidence, suggested his brother Gian Antonio as the more probable, and today we have reached a compromise and ascribe these brilliant evocations of Venetian life to collaboration between the brothers.

14

Genre

It was the eighteenth century that allowed genre painting, the recording of episodes from everyday life, to emerge. Backgrounds or detached portions of compositions had previously 'supported' the main theme by depicting by-play of varying interest; take, for instance, the figures of the Queen's *aposentador* and the artist himself in Velázquez's '*Las Meninas*' or the kitchen staff in Tintoretto's 'Last Supper'. But these are not genre paintings, in which the activities or relaxations of everyday life are the purpose of the composition.

Genre painting of low life was nothing new in Italy, for Ceruti of Brescia had produced such studies, with considerable art, in the first quarter of the century, and Marco Ricci had selected the subject of an operatic rehearsal for a painting in England even earlier. It is usual to regard Pietro Falca, called Longhi (1702–85), as the greatest exponent of genre painting of the century, but in the praise that has been lavished on him, the far more artistic and sensitive work of Chardin in France is forgotten. Perhaps snobbery had something to do with it: Ceruti painted mostly the dregs, Longhi the froth and Chardin the bourgeoisie in the middle. To learn something of everyday life in Venice we have to turn to the drawings and engravings of Gaetano Zompini (1700–78). He recorded the activities of various trades among the poorer classes; true genre as contrasted with the artificial life of the upper classes. The Elder Zanetti showed great interest and is believed to have inspired Zompini's book of engravings, *Le Arti che vanno per via nella città di Venezia*; Zanetti's encouragement was eminently practical, for he took Zompini into his own house and cared for him while he prepared his book.

One of Longhi's teachers, Giuseppe Maria Crespi of Bologna, may have had much to do with Longhi's choice of a speciality, for his own works contain several examples that can be classed as genre. Many of the history painters, in fact, produced an occasional genre picture—not merely a background or subsidiary motif—and this seems to have been particularly the case in eighteenth-century Venice. Piazzetta's 'Idyll' is usually cited as an example, though the question is debatable; but his '*L'Indovina*' in the Venice Accademia is a fine study of a peasant girl who tells fortunes, and deserves to be called a work of art, which can be said of few of Longhi's genre paintings. Domenico, the younger Tiepolo, also produced excellent genre paintings, to which we shall return, though his main work had perforce to be as assistant to his father in the fields of history and decoration. Even Zais the landscape painter introduced genre in the form of peasants dancing, or busy with their daily tasks.

Pietro Longhi is, however, the archetype of eighteenth-century Venetian genre painters. Two facts must always be kept in mind when discussing his work in that field: first, that some of his paintings were produced two, three or more times, possibly by pupils, and secondly, that not every attribution to Longhi is correct, for he had almost as many imitators as Guardi. But, in spite of these excuses, which may apply to certain paintings accepted as Longhis, many regard him as more of a reporter than an artist; Goldoni, in fact, who hailed him as a fellow spirit and worker in the field of realism, praised him as a seeker after truth and not as a painter.

His early works and the occasional portrait or religious picture that he painted after specializing in genre do not show marked ability. The portraits are never very lifelike, except when there is evidence of collaboration with his son Alessandro; his earliest dated essay in history painting was the fresco 'The Fall of the Giants' over the staircase of the Palazzo Sagredo, which is classed as 'clumsy'.[1] His very earliest works are reported to have been painted in collaboration with his teacher Antonio Balestra, but they are, perhaps fortunately, lost. An interesting comparison can be made in the Church of San Pantaleone, where a spandrel on the left has the image of the apostles Peter and Andrew by Pietro Longhi, and one on the right has Thaddeus and Matthew signed by his son Alessandro. I prefer the latter. In the same church, Valcanova, about a quarter of a century ago, attributed other frescoes, including a Madonna and Child with a female saint, to Pietro Longhi. Moschini remarks that it is not a great work and that the colouring is unremarkable.

Longhi's entry into the field of genre painting dates from about 1740, for his 'Concerto' in the Venice Accademia is his first dated genre picture. Thereafter he limited himself to portraying the activities—or lack of activity—of the patricians, with few exceptions. There are three country scenes with peasants in the Pinacoteca Querini-Stampalia, paintings of the rare animals that were exhibited in Venice ('Exhibition of a Rhinoceros' in the National Gallery, London), and the 'Seven Sacraments' in the same Pinacoteca; these last are his nearest approach to art rather than reportage. The 'Concerto' tells us more about the meaning behind his genre paintings: three men on the right are playing the fiddle while in the left background a fat monk and a thin, eager old priest are playing cards; the sixth man is watching the game and the concert's only audience is a lap dog on a stool.

Levey[2] compares Longhi's clumsy drawing and unorganized composition with the Dutchman Cornelis Troost's superior technique and consoles the Longhi enthusiast with the latter's pungency and candour.

It is difficult to explain why he should have been admired and collected by the very people whom we are supposed to see satirized. Were they unconscious of the satire, or did they have a better sense of humour than we suspect? In any case they make a poor showing. Some of Rosalba's Venetian sitters were described as 'vapid'; in that case there is no word for the lack of intelligence, or even life, in the faces of Longhi's patricians. Gioseffi[3] writes of 'a feeling of sweet tedium', but to me they become ever more wooden and fossilized. This impression is heightened by the great numbers of copies and spurious Longhi paintings that survive, the products of even less skilful brushes.

The frozen attitudes and the flatness of the compositions are now conveniently extenuated as the attributes of a primitive, and a primitive is apparently a good thing to be. If so, then Longhi should be called the 'Grandma Moses of eighteenth-century Venice'. It is reassuring to the amateur, who 'knows what he likes—and dislikes' to read what another expert has to say, in much the same vein as Levey: 'These vivid glimpses into Venetian private life, painted in cool pastel colours, have great charm. But do they merit the praise that has often been lavished on them by Italian critics? One examines them in vain for the wit of Domenico Tiepolo, for the exquisite refinement of Chardin, for the vivacity and social criticism of Hogarth. They are in fact little superior to Gabriele Bello's amusing naïveties. Only one picture is of much higher quality— the group of men shooting duck on the lagoon, and this may well be the work of another artist.'[4] With regard to the last, I can only add that the painter, whoever he was, knew nothing of archery, for his duck hunter is holding the half drawn bowstring without an arrow.

Nor can we allow that Longhi was the only practitioner of genre at the time and therefore had to be selected for this type of work by any patron. Haskell[5] goes into some detail about the publisher Pasquali and says that his most enterprising venture was a seventeen-volume edition of Goldoni's works. Particular attention was paid to the hundred or more illustrations by various artists and, at Goldoni's own request, these were no longer to be hackneyed mythological subjects, with Muses and Classical actors' masks, but scenes from his own life. Here was an opening for Goldoni's admired friend Longhi; but no, an artist named Novelli was selected to design plates illustrating the plays, mostly dealing with the comfortable bourgeoisie and 'from no other source—certainly not from the pictures of Pietro Longhi—can we get such a vivid impression of the period'.[6] We are left with the disturbing suspicion that Longhi may have been an inferior interpreter of a commonly practised form of art. Can his success have had anything to do with his personal friendship with Carlo Goldoni? Or even be owed to the support of Gaspare Gozzi, who praised him both in the *Gazzetta* and the *Osservatore*? Gozzi's critical support depended largely on Longhi's discarding the ancient dress so dear to the history painters, Tiepolo for example.*

In every way the opposite to Canaletto, Longhi achieved greater success with Venetians than with foreigners, though Joseph Smith included some of his paintings in the collection he sold to George III, now housed at Windsor. The French would probably have been satisfied with their own, greater artist Chardin and the English with the profounder emotion of Hogarth.

It is amusing to follow Longhi's genre pictures from the 'Concerto' onwards: at about the same time he painted 'The Dancing Lesson', 'The Toilette' and 'The Apothecary's Shop'; all portray human beings, even if uninteresting, and pay some attention to lighting, background and details. But after these his sitters seem to become increasingly vacuous, there is less and less apparent communication between them and more and more tendency to stare 'at the camera' instead of getting on with whatever activity was meant to constitute genre. The best place to follow his progress, or decline, is Venice itself, for he neither travelled nor, as stated, did his pictures sell abroad to any extent. There are six at the Accademia, eight in the House of Goldoni, twenty-nine at the Ca' Rezzonico, seventeen (including a few portraits and an allegory) at the Querini-Stampalia and several others in the Correr Museum. In them we can see the change from the earlier paintings of true genre to the later galleries of dolls with eyes like currants in lumps of dough and attitudes that have the fixed inertia of a 'still' from a moving picture. It is possibly significant that Longhi had been forgotten when the Goncourt brothers revived him; they themselves are noted for doing in literature exactly what Longhi tried to do in painting and their novels have been described as 'picture galleries hung with pictures of the momentary aspects of the world'. Longhi's son Alessandro is noted for a spirit of detached observation in his portraits; perhaps Pietro shared this, indeed I think it very likely, for he shows no sign of empathy towards his subjects.

The fact that Longhi has been called 'The Lancret of the Lagoons' may have something to do with the veneration in which he has been, and still is held. Lancret was one of Watteau's principal followers; Goldoni was made much of by the French and Gaspare Gozzi made much of the new ideas that came from France. As Goldoni and Gozzi were much esteemed in Venice, and by each other,[7] it would not be surprising if Longhi were regarded as representing the Enlightenment and 'we know that Pietro

---

* In this connection we must remember that about a century later Verdi's *La Traviata* had a bad press just because it was staged in modern dress.

Longhi was highly thought of in other advanced circles of Venetian society'.[8] This, you must remember was before the masses overthrew both the aristocracy and the bourgeoisie. A man could still be cultivated by the Venetian upper classes, even if thought to be 'enlightened'.

Plagiarism, as practised by the view painters, was not regarded as a serious offence in genre either. We find many copies of Longhi's pictures, some repeated by him, others by his pupils and still others by outsiders. None of them have improved on the master's expressionless portrayals. It is thought that Longhi had a *bottega*, or studio, where copies were turned out and several 'properties', such as a wall mirror or a picture, strengthen this belief; an example is a picture on the back wall, identical in '*La Visita*' and '*La Cucitrice*'. Of the best known duplicates I would mention the famous rhinoceros, of which two copies are still extant, one in the Ca' Rezzonico, the other in the London National Gallery; at least four were at one time recorded. 'The Geography Lesson' has a version in the Querini-Stampalia Gallery and another in the Civic Museum at Padua. '*La Visita*' may be seen in Milan's Crespi Collection and in the New York Metropolitan Museum. One of 'The Seven Sacraments' is with the others in the Querini-Stampalia Gallery but may also be found in the Uffizi Gallery of Florence and the '*Venditrice di Frittole*' (The Fritter Seller) in the Ca' Rezzonico and the House of Goldoni. Apart from these almost complete duplicates, figures and groups may be used over again as, for instance, a couple in '*Il Burattinaio*' and some versions of the '*Ridotto*' (which Longhi sometimes spells '*Reduto*'). Compare too the grouping and background in 'The Venetian Family' in Verona and 'The Patrician Family' in the Ca' Rezzonico. In addition to all this, we must remember that copies to illustrate books, or for wider circulation in any form, were customarily made with the etching needle; Domenico and Lorenzo Tiepolo reproduced many of their father's works in this way, Canaletto made his own, and many of Longhi's paintings were engraved by his son Alessandro and specialists, among whom G. Flipart, F. Bartolozzi and M. A. Pitteri are mentioned.

Followers of Longhi were many and all but one anonymous. Occasionally one sees reproductions of doll-like figures arranged as though performing some task, such as working in a tailor's shop; they often look like dwarfs or ventriloquists' dummies and are labelled 'School of P. Longhi'. A few are on view in the Mezzanino Falier of the Ca' Rezzonico. Less crude perhaps, but never aspiring to refinement, are the paintings of Gabriele Bella (often spelled Bello), who was active in the second half of the century. Sixty-seven of his small oil paintings are collected in the Pinacoteca Querini-Stampalia, where they hang in serried rows and glorious confusion. Even if of no artistic merit, they serve to illustrate many middle-class activities, leaving the rich to Longhi and the poor to

Zompini. Meticulous titles leave little to the imagination but give us valuable details of contemporary life. Here is the Broglio, that part of the Piazzetta where favours were asked of senators and plots hatched, with one of the gentry arranging his gown; there a procession of masked patricians on St Stephen's day; again, the Doge and Council attending Mass at San Rocco in annual fulfilment of a vow. There is bear-baiting, fist fighting, a 'running'★ of bulls on the Rialto Bridge and a wheelbarrow race; amateur football at Sant'Alvise, for gentlefolk only; the girls' choir singing for the Dukes of the North and (what should be a companion piece) a supper given for them in the Theatre of San Benedetto; the entry of Henri III of France and Poland in 1574. Again, you may see how people walked on the frozen lagoon during January 1708; or the platform put up outside the Church of SS Giovanni e Paolo for the Pope to bless the multitude in 1782; indoor tennis, election of the Doge, presentation of the Doge, the Doge being carried round St Mark's Square scattering largess, as far as the Giant's Staircase in his Palace; a women's regatta; a patrician wedding, in which the bride (unveiled) steps out of her gondola and climbs the church steps between rows of lackeys. Perhaps the most fascinating of this entertaining series is a view of the Piazza with people of all nations, the better dressed in the arcade of the Doge's Palace, clowns, cheap-jacks and charlatans elsewhere and the Punch-and-Judy show almost always a part of Venetian merrymaking.

So much for the full-time genre painters. None of them approached in virtuosity Gian Domenico Tiepolo, whose mother was a Guardi and whose father the artistic genius of the century. Like the rest of art appreciation, personal taste is everything—except that part which is dictated by fashion and prejudice; why else, for instance, do three of my French authorities (Bailly, Jonard and Monnier) stress Longhi's works for their art as well as their content, and omit all reference to Domenico Tiepolo, while a fourth (Chastel) mentions him once, only to remark that those genre scenes in the Ca' Rezzonico do not attain a high level? We are inevitably brought back to 'I know what I like' and a healthy scepticism of the judgment of others.

Giovanni Domenico Tiepolo (1727–1804) was born within a few years of Bernardo Bellotto and Alessandro Longhi. Together with Guardi they comprise the last major painters of the Venetian decadence, for to all intents the great revival of the eighteenth century died at the same time as Algarotti, in 1764. Tiepolo and his sons were in Madrid, Bellotto in Dresden, Guardi in obscurity. When Domenico came back from Madrid, on his father's death there in 1770, he did little more than produce etchings of the master's works and decorate with frescoes the family villa at Zianigo. We have to rely on inference for the little we know of his life; among the

★ Compare the Spanish word '*corrida*'.

few reports that we have, Algarotti remarked that Domenico, at sixteen, was working with his father and four years later had painted the fourteen Stations of the Cross in the Church of San Polo; they are now collected in a separate room, the lighting is adequate, which is rare in a Venetian church, and one is left alone; everything, in fact, to promote appreciation. One's first reaction is to deny that a lad of twenty could have painted this moving story; one's next is incredulity that the painter of so many genre scenes with clowns could reach such heights of emotion. Perhaps that is why I prize him as the best of the genre painters, for he is the only one who shows evidence of feeling.

Honour's reaction is that the series shows remarkable maturity and that 'the seventh and tenth are particularly poignant in their dramatic simplicity'.[9] But Honour and I are in the minority; within two years of their completion the '*Via Crucis*' series was being criticized: Pietro Visconti[10] wrote, 'all the figures wear different costume—some Spanish, some Slav and some are just caricatures. And people say that in those days that sort of person was not found and that he has painted them in that way only out of personal whim' and Haskell adds that one at least of *Longhi*'s admirers made it quite clear that he liked him just because of his rejection of whimsy.

The 'caricatures' are just what make the Passion story so real in Domenico's paintings and Longhi is congratulated for not possessing, or at least for not showing that he possessed the sympathy of the competent genre painter. When Domenico was in Madrid over twenty years later he painted another series of 'Stations of the Cross', now in the Prado. According to Pallucchini[11] it marks a regression to the juvenile error of trying a field unsuitable for his talents; he remarks further that the San Polo series is a failure and showed that religious drama was unsuited to Domenico's gifts. Lest you think that all 'informed' comment was adverse I must add that La Lande thought Domenico the best of the 'surviving' painters.* A better critic, Gioseffi[12] refers to Domenico as 'of considerable stature', an artist of a strong, outspoken type.

With regard to the few Tiepolo paintings in which the authorship is disputed, it is not my business here to give my vote for what was G. B. Tiepolo and how much Domenico. In reviewing the latter's history paintings—even their dates, apart from those at San Polo, are uncertain—it is worth noticing that he had a few individual commissions while assisting his father in Würzburg (1751–3), that he later helped him with the Palazzo Labia and other undertakings, and that he accompanied him to Madrid on his last journey; a good son, and one who developed his own style, in spite of his father's help.

* La Lande's journey was in 1765–6 and his book was published in 1790, so it is difficult to know exactly what epoch he is discussing; he adds that Domenico is in Madrid, which narrows the time to no later than 1770.

As our business is with genre painting I shall confine myself to discussing the frescoes in the guest-house (*foresteria*) at Villa Valmarana, Vicenza and those from the Tiepolo family villa at Zianigo, which are now in the Ca' Rezzonico. They have certain features in common: the draughtsmanship that is always noticeable and occasionally emphasized, the use of light and air or at least the knack of drawing attention to them, and a liking for back views of figures. The first two are in his father's tradition; the last is a method by which Domenico seems to have heightened the sense of depth in a picture and shown as such most convincingly in a fresco of 'Two Peasant Women' at the Villa Valmarana. I have stood before this and, with considerable effort, used my imagination to see the same two women coming towards me, and the result was immediately to bring the background nearer. The 'trick' was acquired early, for it is found in thirteen of his San Polo 'Stations of the Cross'.

When Tiepolo the Elder was commissioned to paint the walls of the Villa Valmarana, outside Vicenza, Domenico was given the decoration of all but one room in the *foresteria*. The pictures stand out today as vividly as they did in 1757, when he signed and dated one of them. The *chinoiserie* room reflects and perhaps caricatures the prevailing vogue for things oriental. It is a tribute to the adaptability of a great artist. Knowing nothing of China or the Chinese, Domenico has managed to convey the Rococo idea of *chinoiserie*; what matter if the humble peasant woman's dress is of lustrous silk? Or if the statue of a goddess, in a land where there were no goddesses, shows a tendency to bulge in a country where bosoms were invariably suppressed? It is fantasy, but it is also art.

The two country scenes, 'The Peasants' Meal' and 'Peasants Reposing', which appear together, represent a departure from tradition which is hard to pinpoint; it may be the quality of the light, or the semi-diagrammatic treatment of trees and background, but there is something highly individual in both scenes. The only other painting I can recall, where the same effect is obtained, is Bazille's '*Réunion de Famille*' in the Louvre (Jeu de Paume). A further thought inspired by the clear background in these two frescoes is the resemblance they have to scene painting and this leads one to wonder whether the backgrounds are ideal, that is to say *capricci* in the best style. Certainly they are extraordinarily effective in their composition and this makes me suspect that Nature may have been assisted. The last stylistic procedure is one which was coming more and more into fashion, the use of heavy impasto; Domenico used it for highlights, especially on the white costumes of his clowns—Guardi did the same with clouds in some pictures—and occasionally produces a 'chalkiness' with which his father has been unjustly credited.

It is when we come to the Carnival scenes in the *foresteria* that we feel we are back in Venice. *Baute* and masks and swirling skirts, and everywhere

the *Pulcinella*, those clowns with beaky masks and tapering, brimless hats*
that the Tiepolos loved. There is no doubt that it was the costume of
revellers and of professional clowns and the elder Tiepolo has two genre
paintings of them, '*Pulcinella colpevole*' and '*La Cucina di Pulcinella*'.† On
the *trompe-l'œil* painted staircase is the magnificent figure of a Negro—
painted by G. B. Tiepolo; what a testimonial to the affection that existed
between the collaborators! But it occasionally makes attribution difficult.
Thus the Louvre has two small paintings by the Elder, 'The Minuet' and
'The Charlatan', which are possibly joint products; at least they do not
figure in the complete catalogue of G. B. Tiepolo's paintings.[13] The
modelling and the gorgeous colours are certainly suggestive of G.B., but
the subjects and their treatment are characteristic of Domenico.

In 'The Minuet' the scene is laid in the courtyard of a house, with a
glimpse of the sea or lagoon; the lady of the house is seated on her
balcony, coffee cup in one hand, fan in the other. Heads peer over the wall,
watching the dense throng inside that presses the musicians into a corner
so closely that they are almost deprived of the use of their arms. In the
foreground a young woman, unmasked, dances, delicately holding out the
panniers of her brilliant golden skirt. Facing her, and therefore almost one
of Domenico's back views, is a young gallant whose style of dancing is
more rustic. Among the onlookers are masked, half-masked and unmasked
men and women; grotesques, including three beak-nosed *Pulcinella* can be
made out and on the extreme right is part of what can only be a *quacchero*,
one of the Quakers the Venetians were fond of caricaturing. Every face,
indeed every movement is expressive; a dozen actions are taking place
simultaneously and so realistic is it all that we almost hear the last fitful
strains of the orchestra as the pressure stops their playing. Giambattista or
Domenico?

Their collaboration is accepted in the '*Consilium in Arena*' at Udine,
presumably painted while they were there in 1759. It depicts the election
of Count Filippo Florio, at his second attempt, to the Order of the Knights
of St John. Here the by-play is typical of Domenico, as are the fantastic
touches, such as the presence of two turbanned men among the bystanders
and the private conversations that go on in the audience at any meeting;
but the concept and the sense of drama afforded by the main action are
consistent with the work of Giambattista.

Levey's[14] comments on the pastoral scenes of the frescoes at Villa Valmarana are so apposite that I must quote one of them: '... a type of
pastoral never attempted before, balancing as it does on a razor's edge

---

* A costume strangely like that worn for protection by physicians during medieval
plague epidemics.
† The second is in the Cailleux Collection in Paris; the other is lost, but was known until
1934.

between naturalism and idealization. It is a fresco of a siesta that will never end: where the trees, half touched by premature autumn, will never lose their leaves.' Did he too, I wonder, feel the spell of the Grecian urn, as Keats felt it when he wrote:

> Ah, happy, happy boughs! that cannot shed
> Your leaves, nor ever bid the Spring adieu;
> And, happy melodist, unwearied,
> For ever piping songs forever new . . .

I see nothing strange in the fact that Goethe, like most Europeans knowing only the name Tiepolo, thought that the best frescoes at Valmarana were those which we now know to be Domenico's, so clear, so jocund and so witty.

Apart from genre scenes in other countries, Domenico's liveliest are the frescoes he painted in the family villa, now carefully mounted on canvas and shown at the Ca' Rezzonico. Here he could really let satire guide his brush, and he brings to life, as no one but possibly Guardi could, the topsy-turvy world of *settecento* Venice. Here is his second version of 'The New World', the crowd waiting each his turn to see the diorama views of America. Mostly back views, naturally, though now not needed to create the illusion of depth; at the peep-hole a man holds up his son to look at the marvels, while he himself talks to a neighbour in the crowd; the showman with his pointer stands on a stool; a *Pulcinella* on the left balances an aristocratic pair on the right, the man surveying the scene through his quizzing glass with an air of boredom. In the privacy of his home Domenico could give rein to his satire. Irony pours out, whether it is in the antics of clowns,* in ridiculing mythological subjects or more up-to-date ones, 'The Evening Stroll', 'The Minuet', 'Carnival Nights'; all the characters are enjoying themselves and Domenico does not grudge them their fun; he just shows us how they behave and leaves us to make our comments. Just as Longhi did, for that matter, but here there is no feeling that there is a body upstairs.

---

* Note the artistry with which his masked and humped clowns portray their feelings, simply by their attitudes.

15

The Master

To be compared with the giants of Venetian Renaissance painting during his lifetime was the enviable and well-deserved lot of Giambattista Tiepolo (1696–1770). Unlike Sebastiano Ricci he aspired to emulate Titian, Veronese and Tintoretto without imitating them and was rewarded with not only fame, but the respect that was so dear to his exalted spirit. For Tiepolo, though his surname was that of an old patrician family,* was the son of a merchant-shipowner; but his life and work reflected both his nobility of soul and his aristocratic prejudice.

He was left an orphan, but not by any means destitute, at the age of one and became a successful artist early in life. He learned the elements of painting from Gregorio Lazzarini, who was important in Venice at the time but unable to rid himself of seventeenth-century traditions. Lazzarini is said to have shown young Tiepolo how to produce the iridescent effects of colour, but his teacher could never have dreamed to what purpose his pupil would put it, or how he would improve on it. His first recorded work was a 'Passage of the Red Sea' displayed at the Fair of San Rocco and much admired; its whereabouts today are not known. Leaving 'Time and Death' of the same year as a doubtful attribution we come to the third work of 1716, 'The Sacrifice of Isaac', which fills an over-arch and spandrels in the Church of Ospedaletto. Full use is made of the awkwardly shaped area allotted to the work and the plasticity of the figures reminds us that Tiepolo was an admirer of Piazzetta. He learned much from him and more from studying paintings of Titian and Veronese: the glowing colours, the sumptuous robes and the sensuous lines that would soon appear in his paintings.

He was entered in the roll of the painters' guild and fully independent when in 1719 he married Cecilia, sister of the Guardis. In this account I

---

* For example, the mother of Counts Gaspare and Carlo Gozzi was a Tiepolo. Giving an example of patrician reticence and fortitude, Molmenti[1] tells of a Senator Tiepolo, who broke his arm through his and his gondolier's combined clumsiness; he made no complaint and referred to the accident only when his valet came to undress him, saying 'Be a little gentle, please; my right arm is broken in two.'

must limit myself to a few milestones in his triumphant career. We begin with the year 1724, in which he painted his first 'skyscape', as I should like to call it. The 'Apotheosis of St Teresa', a ceiling fresco in the saint's chapel in the Church of the Scalzi, was probably his most important assignment before his first visit to Udine. It was painted at about the same time as Piazzetta's only fresco in the Church of SS Giovanni e Paolo and their comparison is instructive. See how Tiepolo has captured an ethereal quality, which still allows figure outlines to be seen and employs the plasticity of *chiaroscuro* without the dark background so necessary for Piazzetta's effects; the result is that Tiepolo paints figures that are at home in the heavens, while Piazzetta's might at any moment fall on the observer's head.

To emphasize the difference, we have Tiepolo's 'St Dominic in Glory' at the Venice Accademia, Piazzetta's own subject, more than ever underlining the difference between the masters. What makes this feat of Tiepolo's the more remarkable is that his 'St Dominic' is in oil, whereas fresco work brought out his best qualities. The work is said to have marked the beginning of Tiepolo's collaboration with Gerolamo Mengozzi-Colonna, an expert in architectural perspective; this is the last picture in which we should expect such help to be necessary, until we notice that on a flat canvas he has painted a scene which leaves you convinced that you are looking into a dome. Another corollary is that ceiling frescoes, in which Tiepolo excelled,* require the use of *sotto in sù* views of the face. This little problem seems to have fascinated Tiepolo and he seems to have played with it in many oils and frescoes where it was not strictly required to indicate the observer's position.

He must have left for Udine shortly after painting these works, for his frescoes there are dated 1726. He had been invited by the Patriarch of Ravenna, Dionisio Dolfin, and his chief work was to decorate the Cathedral with frescoes; these include at least one of those heavenly scenes of angels and *putti* disporting themselves. He was already a master at this type of ceiling painting, depicting sculptured figures with all the attributes of matter and the appearance of weightlessness. From the Cathedral he went on to decorate the Archbishop's Palace, then called the Palazzo Dolfin; his frescoes are breath-taking in their scope and invention; the superb technique may by now be taken for granted. 'The Angel appearing to Sarah' is an example of Tiepolo's vivacity, 'Rachel hiding the Idols' a masterpiece of composition, with a genre scene for balance on the left. Here observe the peasant girl and you will appreciate his partiality to the sculptured form and his knack of producing it against a light background;

---

* Tiepolo did not invent the 'Tiepolesque ceiling', of which the St Teresa is the first example. It can be traced back through Correggio to Mantegna in the fifteenth century.

and in view of what I shall say about models, observe that the Abraham receiving the angels is not the Abraham of the San Rocco canvas.

It is said that Tiepolo's palette lightened during his travels and these were frequent enough to give him adequate opportunity. Scarcely had he returned from Udine when he was summoned to Milan, where he decorated two palaces. Then came two visits to Bergamo, where he decorated part of the ceiling of the Colleoni Chapel; I feel that the 'Virtues' on the pendentives of the dome are more in the Piazzetta style which he had been shaking off, though the colours are gorgeous and authentically Tiepolo.

By 1736 he was known in Central Europe and in that year Count Tessin, the Swedish Ambassador, tried to employ Tiepolo to decorate the royal palace of Stockholm. Finding the artist's prices too high he compromised by buying for himself the recently completed 'Danae and Jupiter', which is now in the University Museum, Stockholm. The refusal of a royal patron gives us an idea of how successful Tiepolo had become and, here we glimpse the mercantile strain in his ancestry that he knew the value of his work. He found a spell at home congenial, painted sacred subjects for Udine and the stupendous frescoes on the ceiling of the Gesuati Church in Venice; the largest of these, 'The Institution of the Rosary', reminds us of the possible influence of Fumiani, with its vertical perspective up a flight of stairs. He has also used a common trick of the decorators, designed to give a feeling of reality: but instead of a leg or the hem of a robe trailing over the decorated border, Tiepolo has inserted the bodies of the Albigenses being consigned to the depths. And amid all this activity he still found time for another visit to Milan.

Meanwhile his fame was increasing. No family of any standing could afford to be without his services and he, a pillar of the Old Order, which remained stationary when not moving backwards, was glad to perpetuate the glories of the patricians, new or old, and of advocates, who ranked next to the nobility in the Golden Book. It was now that Algarotti took him up and, in 1743, commissioned 'The Banquet of Cleopatra' which Tiepolo had almost certainly started for Joseph Smith.[2] In 1744-5 he decorated the Barbarigo Palace—a timid commission on the part of the owners, who asked for allegories and had their coat of arms reproduced only once. Other families were less modest. The frescoes in the Labia Palace—possibly the finest of all Tiepolo's masterpieces—embody a delicate compliment to the fair and flighty Maria Labia, whom he pictures as Cleopatra; in the Barbaro Palace he painted an 'Apotheosis' of the family, not of course to be taken as accession to divinity, but simply exaltation, and at the same time a canvas entitled 'The Apotheosis of Francesco Barbaro', now in private ownership in Paris.

At about the same time he executed his one commission for the government, the representation of 'Venice receiving the Homage of Neptune' for the Hall of Four Doors in the Doge's Palace, and now in the Sala degli Scudieri; it is yet another in his best style and indeed he seems to have reached the zenith of his powers, a place he was to retain during another twenty years' flawless work. The ridiculous nature of this last commission escaped him; Venice was lapsing into financial ruin, chased off the sea by the Turks and surpassed by her mercantile rivals; and still Neptune had to be shown offering his riches to the Imperial Dame, as Pope called the lesser luminary Juno. Tiepolo saw nothing absurd in it for he was a Venetian die-hard, honoured to exalt a crumbling state and proud to flatter its effete nobility. But all his sentiment could not blind his artist's eye: the portrait of 'A Procurator', by some believed to be Giovanni Querini, shows the gorgeous robes and flowing wig of a man below middle height, whose face reveals obstinacy instead of strength. This hangs in the Pinacoteca Querini Stampalia.

But not all his patrons wanted bombast. Leonardo Valmarana, whose villa at Vicenza was decorated by Tiepolo and his son Domenico, was more modest than most patricians and served to counterbalance the *nouveaux riches* Rezzonico. When Aurelio Rezzonico's son Lodovico was to marry Faustina Savorgnan nothing would do but to have Tiepolo commemorate the event in an allegorical fresco in the Palazzo Rezzonico. There, on the ceiling of the ballroom, you can see the bridal pair riding in the chariot of the sun, accompanied by Apollo, while Fame trumpets forth the event. As if anyone cared. More extraordinary is 'The Apotheosis of the Pisani', where the whole family is immortalized on the ceiling of the ballroom of the villa at Strà, even down to little Almorò in his mother's lap, while the Blessed Virgin is being invoked for her blessing. Some patricians could afford these extravagances, those I have mentioned, the Soderini, the Contarini and other besides, and Tiepolo did a great service to Art in putting up his prices, for it is easier to grasp a picture's cost than its value.

But we are going ahead too fast and have reached Tiepolo's last major work before his final departure from Venice.

Twelve years before this sad event he was commissioned by the Prince-Bishop, Carl Philipp von Greifenklau, to decorate the Kaisersaal, the great hall of the Palace, or Residenz, of Würzburg. It had just been built in German Rococo style by Balthasar Neumann; Tiepolo's frescoes were precisely complementary to the new art. After much consultation and preliminary sketching by Tiepolo, his sons Domenico (aged 24) and Lorenzo (14), and the Germans G. A. Urlaub and L. A. Flachner, the scheme of decoration was decided during the winter of 1750: the main theme is Apollo conducting Beatrice of Burgundy, the (second) bride of Frederick Barbarossa to her wedding—the chariot and team of greys was to be used again in the Rezzonico Palace—and the vast main area is filled with allegories, becoming darker as they approach the frame. This last is built up with stucco in order to allow parts of the scene to cross over, clouds, a bird and a detail, vaguely erotic, of the River Main and a nymph. There is a doublet in the Palazzo Clerici, Milan, about three inches less erotic.

The theme was chosen because the first Prince-Bishop of Würzburg, Harold by name, had been picked for ordination by Barbarossa and the line of nonentities had continued for six hundred years, to be rescued from oblivion by Neumann and Tiepolo. On the walls are 'The Marriage of Barbarossa' and 'The Investiture of Bishop Harold', painted with equal grace, and between the windows are ten allegorical figures in grisaille, which can be attributed to Domenico with certainty. Later, Domenico was to do eight more grisailles in the same style for the Oratorio della Purità at Udine, and some near *trompe-l'œil* to imitate stucco moulding.

So successful was the work in the Kaisersaal and so harmonious its combination with the magnificent Rococo architecture that Tiepolo was commissioned to stay on and decorate the grand staircase in the same palace. He chose 'Olympus' as his subject and portrayed the gods rendering homage to the egregious Prince-Bishop, whose portrait, one of the few I know by Tiepolo, is supported by Fame, who is blowing his trumpet for him. Round the edges of the great ceiling fresco are the four continents: Europe, with the Prince-Bishop floating above and portraits of Tiepolo and Domenico thrown in for good measure; Asia, with a caparisoned elephant and pilgrims on the way to Jerusalem; Africa, with a voluptuous Negress (who defies Nature by having deep red lips), camels and parasols; and finally America, to complete the four quarters of the earth, with a buxom Red Indian lady supervising various tasks while sitting on an alligator and surrounded by drums, turbans and antlered deer. The wonder of it all is that every figure, every animal seems to have been specially selected for careful treatment; nothing is hurried or skimped and all is bathed in Tiepolo's heavenly radiance, for which we forgive him his biological errors.

In Venice again, Tiepolo was asked to decorate the ceiling of the newly completed Church of the Pietà and was paid only 500 zecchini; he is said to have accepted it gravely and then to have lent the church three times that amount to help them out with the rest of the decoration. He was able to complete one more superb series of frescoes, the medium that best suited his rapid style, his sure touch and his rich palette. The Villa Valmarana ai Nani* marks a reaction against the grand manner. Here he could indulge the lyrical side of his nature, which had appeared in his

---

* So called to distinguish it from the Palazzo Valmarana in Vicenza and the town hall of Altavilla, about six miles away, which was also a Villa Valmarana.

biblical scenes for the Palazzo Dolfin in Udine and in the Cleopatra series, including those oils that were not designed for the Palazzo Labia and are now in Melbourne (Australia), Milan, Archangel or Leningrad.

At Valmarana, for the unassuming but appreciative owner, episodes were chosen from four romantic works, the Iliad, the Aeneid, Tasso's *Gerusalemme Liberata* and Ariosto's *Orlando Furioso*. Tiepolo is here in his happiest vein; his son is working in the *foresteria* and from time to time each lends a hand in the other's work. Nor must we forget Mengozzi-Colonna, whose architectural contribution gives the action a suitable frame. Here, I feel, Tiepolo was happy, perhaps I should say specially happy, for his temperament was never melancholy. How he must have enjoyed seeing those legendary heroes and their ravishing females come to life under his brush! Never have forms seemed so sculptured, never have colours assumed such pastel shades; and never, it is safe to say, has even Tiepolo suffused his scenes with so much light.

The drama of the scene is enhanced by the touches of genius that seem so effortless. Calchas the priest is about to kill Agamemnon's daughter Iphigenia, who is reclining on the sacrificial altar; suddenly faces are turned towards a cloud, on which two *putti* are bringing the deer that is to substitute for Agamemnon's daughter. In the background a standard ripples with the first breeze that Artemis sends in acknowledgement of the sacrifice.★ But on the right, where the sight of this sudden salvation is still hidden, a warrior, Agamemnon himself, hides his eyes with his cloak, and to break the stark lines of the columns that frame the action, a spectator's hand has crept round the shaft of one and this hand alone conveys the tension of that awful moment.

Nothing can impart the majesty of Giambattista's frescoes as well as Goethe's remarks, when he had seen the decorations in the villa and the guest-house. He knew nothing about Domenico; Tiepolo was the name of Italy's greatest living artist and even though the name Tiepolo connoted *two* people, the world thought of one man only. Hence it is highly significant that Goethe should classify the frescoes at the Villa Valmarana as the 'sublime' and the 'natural', where we, complacent with the knowledge that others have given us, say 'Giambattista' and 'Domenico'. Each partner took his release from vast glorifications in his own way: Giambattista became lyrical, Domenico idyllic and whimsical.

For Venice the end came in 1762 when Tiepolo, now feeling old and tired, was invited to Madrid to decorate the royal palace; unwilling to travel again, he was practically forced to accept the commission by the

---

★ The Greek host was unable to sail against Troy for lack of a favourable wind. This was interpreted as a sign of displeasure on the part of Artemis, who could be appeased only by the sacrifice of Agamemnon's daughter. A later and kinder version has the goddess send a substitute deer at the last minute and waft the reprieved princess to Tauris in the Crimea.

Venetian government, true to its policy of universal appeasement. Before leaving he had begun a portrait of his friend Algarotti, but this had to be left unfinished, so important was it for Venice to prevent the hostility of another tottering state. He left with his sons less than six weeks after Goldoni's move to Paris, and by 1764 had completed and signed another vast ceiling fresco, that of the throne room. Another apotheosis, of course; it is said to have been planned while Tiepolo was exalting the Pisani family at Strà.

The execution suffered the usual stoppages in the hard winters of central Spain and something of the fire of the old Tiepolo is lacking; nevertheless, all are agreed that 'The Glory of Spain' is a tremendous achievement and we should undoubtedly consider it his masterpiece in grandeur, had we not seen the Kaisersaal in Würzburg. As usual, there is a surfeit of allegory, which has to be painstakingly disentangled, most of it in glorification of Charles III; then there are the regions of Spain, with their typical products; America with its diverse populations; a digression for the gifts brought back by Columbus and a rapid transition to mythology, with marine divinities, ships and giant fish. The whole design is permeated with personifications of Fame, Virtue, Peace, Justice and above all the usual cloud of *putti*, tumbling in the buoyant aether.

The successful completion of this majestic project led to two smaller commissions, the ceiling frescoes of the Guard Room, or *Salón de Alabarderos*, and of the *saleta*, or anteroom to the Queen's apartments; the former had as its subject 'The Apotheosis of Aeneas', the latter 'The Apotheosis of the Spanish Monarchy'. To describe these works, imposing though they are, would be tedious; even to examine adequately all three at one visit is almost impossible. Then came seven altarpieces for the Royal Palace Chapel at Aranjuez, and all the time Tiepolo and his sons were working on canvases that are now, at least the greater part of them, in the Prado. Rafael Mengs, the apostle of Neo-Classicism, worked on other rooms at Madrid while the Tiepolos were busy in the Throne Room; he had the support of the King's Confessor and behind the scenes there was rivalry between the partisans of the two artists. It seems unlikely that any bitterness spread to the painters themselves; Mengs showed the greatest admiration for Tiepolo's work and two such great-souled artists would surely be above petty jealousy. No sooner was Tiepolo dead, however, than his altarpieces were replaced by those of Mengs.

Tiepolo's style cannot easily be described, for two personalities are often evident: on the one hand we have the grandiloquent supporter of monarchs, prelates and patricians; on the other a realist with a sense of humour, or at least fun, which are surely attributes of any careful observer. Most critics agree in selecting his outstanding works and I have tried to include a mention of them; personal taste is, however, another matter and my preferences may possibly persuade some traveller to spend an extra minute deriving pleasure from a less known work.

Of the more famous, no one should omit the 'Cleopatra' sequence in the Palazzo Labia in Venice and the frescoes of the Villa Valmarana outside Vicenza. Of the personal and not necessarily reasoned preferences, I would choose 'Abraham visited by the Angels' at the Scuola di San Rocco, for a reason which will become apparent when I write about Tiepolo's models; 'The Angel appearing to Sarah' in the Archbishop's Palace at Udine pleases everyone who is beginning to feel that serious art is weighing them down. The contrast between the wizened, almost toothless old lady, hope and doubt chasing each other across her features, and the winged angel, all smooth skin and muscle, is one of Tiepolo's *tours de force*. Surprise has been expressed that he should give so much of his genius to a scene that is not even biblical; I am sure that he would never have dreamed of a comic 'Annunciation', but if he had, what a triumph of ridicule and heresy he would have achieved! Then I love one of his three works in the Civic Museum of Padua, 'St Paul (now believed to be St Patrick) heals a possessed man', if only for the faces of the onlookers.

Lastly (and if I listed all the Tiepolo paintings that have thrilled me, I would catalogue all those I have seen) I choose the 'Apotheosis of St Teresa' in her chapel in the Church of the Scalzi (the Barefoot Carmelites); such maturity in such an early work is surely worth more than a glance. Observe the balance of the composition and the freshness with which he endows the regular device of a pyramid of figures with the Saint at the apex, the light and colour and, above all, the subject that makes this fresco so superior to all the apotheoses of nonentities. Remember that this miracle of light and buoyancy was painted at about the same time as Piazzetta's only fresco, in which it is St Dominic who is being received in Heaven, and you will esteem still more the genius of a man not yet in his thirties.

The question of old and new styles has led to difficulties. Where many saw in Tiepolo a new interpreter, we have his own statements that he wanted to paint only in the old style; the heavy, Baroque period of Louis XIV had passed away with its chief patron and the whole of Europe shared France's relief at the return of frivolity, all, that is, except an old guard that included the Venetian patricians. 'We have to paint for the people with money,' said Tiepolo once, but, also, 'the mind of the painter must always reach out to the Sublime, the Heroic, to Perfection!'[3] And thus he still managed to paint in the grand style, but with a difference. His sculptured forms and grandiose concepts take us back, not to the ponderous artists of the *seicento*, but to those of the Renaissance; from Veronese he took the gorgeous pageantry and glowing colours and from

Tintoretto the Classical backgrounds, with Mengozzi-Colonna's help; perhaps part of his uncanny ability to flood the firmament with light came from his use of a pale buff priming instead of the more usual red. Then, I feel sure, his speed helped to make his drawing more certain; others would have to work painstakingly to attain the effect they needed, but with Tiepolo brain and hand worked in unison. Even when the drawing is not as accurate as we could wish, as, for instance, when he gives us an obese Rinaldo abandoning Armida in the Villa Valmarana, the effect of the scene is not spoiled; there is a freshness and spontaneity about his idyllic work which is absent from that of his contemporaries. In all his work, however, there is what Berenson called 'the quality of force' and the same critic's summary is too good to be omitted: '... Tiepolo's feeling for strength, for movement, and for colour was great enough to give a new impulse to art.'

His contemporaries were by no means so enthusiastic. Joseph Smith took little interest in his work[4] except possibly for the 'Cleopatra' painting he ordered and relinquished and, perhaps in consequence, Tiepolo never became popular in England; Phillips[5] believes he was not even known there. In any case 'popish' glorifications and grandiose mythological subjects were appreciated less there than in the rest of Europe. Gaspare Gozzi was of course a poet and a writer above all, but it still comes as a shock to read that he considered Longhi's realism greater than Tiepolo's. Did no one ask, 'Who wants realism?'

An important exception was Algarotti; opinions about him differ, but this at least must be set to his credit. It was Algarotti who spread Tiepolo's fame through Europe. It was Algarotti who enjoyed a personal friendship and praised his '... delightful colours and incredible freedom of brush-strokes'[6] and paid due homage to his *brio* and fantasy. Algarotti's correspondence is full of Tiepolo; when he came back to Venice in 1743 to buy paintings for Frederick Augustus III he commissioned a history painting, now lost, from Tiepolo. He wrote frequently to Count von Brühl, praising the painter and boasting of their friendship, and the two friends were regular correspondents when separated.

I cannot agree with Phillips that Tiepolo was not much thought of in France, for Haskell[7] mentions some of his French admirers. It is true that they had Boucher and that Tiepolo did little in the way of erotic painting, which was so popular, but there are many references by Frenchmen, Saint-Non, Mariette, Bergeret and Fragonard,[8] which are distinctly favourable. When Phillips adds that 'even Napoleon's robbers did not take any of his work' I can only suggest that it was because their guide-books were not up to date. We know that in Spain the French used the Rev. Joseph Townsend's travel book as a guide to both the country and its art treasures, and Townsend does not mention Tiepolo; a previous,

French traveller, the Baron de Bourgoing, mentions him only once, as '... a Venetian called Tiepolo'. 'Napoleon's robbers', who stole for themselves as much as for their Emperor, are known to have had lists of the masters whose works would be welcome in Paris or profitable to themselves.

Tiepolo's reputation in France would not reach its proper height until Delacroix realized his importance twenty years after the fall of Napoleon; but in 1754 the Marquis de Vandière, royal surveyor in Paris, wrote to Rome asking that someone be sent to copy Tiepolo's frescoes in the Villa Contarini; and in 1760 Tiepolo made a present of a painting to Louis XV, whose gratitude was golden. Delacroix, who enjoyed considerable respect, transmitted Tiepolo's fame to the Impressionists and today we can appreciate him for what we see, without having to bother about Romanticism or Neo-Classicism or any other 'isms'.

Of his private life we know less than we should like. His large family gave him an affectionate home and his good nature amply rewarded them; this, by the way, is surprising in the case of a man so afflicted with gout. The stories whispered about his beautiful model Cristina are thought to have been inventions, though anyone who has seen her in Tiepolo's paintings could hardly blame him had they been true. But '*Il buon Tiepolo*', or 'Tiepoletto' as he was affectionately called, remained a dutiful husband and even if he took Cristina to Madrid and left his wife Cecilia in Venice, it was because the latter elected to stay on account of her health; there is no support for the malicious rumour that Cecilia was an inveterate gambler.

Cristina will be familiar to all who have taken an interest in Tiepolo's paintings; amid all the apotheoses he glorified the blonde gondolier's daughter with the aristocratic air, as the Blessed Virgin, assorted saints, Iphigenia, Cleopatra (at the Palazzo Labia) and sometimes among the crowd in his larger creations. Other models, now nameless, spring to mind: the old man as 'Abraham receiving the Angels' in the Scuola di San Rocco, whom we recognize as an inhabitant of the Ghetto, though he looks much older as St Philip Neri, in the church of that name. Sarah makes another appearance as the *dueña* of Pharaoh's daughter, while Moses is being picked out of the Nile.[9] And the youth who is Rinaldo in the Villa Valmarana is an angel in 'The Stigmata of St Francis'.[10] And many, many more; so many, in fact, that a prolonged study of Tiepolo makes you feel like one of a family.

For a man who believed wholeheartedly in Venice's *ancien régime*, a sense of humour comes as a surprise. We have laughed at Sarah in her 'Annunciation', but I have said nothing about Tiepolo's *putti*. They are very special *putti*. Where others paint them as a lot of lazy, useless excuses for filling blank spaces, Tiepolo allows them their own function. In the

Scuola dei Carmini they are really kept busy, one bringing the scapulary which the Blessed Virgin is about to bestow on St Simon Stock, another the book of the Scuola. In Madrid a *putto* brings the laurel wreath to crown Cristina, I mean the 'Glory of Spain'; in the Civic Museum of Udine a *putto* is flying a kite shaped like a bat; elsewhere they have butterfly wings and in 'The Rape of Europa' in the Venice Accademia a *putto* is standing on the edge of a cloud, peeing into the empyrean.

If Tiepolo was a rapid painter, and he claimed to complete a picture while others were mixing their colours, it was only after much thought had gone into preparation. His *modelli*, or preliminary oil paintings, are almost innumerable and to be found in many countries. But the first stage was the drawing and in Britain the Victoria and Albert Museum has a large number,[11] while the Pierpont Morgan Library in New York has the famous Cheney–Algarotti Album. As we might expect from one whose outlines show such a sure touch, his drawings are equally confident; it therefore comes as a surprise to read that Henri de Chennevières suggested in 1898 that G. B. Tiepolo was no great draughtsman and that 'no great Venetian has drawn much'. In his drawings we can follow the development of his ideas on sculptural forms, which coincided with the sculptors of Venice imitating pictures in their low reliefs.

In 1743 we see the influence of Algarotti who, as mentioned, was visiting Venice on a buying expedition. The *Uomo universale* was insistent on accuracy in Classical history painting and in these drawings we see the various stages of the development of the 'Cleopatra' series, including the changes that Algarotti proposed. Here too is a study for the Roman military uniform, obviously for his history paintings. The 'Cleopatra' series are all dated after 1743; paintings of Romans from before Algarotti's visit, such as the frescoes of the Palazzo Dugnani, Milan, are even more inaccurate than Algarotti's ideas. The frescoes in the Villa Cordellina at Montecchio Maggiore are from the year of Algarotti's visit and show not only his, but Veronese's far more important influence. In the Victoria and Albert collection we also obtain much information about the 'Cleopatra' series, with an account of its various versions, from which we can deduce much of Algarotti's influence. I like best the drawings for the Villa Valmarana frescoes and one of them, of Angelica staunching the wounds of Medor is particularly lifelike and refutes Chennevières' accusation.

The Tiepolo etchings, and this includes a large number by Domenico and Lorenzo, are a mine of information and of unanswered questions. Aldo Ricci's recent work underlines the risk of being dogmatic in a field where fresh information is liable to turn up at awkward moments. The Elder Tiepolo produced two series, the '*Scherzi di Fantasia*' and the '*Capricci*', which are less known than his paintings but are worth studying by those interested in his lighter moods; it is interesting to recall that the Elder Zanetti was the first to publish G. B. Tiepolo's etchings, possibly in 1743.

Tiepolo stands at the summit of Venetian achievement in the Decadence. For breadth of vision, vastness of concept, consummate imagination and perfection of technique he stands alone. During his lifetime his name was synonymous with Italian painting in the principal states of Central Europe. As a man he achieved what we would all wish to have, the respect of his fellow-men and his reward was mankind's greatest blessing, a sudden and unexpected death. The last entry in his record deals with the dispatch of valuable presents to his wife.

Epilogue

In 1793, after the execution of Louis XVI and Marie Antoinette, all Europe was in arms against Revolutionary France; all, that is, except Switzerland, Denmark and Venice. They were not to profit by their forbearance. Venice's century of avoiding entanglements in Europe resulted in the total lack of friends. In 1796 the forces of the Republic under Bonaparte fought a series of battles with the Austrian armies in Northern Italy, including Venetian territory, without any thought of respecting the neutrality of La Serenissima. On the contrary, as early as February hostility was shown by French accusations of Venetian partiality for the Austrians. It is likely that the Austrians were the first to violate Venetian territory by occupying Peschiera before their hasty withdrawal towards the Tyrol; but the French were not far behind and established themselves in various towns of the Veneto.

The feeble resources of Venice were powerless to prevent either of the combatants from trespassing on her lands, and 1797 saw the Austrians again invading them, occupying Osoppo and Palmanova on 3 March. By 5 April Napoleon, now at Judenburg, was thinking of giving Venetian possessions to Austria, and to prepare the scene needed an excuse for a quarrel with La Serenissima. On 15 April he sent an ultimatum to Venice, by Junot and Lallement, in which he expressed his displeasure at two events: that the Venetians had allowed the Comte de Lille, the future Louis XVIII, to stay in Verona; and that they had allowed Imperial (i.e. Austrian) troops to occupy the citadel of Peschiera. The Venetians replied helplessly that, being without the means of defence, they could hardly stop the Austrians.

When the Austrians had been routed, the Venetian Council plucked up courage, sent a message of congratulation to Napoleon with a bill for damage done to Crema and Brescia. In an access of rage, calculated rage according to many, the French general shouted that it was not for them, but for him to make complaints, in view of their acts of hostility; he would burn Verona, he would occupy Venice immediately.

Verona had been occupied in 1796, but was not burned down now or later. But on 17 April 1797 the populace of Verona rose against the French garrison, massacred all who were without arms and then began fighting among themselves, liberators versus conservatives, while the French bombarded both impartially. It took the French six days to recapture the town and institute the usual mass reprisals.

On 20 April a French frigate, the *Libérateur d'Italie*, sailed into the lagoon without permission;* Domenico Pizzamano, commander of the Fort of Sant'Andrea, fired on her, then sent to board her. There was a savage hand-to-hand fight, during which the French captain Laugier was killed and the crew taken prisoner. The French ambassador immediately protested and demanded the arrest of Pizzamano, the release of the French prisoners and the restitution of the frigate. The Doge and Council, sunk in the mire of appeasement, could only obey. But on 18 April—note the date, two days before the '*Libérateur*' episode—Napoleon had signed the preliminaries of the armistice of Leoben, which contained a secret clause ceding the *terraferma*, Istria and Dalmatia to Austria in return for French gains on the left bank of the Rhine. The little Corsican was beginning to dabble in politics. Perhaps he did not yet know that Barras in Paris, in return for a bribe of 700,000 lire, had promised to respect Venetian independence; perhaps he didn't care.

A week later a deputation arrived from Venice, confident that they could preserve their country's status as a non-combatant. Napoleon once more accused the Republic of perfidious behaviour: they had not released their political prisoners (there were none), they had not disarmed the insurgents of the *terraferma*, they had not expelled the British diplomatic corps and consequently had put themselves in a state of war with France. At all costs he had to justify the bargain he had made with Austria. 'I have 80,000 men and twenty gunboats,' he shouted, 'I want no more of your Inquisition, I want no more of your Senate, I shall be an Attila to the State of Venice!' It was noted that, with characteristic coarseness, he used '*non voglio*' instead of the usual and more polite '*non vorrei*'. He summoned the unfortunate envoys to luncheon and bombarded them with contemptuous references to their antiquated system of government, their police supervision, their tyranny, their 'tombs' (*I Pozzi*) and 'Leads', their Bridge of Sighs and, in short, all their medieval survivals in an Age of Enlightenment. Fortunately the envoys left before news came of the fate of the *Libérateur*.

On 1 May the Grand Council sent another deputation to Napoleon; he refused to receive them but issued a declaration of war based on fifteen counts. The next day saw the French army on *terraferma* busily pulling down or defacing coats of arms and other insignia on private houses.† On 12 May the Grand Council held its last meeting; the Doge offered his resignation and the councillors remembered how he had told them some

---

* The previous July, Venice had acquainted the belligerent powers with her decision to refuse access to ships of war.

† Similar damage perpetrated in Malta a year later is still visible in Valletta.

days before: 'Tonight we are no longer safe in our beds.' The government of La Serenissima voted itself out of existence and Caterina Dolfin Tron remarked that the Lion of St Mark had changed into a goose.

When a provisional representative government on French lines was accepted, a cry of *'Viva la libertà!'* went up from the Jacobins; the people of Venice countered with *'Viva San Marco!'* On the 20th the statue of Liberty replaced the winged lion as the emblem of Venice, and on the 29th the Committee of Public Safety (copied from the more sinister one in Paris) decreed that all emblems of the Lion remaining in the city should be pulled down. A week later, on Napoleon's order, the insignia of the Republic, including the Golden Book, were burned and the ashes scattered. The last *Bucintoro* followed. In August the standard of the Venetian Republic was hoisted for the last time. It was in Perasto, Dalmatia, and the Yugoslavs were therefore the last to remain loyal to their overlords of 367 years.

On 17 October Venice, to whom Napoleon had promised a democratic constitution, was ceded to Austria by the Treaty of Campo Formio and finally lost her liberty, but not before many of her art treasures, including the famous horses of St Mark, had been sent to Paris. Venice was by no means the only city to mourn her losses; a superficial acquaintance with Italian will enable the reader to appreciate the pun that was current at the time: *'Non tutti francesi sono latroni, ma BUONA PARTE'* (Not all French are thieves, but a good part). Meanwhile a Tree of Liberty had been erected and a plebiscite taken on adopting a democratic government: of 23,500 votes, 10,000 were against the motion. But looting and destruction went on and the French, not content with trading the *terraferma* and capturing Venice as an enemy capital, now dismantled the guns in the Arsenal and sent them to the Ionian Islands, which they retained. So the Austrians, too, were swindled. Not once, but again; for the inevitable crushing defeat they sustained in 1805 at Ulm and Austerlitz led to the Treaty of Pressburg, at which the Emperor Napoleon added the Pearl of the Adriatic to the Iron Crown of the Lombards, just another piece of Bonaparte headgear.

*   *   *

Now consider whether Venice's immorality played any part in her fall. Were Parma, Milan, the Papal States, Holland, Spain and Portugal also degenerate? Had she been as chaste as ice, as pure as snow, she would still have been treated as nothing more than a counter in a deplorable bargain. But La Serenissima had enjoyed a long, full life and in her last century showed the world how far she could advance along the road of civilization.

Epilogue

Her passing was not the occasion for perfunctory signs of grief, but for a
real sense of loss.

> And what if she had seen those glories fade,
>   Those titles vanish, and that strength decay—
> Yet shall some tribute of regret be paid
>   When her long life hath reach'd its final day:
> Men are we, and must grieve when even the shade
>   Of that which once was great is pass'd away.

Notes

Chapter 1   What went before

1. Damerini, see *Fondazione*. . . .
2. Discussing Kurt Weitzmann's 'Studies in Classical and Byzantine Manuscript Illumination', the anonymous reviewer of the *Times Literary Supplement* (7 Jan., 1972) writes of the Macedonian renaissance of the tenth century: 'He shows that it was a true renaissance in the sense that both artists and scholars made a particular effort to recapture the glories of the classical heritage.'
3. De Brosses, cited by Jonard, Chapter 4.
4. Molmenti I/2.
5. Cited by Molmenti I/8.
6. Ademollo, cited by Molmenti II/99.
7. Casanova, *Mémoires* IV, Chapter 15.
8. Damerini, see *Fondazione*. . . .
9. Casanova I/Chapter 6.
10. Molmenti I/228.
11. Molmenti I/16.
12. Acton, p. 54.
13. De Brosses.
14. A. Bailly, p. 332.

Chapter 2   Grand Tourists

1. N. Jonard, Chapter 4.
2. Monnier, p. 329.
3. J.-J. Rousseau, in a letter to Mme de Besenval about the French ambassador, Count de Montaigu, called it 'one of the most immoral of cities'. Addison complained chiefly of the 'filthy double meanings' in the popular comedies.
4. G. Trease.
5. M. Levey (1959).
6. E. Gibbon, *Autobiographies*.
7. G. Trease.
8. G. Lorenzetti.
9. (a) The Durants (W. & A.) IX/ 210, (b) G. Paston, (c) Wortley Montagu: collected letters and works by her great-grandson, Lord Wharncliffe.
10. The Durants LX/212.
11. E. M. Phillips.
12. A. Eeles: *Canaletto*, Hamlyn, 1967.
13. R. J. Charleston.

Chapter 3   Daily Life

1   Molmenti I/129.
2. '. . . tous les honneurs, et elle les reçut avec cette aisance et cet usage du monde qu'on ne connaît qu'en France et même que dans la meilleure société, à l'exception

pourtant de quelques provinces où la noblesse, qu'on appelle à tort la bonne société, laisse un peu trop percer la morgue qui la caractérise'—Casanova, *Mémoires* II, Chapter 10.

3. H. Piozzi.
4. Albergati, *Il saggio amico*, Act 2, sc 2; cited by Molmenti II/116.
5. *Mémoires* III, Chapter 6.
6. C. Gozzi, *Memorie inutili.*
7. Cited by Molmenti II/78.
8. Sir J. Frazer.
9. *'Perfin seduta sul bidet'*, Damerini, see *Fondazione.* . . .
10. Casanova, *Mémoires* III, Chapters 4 & 5.
11. Molmenti II/121.
12. Casanova, *Mémoires* III, Chapter 6.
13. Casanova, *Mémoires* III, Chapter 1.
14. Molmenti II/84.

Chapter 4   A Diversity of People
1. Cited by Molmenti I/183.
2. G. Trease.
3. Molmenti I/140.
4. Molmenti II/99–104.
5. Casanova, *Mémoires* II, Chapter 1.
6. H. Piozzi.
7. Cesare Musati, cited by Molmenti I/207.
8. e.g. Samuel Sharp.
9. Cited by Molmenti I/213.
10. C. Diehl.
11. G. Marangoni, p. 91.
12. T. Talbot Rice, p. 158.
13. Molmenti I/102.
14. G. Lorenzetti.

Chapter 5   Some Entertainments
1. A. Bailly, p. 329.
2. C. Diehl.
3. Molmenti I/109.
4. Venice Accademia.
5. G. Marangoni p. 182.
6. Bragadin, see A. Fanfani.
7. N. Jonard, Chapter 10.
8. Gouvar, see G. Damerini.
9. National Gallery, London.
10. Molmenti I/147 gives full particulars. The artist was named Vierney and the medal was struck in Nürnberg.

Chapter 6   The Spirit
1. P. Monnier, Chapter 5.
2. M. Marcazan.
3. F. Haskell, p. 328.
4. F. Viglione.
5. P. Hazard, p. 275.

6. P. Monnier, Chapter 5.
7. R. Chiarelli, p. 30.
8. a) *Storia della Medicina.*
   b) Anon: 'An Authentick Account . . .'

Chapter 7   *Viva Goldoni!*

1. C. Burney, see Glover.
2. It can be found in his collected works by the first line: '*Io vi vorrei pur confortare . . .*'

Chapter 8   *Evvivan i Sassoni!*

1. D. Valeri (1960), see *Fondazione.* . . .
2. P. J. Grosley, cited by Della Corte.
3. C. Burney, see Glover.
4. Casanova, *Mémoires* II, Chapter 10.
5. E.-A. Cicogna, see Della Corte.
6. C. Goldoni, Black's translation.
7. Casotti, see Della Corte.
8. P. J. Grosley, cited by Molmenti I/170.
9. C. Goldoni, see Durants X/240.

Chapter 9   Architecture

1. A. Fanfani, see *Fondazione.* . . .
2. E. Cicogna, MS notes on Venetian churches (1824–45) at Correr Museum.
3. Molmenti I/71.
4. D. Valeri, see *Fondazione.* . . .
5. E. Bassi, p. 298.

Chapter 10   Sculpture and Minor Arts

1. A. Chastel, see *Fondazione.* . . .
2. Molmenti I/69.
3. T. Hodgkinson.
4. H. Honour, p. 162.
5. H. Honour, p. 165.
6. E. Bassi, p. 328.
7. H. Honour, p. 140.
8. H. Honour, p. 155.
9. Molmenti I/92.
10. E. C. Munro, p. 280.
11. The Durants IX/304.
12. Molmenti II/12.
13. E. M. Phillips.
14. A. Chastel, see *Fondazione.* . . .
15. A. Coleridge.
16. H. Honour, p. 172.
17. R. J. Charleston.

Chapter 11   History Painting

1. Monnier, Chapter 7.
2. Casanova, *Mémoires* I, Chapter 6—'. . . mon frère François, qui était en pension chez un peintre nommé Guardi. . . .'
3. De Brosses.
4. E. Croft-Murray.

5. P. & L. Murray.
6. J. Steer.
7. R. Wittkower.
8. E. M. Phillips.
9. M. Levey (1959), p. 22.
10. In the National Gallery.
11. G. Vertue, cited by Haskell, p. 280.
12. D. Gioseffi (1960).
13. H. Honour, p. 180.
14. M. Levey (1959), p. 25.
15. F. Haskell, p. 286.
16. D. Gioseffi (1960).
17. F. Haskell, p. 297.
18. M. Levey (1959) p. 40.
19. Cited by F. Haskell, p. 351.
20. The National Gallery. Catalogue No. 6279.
21. D. Gioseffi (1960).
22. D. Gioseffi (1960).
23. F. Haskell, p. 351.
24. M. Levey (1959), p. 122.
25. R. Pallucchini (1934).
26. F. Haskell, p. 355.
27. F. Haskell, p. 336.

Chapter 12   The Portrait and Landscape Painters
1. a) V. Moschini.
   b) G. Fiocco (1923).
2. H. Honour, p. 93.
3. M. Levey (1959), p. 135.
4. M. Levey (1959), p. 158, 160. Levey describes the subject as Jacopo Gradenigo.
5. Molmenti II/113.
6. D. Valieri, see *Fondazione. . . .* We do not have to agree.
7. M. Levey (1959), p. 26.
8. Civic Museum, Bassano.
9. See *Country Life*, Nov. 25, 1971, p. 1446, fig. 2.
10. Royal Collection, Windsor Castle.
11. F. Haskell, p. 328.

Chapter 13   The View Painters
1. M. Levey (1959), p. 70.
2. Bristol City Art Gallery.
3. Victoria & Albert Museum, Print Room & Jones Collection.
4. National Gallery, No. 127.
5. M. Levey (1971), p. 120.
6. National Gallery, No. 942.
7. See R. Pallucchini & G. F. Guarnati.
8. National Gallery, No. 937.
9. National Gallery, No. 938.
10. National Gallery, Nos. 2515, 2516.
11. In the Victoria & Albert Museum.
12. See 'Ist. Ital. . . .', 'Guardi'.
13. D. Gioseffi (1956).

14. F. Haskell, p. 374.
15. G. Marangoni, p. 13.
16. a) G. A. Simonson.
    b) Various drawings in the Print Room of the Victoria & Albert Museum.
17. Count Seilern Collection, London.
18. Lord Butler Collection, Cambridge.
19. M. Levey (1959), p. 103.
20. National Gallery, No. 2523.
21. National Gallery, No. 2522.
22. See note 19.
23. G. Fiocco (1923).

Chapter 14   Genre
1. F. Haskell, p. 265.
2. M. Levey (1959), p. 112.
3. D. Gioseffi (1960).
4. H. Honour, p. 94
5. F. Haskell, p. 337.
6. F. Haskell, p. 338.
7. L. D'Ambra, pp. 164-5.
8. F. Haskell, p. 323.
9. H. Honour, p. 207.
10. P. Visconti, see Haskell, p. 323.
11. R. Pallucchini (1960).
12. D. Gioseffi (1960).
13. G. Piovene & A. Pallucchini.
14. M. Levey (1959), pp. 128-9.

Chapter 15   The Master
1. Molmenti II/75.
2. F. Haskell, p. 352.
3. *Nuova Venetiana Gazetta* (Gozzi) 20/3/1762.
4. F. Haskell, pp. 309, 315.
5. E. M. Phillips, p. 299.
6. F. Haskell, p. 354.
7. F. Haskell, p. 257.
8. G. Piovene & A. Pallucchini, pp. 10, 11.
9. Edinburgh: National Gallery of Scotland.
10. London: Seilern Collection.
11. See Knox.

Sources

ACKERMAN, J. S.: *Palladio*, London: Penguin, 1966.

ACTON, LORD JOHN: *Lectures on Modern History*, London: Fontana, 1960.

ADDISON, J.: *Remarks on several Parts of Italy*, etc. 2 vols., London: n.p., 1726.

ANON.: *An Authentick Account of the Mesures and Precautions used at Venice by the Magistrates of the Office of Health*, etc. London: Edwin Owen, 1752.

BAILLY, A.: *La Sérénissime République de Venise*, Paris: Fayard, 1946.

BASSI, E.: *Architettura del Sei e Settecento a Venezia*, Naples: Ediz. Scientifiche Ital., 1962.

BECKFORD, P.: *Familiar Letters from Italy*, 2 vols., Salisbury: J. Easton, 1805.

BERENSON, B.: *Italian Painters of the Renaissance*, London: Phaidon, 1952.

BRINTON, S.: *Venice, past and present*, London: The Studio Ltd., 1925 (Special Spring number of *The Studio*).

BRION, M.: *Venice*, London: Elek, 1962.

BROSSES, PRESIDENT C. DE: *Voyage en Italie* (read in Spanish translation by N. Samerón García, 3 vols., Madrid: Calpe, from French 2nd ed. of 1861).

BRUNETTI, M. ET AL.: *Venice*, London: Zwemmer, 1965.

CASANOVA, J. J.: *Mémoires*, 8 vols., Paris: Garnier, n.d.

CATALOGO DELLA MOSTRA.: *La Pittura del Seicento a Venezia*, Venice: Alfieri,1959.

CESSI, F.: *Tiepolo*, London: Thames & Hudson, 1971.

CHAMBERS, D. S.: *The Imperial Age of Venice*, London: Thames & Hudson, 1970.

CHARLESTON, R. J.: 'Souvenirs of the Grand Tour', *Journal of Glass Studies*, I: 63 (1959).

CHASTEL, A.: see *Fondazione* . . .

CHATFIELD-TAYLOR, H. C.: *Goldoni. A Biography*, New York: Duffield, 1913.

CHIARELLI, R.: *Verona*, Florence: Arnaud, 1962.

CLIFFORD, J. L.: *Hester Lynch Piozzi (Mrs. Thrale)*, Oxford: Clarendon Press, 1941.

COLERIDGE, A.: *Chippendale Furniture: The Work of Thomas Chippendale and his Contemporaries in the Rococo Style*, London: Faber & Faber, 1968.

CROFT-MURRAY, E.: 'Decorative painting in England', London: *Country Life*, 1971.

D'AMBRA, L.: *L'Autore delle Duecento Commedie (Carlo Goldoni)*, Bologna: Zanichelli, 1943.

DAMERINI, G.: see *Fondazione* . . .

DELLA CORTE, A.: see *Fondazione* . . .

DIEHL, C.: *Venise*, Paris: Flammarion, 1915.

DRAGO, A.: 'La Princesa Tarakanova', *Historia y Vida* (Barcelona & Madrid) I: 82 (1968).

DURANT, W. & A.: *The Story of Civilization*, 10 vols., New York: Simon & Schuster. London: Angus & Robertson.
    IX: *The Age of Voltaire*, 1966.
    X: *Rousseau and Revolution*, 1967.

EELES, A.: *Canaletto*, London: Hamlyn, 1967.

FANFANI, A.: see *Fondazione* . . .

FIOCCO, G.: *Francesco Guardi*, Florence: Battistelli, 1923.
    Venetian Painting of the Seicento and Settecento, Florence: Pantheon Press, 1929.

FONDAZIONE, GIORGIO CINI: *La Civiltà Veneziana nel Settecento*, Florence: Sansoni, 1960.

FRAZER, SIR J.: *Folklore in the Old Testament* (abridged ed.) London: Macmillan, 1923.

GIBBON, E.: *The Decline and Fall of the Roman Empire.*
Autobiographies, London: Murray, 1896.

GIOSEFFI, D.: *Pittura Veneziana del Settecento*, Bergamo: Ist. Ital. d'Arti Grafiche, 1956.
Canaletto and his Contemporaries, London: Batsford, 1960.

GLOVER, C. H.: *Dr. Charles Burney's Continental Travels; 1770–1772*, Glasgow: Blackie & Son, 1927.

GOAD, H.: *Language in History*, London: Penguin, 1958.

GOETHE, J. W. VON: *Briefe aus Venedig*, Hamburg: Rohse, 1964 (limited ed.). Most of this contained in *Italian Journey* (trans. from *Italiänische Reise* by W. H. Auden and Elizabeth Mayer) London: Collins, 1962.

GOLDONI, C.: *Mémoires*, Venice: Visentini, 1883. English trans. by J. Black, 2 vols., London: Henry Colburn, 1814.
See also Kennard & Chatfield-Taylor.
Four Plays (introduction by F. Davies), London: Penguin 1968.

GOZZI, C.: *Memorie inutili*, 2 vols., Bari: n.p. 1910.
Fiabe Teatrali, n.p., n.d.
Guardi, Bergamo: Ist. Ital. d'Arti Grafiche, 1957.

HALE, J. re Pullan, B.: *Rich and Poor in Renaissance Venice* (London: Blackwell, 1972) *The Listener*, 27.7.72.

HASKELL, F.: *Patrons and Painters*, London: Chatto & Windus, 1963.

HAZARD, P.: *La Pensée européenne au xviiie siècle, de Montesquieu à Lessing*, Paris: Boivin, 1949.
Trans. J. Lewis May: *European Thought in the Eighteenth Century*, London: Penguin, 1965.

HODGKINSON, T.: *Two Garden Sculptures by Antonio Corradini*, Bull. Vict. & Albert Mus. 4:37 (1938).

HONOUR, H.: *The Companion Guide to Venice*, London: Collins, 1965.

JONARD, N.: *La Vie quotidienne à Venise au xviii Siècle*, Paris. Italian trans. by Aldo Devizzi, Milan: Martello, n.d.

KENNARD, J. S.: *Goldoni and the Venice of his Time*, New York: Macmillan, 1920.

KNOX, G.: *The Catalogue of the Tiepolo Drawings in the Victoria and Albert Museum*, London: H. M. Stationery Office, 1960.

LEVEY, M.: *Painting in XVIII century Venice*, London: Phaidon, 1959.
National Gallery Catalogues: *The Seventeenth and Eighteenth century Italian Schools*, London: Trustees of the National Gallery, 1971.

LORENZETTI, G.: *Le Feste e le Maschere Veneziane*, Venice: Ferrari, 1937.

McCARTHY, M.: *Venice Observed*, London: Heinemann, 1956.

MARANGONI, G.: *Giorno per giorno, tanti anni fa*, Venice: Filippi, 1971.

MARCAZZAN, M.: see *Fondazione* . . .

MARIETTE, J-P.: *Abecedario*, Paris: de Chennevières & de Montaiglon, 1851–60. Cited by Monnier.

MASI, E.: *Lettere di Carlo Goldoni*, Bologna: n.p., 1880.

MASSON, G.: *Italian Villas and Palaces*, London: Thames & Hudson, 1959.

MAZZOTTI, G.: *Ville Venete*, Rome: Bestetti, 1957.
Palladian and other Venetian Villas, London: Tiranti, 1959 (largely from previous reference).

MICHEL, A.: *Histoire de l'Art*, VII/2, Paris: Armand Colin, 1924.

MIKES, G.: *East is East*, London: André Deutsch, 1958.

MOLMENTI, P.: *Venice: the Decadence*, 2 vols. (trans. H. F. Brown from the original

Italian *La Storia di Venezia nella vita privata dalle origini alla caduta della repubblica*, Bergamo, 1908). The original work is in 3 vols., of which the third comprises these two. London: Murray, 1908.

MONNIER, P.: *Venise au xviiie Siècle*, Paris: Perrin, 1937.

MONTESQUIEU, CHARLES DE SECONDAT, BARON DE: *Voyages*, Bordeaux: Gounouilhou, 1894.

MORAZZINI, G.: *Giovanni Battista Piranesi*, Rome: Alfieri & LaCroix, 1922.

MORRIS, J.: *Venice*, London: Faber, 1960.

MOSCHINI, V.: *Pietro Longhi*, Milan: Martello, 1956.

MUNRO, E. C.: *The Golden Encyclopaedia of Art*, New York: Golden Press, 1961.

MURRAY, P.: *Piranesi and the Grandeur of Ancient Rome*, London: Thames & Hudson, 1972.

MURRAY, P. & L.: *A Dictionary of Art and Artists*, London: Penguin, 1959.

NIERO, A.: *La Chiesa dei Carmini*, Venice: n.p., 1965.

PALLUCCHINI, R.: *L'Arte di Giovanni Battista Piazzetta*, Bologna: Maylender, 1934.
  La Pittura Veneziana del Settecento, Venice: Istit. Col. Culturale, 1960.

PALLUCCHINI, R. & GUARNATI, G. F.: *Le Acquaforti di Canaletto*, Venice: D. Guarnati, 1945.

PASTON, G.: *Lady Mary Wortley Montagu and her Times*, London: Methuen, 1907.

PHILLIPS, E. M.: *The Venetian School of Painting*, London: Macmillan, 1912.

PHILOSOPHER (Anonymous): *Lettera d'un filosofo osservatore su gli spettacoli pubblici di Venezia con la descrizione della Regata*, Venice: n.p., 1791.

PIGNATTI, T.: *Tesori di Ca' Rezzonico*, Milan: Martello, 1965.
  Venice and its Art Treasures, Venice: Ardo, n.d.

PIOVENE, G. & PALLUCCHINI, A.: *L'Opera completa di Giambattista Tiepolo*, Milan: Rizzoli, 1968.

PIOZZI, MRS. H.: *Glimpses of Italian Society*, London: Seeley & Co., 1892.

Queini-Stampalia, Pinacoteca, Catalogue: Venice: Zanetti, 1925.

RICCI, A.: *The Etchings of the Tiepolos*, London: Phaidon, 1972. Reviewed in *Times Literary Supplement*, 31.3.72.

RICE, T. T.: *Everyday Life in Byzantium*, London: Batsford, 1967.

ROUSSEAU, J.-J.: *Confessions*, English trans., London: W. Glaisher, 1925.

RUSKIN, J.: *The Stones of Venice*, London: Dent, 1852–3.

SEMENZATO, C.: *La Scultura Veneta del seicento e del settecento*, Venice: Alfieri, 1966.

SHARP, S.: *Letters from Italy*, 3rd ed., London: Henry & Cave, 1767.

SIMONSON, G. A.: 'Guardi's Pictures of the Papal Benediction in Venice', *Burlington Mag.* 36:93 (1920).

STEER, J.: *Concise History of Venetian Painting*, London: Thames & Hudson, 1970.

Storia Della Medicina Italiana, vol. 28, Bologna: Forni (originally) 1848.

TREASE, G.: *The Grand Tour*, London: Heinemann, 1967.

VALCANOVA, F.: *The Treasures of the 'Accademia' Picture-Gallery in Venice*, Milan: Martello, 1966.

VALERI, D.: see *Fondazione* ...
  I Tesori. Il Settecento Veneziano a Ca' Rezzonico, Florence: Sadea, 1966.

VIGLIONE, F.: *L'Algarotti e l'Inghilterra*, Naples: Stab. Tipog. Jovene, 1919.

VOLTAIRE, F-M. AROUET DE: *Candide*, English trans. John Butt, London: Penguin, 1947.

WALPOLE, H.: *The Yale Edition of Horace Walpole's Correspondence*, Ed: W. S. Lewis, vol. 15, London: Oxford Univ. Press & New Haven: Yale Univ. Press, 1952.

WHARNCLIFFE, LORD (W. M. THOMAS): *The Letters and Works of Lady Mary Wortley Montagu*, 2 vols., 2nd ed., London: Bell & Sons, 1887.

WITTKOWER, R.: *Caracci Drawings at Windsor Castle*, London: Phaidon, 1952.

WORTLEY MONTAGU, see Wharncliffe.

Index

Names prefixed by
*San, Sant', Santa and SS are all indexed as if
appearing under Saint*